Blaise de Monluc

Blasij Monluci Franciæ Mareschalli.
Vera Effigies

Blaise de Monluc
A Soldier of France During the Habsburg–Valois War & Wars of Religion, 1521-74

A. W. Evans

LEONAUR

Blaise de Monluc
A Soldier of France During the Habsburg-Valois War & Wars of Religion, 1521-74
by A. W. Evans

First published under the title
Blaise de Monluc

Leonaur is an imprint
of Oakpast Ltd

ISBN: 978-1-78282-539-5 (hardcover)
ISBN: 978-1-78282-540-1 (softcover)

http://www.leonaur.com

Contents

Introduction

On a fine morning in the early years of the sixteenth century, a young Gascon gentleman mounted upon a Spanish horse, might have been seen riding forth from his father's estate of Monluc, near Nerac, bound for the Italian wars. His heart was as light as his purse, for Italy held out golden hopes to all who aspired to win fame and fortune at the point of their swords. This was the case with our young adventurer. He belonged to a noble but impoverished family, and had nobody but himself to depend upon, but with true Gascon intrepidity he left the paternal roof-tree without ever a thought of the possibility of failure. Fifty years later, the same adventurer, now a marshal of France and an ex-Governor of Guyenne, 'maimed by wounds in almost all his limbs,' and 'without strength or hope ever to be cured of that great Harquebuz-Shot in his face,' sat down to dictate the story of his adventures. The *Commentaires of Blaise de Monluc* have long been recognised in France as not only a valuable contribution to history but as one of the best books of adventure that have ever been written.

Full of life and movement, without literary artifice or pretensions, these memoirs give us an admirable picture of a successful souldier of fortune in the sixteenth century. Monluc himself is visible in every page. We see his Gascon temperament, to which, as Cotton says, 'bragging was as natural as bravery,' thirsting for military glory but not blind to the main chance, proud, active, and vigilant, thinking the profession of arms the noblest in the world, dreaming of imaginary battles at night after having fought in real ones by day, and filled with a feverish restlessness from the moment he conceived a project until he carried it into execution.

But if 'the Souldier's Bible,' as Henri IV called the *Commentaires*, has met with justice in France, the power that decrees the fate of books has not dealt generously with the English translation. About a hundred years after Monluc's death English readers were presented with a folio volume bearing the title-page reprinted opposite.

This inviting appeal seems to have met with scant response from the hesitating purchaser, and Charles Cotton—for he was the translator—failed to rouse in his contemporaries any interest in the career of 'the greatest souldier of a subject that ever was in France.' His translation, which has never been reprinted, is marked as 'scarce' when it appears in a second-hand bookseller's list, and it is with the design of calling attention to a volume of singular interest that the following extracts have been reprinted.

Blaise de Lasseran-Massencôme, Seigneur de Monluc, (the word has frequently been written Montluc, but its derivation from *bonus lucus* shows that the proper form is Monluc), was born about the year 1502 at Sainte-Gemme, between Condom and Fleurance, in the heart of Gascony. His father, Francois de Monluc, belonged to the family of the Montesquious, but had lost most of his property, an evil aggravated by the fact that he had to provide for eleven children. Blaise was the eldest of these, and he was soon compelled to learn that if he was to make his way in the world it could only be by his own exertions. He tells us:

> Although I myself am a gentleman by birth, yet have I notwithstanding been raised to that degree of honour wherein I now stand, as leisurely, and as much step by step, as any the poorest souldier who has served in this kingdom these many years. For being born into the world the son of a gentleman, whose father had made sale of all his estate, to only eight hundred or a thousand *livres* yearly revenue, and being the eldest of six brothers that we were, I thought it principally concerned me to illustrate the name of Montluc (which is that of our family) as I have also done with as much peril, and as many hazards of my life, as souldier or captain ever did.

Monluc tells us little of his early years, but from what we know of the small Gascon noblemen of the time we can easily form a picture of the household. The family had more pride than pence, and, as each fresh mouth came to demand its share, the father must have been at his wit's end to secure even a bare subsistence. Black bread and not too much of it was the fare, but poverty and plain living have nourished a fine crop of distinguished souldiers as the annals of many an English vicarage could prove. A lucky chance gave the boy such education as

THE
COMMENTARIES

OF

Messire Blaize de Montluc

MARESCHAL

OF

FRANCE

WHEREIN ARE DESCRIB'D

All the Combats, Rencounters, Skirmishes, Battels,
Sieges, Assaults, Scalado's, the Taking and Surprizes
of Towns and Fortresses; as also the Defences of the
Assaulted and Besieged:

With several other Signal and remarkable Feats of War, wherein this great and renowned Warriour was personally engag'd,
in the space of fifty or threescore years that he bore Arms under
several Kings of *France.*

TOGETHER WITH

Divers Instructions, that such ought not to be ignorant of, as propose
to themselves by the practice of Arms, to arrive at any eminent degree of
Honor, and prudently to carry on all the Exploits of War.

Cicero. M. Marcello, Epist. 8, l. 4.

*Omnia sunt misera in Bellis civilibus, quae Majores nostri ne semel
quidem, nostra aetas saepe jam sensit: sed miserius nihil, quam
ipsa victoria: quae etiamsi ad meliores venit, tamen eos ipsos fero-
ciores, impotentioresq; reddit: ut, etiamsi naturâ tales non sint,
necessitate esse cogantur. Multa enim victori, eorum arbitrio,
per quos vicit, etiam invito facienda sunt.*

LONDON

Printed by *Andrew Clark,* for *Henry Brome,* at the Gun at
the West End of *St. Pauls.* MDCLXXIV.

was then available, and set his feet upon the first rung of the ladder he was to mount.

Through the kind offices of a Gascon neighbour, François de Monluc was enabled to place his eldest son as a page in the household of Duke Antoine of Lorraine. There Monluc learned to read, to sign his name, and to handle his weapons. He also learned, we can believe with more ease than reading and writing, the history of some of the great souldiers of the past generation. Lorraine was then filled with memories of the great struggle of forty years before, when Réné of Lorraine had defeated Charles the Bold. Monluc's imagination was fired by what he heard, and he eagerly drank in the stories, which the survivors of the siege of Nancy used to tell, of how the besieged had kept themselves alive on a diet of dogs, cats, rats, and mice, and of the fame that their stubborn resistance had brought them. He heard, too, that it was his fellow Gascons who had most distinguished themselves, and there were dim rumours of a Gascon captain who had crossed the seas and taken service under the Grand Turk, calling himself Armagnac Pasha, in memory of his native province. We may well think that these tales, repeated around the fireplace in the great hall of the Castle of Nancy, came back into Monluc's mind during the memorable days of his own defence of Siena.

When his time as page was ended, he was, according to the usual custom, given a place as archer in the duke's company of souldiers. The company was commanded by no less a personage than the Chevalier Bayard, but the main body was then in Italy with the duke, and Monluc formed one of a small detachment left at home to keep order in the duchy. This inaction was little to his mind. 'Enflamed with the report of the noble feats of arms every day performed in Italy, which in those days was the scene of action,' he 'was possessed with a longing desire to visit that country.' He left Lorraine, returned to Gascony, persuaded his father to give him a little money and a Spanish horse, and thus equipped, set out like another d'Artagnan upon the road to Italy.

About a day's journey from home, Monluc turned aside to visit the Sieur de Castlenau, 'an antient gentleman who had long frequented Italy,' and to benefit by the experiences of the old campaigner. The conversation raised his ardour to boiling point 'and without longer abode, or staying anywhere longer than to refresh himself and his horse, he passed over the Alps,' and took his way 'directly to Milan.' At Milan he found two of his mother's brothers, Gaxiot and François de Mondenard, men of considerable reputation in the army, who gave their nephew a hearty welcome, and obtained for him an archer's place in the company of Thomas de Foix, Sire de Lescun, the younger brother of Lautrec the commander-in-chief of the army. The position of archer as Monluc does not omit to tell us, was 'a place of great repute in those days, there being in those times several lords and great persons who rode in troops, and two or three who were archers in this.' But he adds, with the regretful backward glance of a veteran, 'since that time discipline is lost and grown degenerate, and all things turned upside down, without hopes that any man now alive shall ever see them restored to their former estate.'

Monluc's first experiences of war fell far short of his dreams. Lautrec's campaign in Milan was disastrous, and instead of the victories to which our young Gascon looked forward he had to learn what it was to belong to a beaten army. That he had his share of the fighting is evident from the fact that five horses were killed under him during the twenty-two months the campaign lasted. At Bicoque he fought on foot, side by side with the future Constable de Montmorency, and when the remnant of Lautrec's army evacuated Italy he had to return with his company to keep garrison in Gascony.

An attack upon Bayonne by the Imperial forces under the Prince of Orange, gave Monluc his next opportunity. With some difficulty he obtained leave of absence from his company and volunteered as an ensign in the defending army which Lautrec was organising. A mistake made by his immediate superior, Captain Carbon, at St Jean de Luz, jeopardised the army, but Monluc together with six Gascon arquebusiers who happened to be in his company, averted the danger. Lautrec, a general usually sparing of his praise, sent for the young ensign, entertained him 'as he would any gentleman in the kingdom,' and dismissed him with the words, 'Monluc, my friend, I will never forget the service you have this day performed the king; but will be mindful of it so long as I live.' Monluc says:

> This was the first action I was ever in in the quality of a commander, and from whence I began to derive my reputation.

He had served his apprenticeship to the trade of arms and his first success was exhilarating. The love of battle was in his veins. 'At such kind of banquets, my body, methought, did not weigh an ounce, and I fancied that I did not touch the ground.' When, a few months later, Lautrec gave him the command of a company, he could feel that he was on the way to realise his dreams.

It would be impossible to give an account here of all the expeditions in which Monluc had a share. Occasions for proving his metal were not long to seek, for it was the period of the prolonged duel between Charles V and Francis I—'an emulation that has cost the lives of two hundred thousand persons, and brought a million of families to utter ruin; when after all neither the one nor the other obtained any other advantage by the dispute, than the bare repentance of having been the causers of so many miseries, and of the effusion of so much Christian bloud.' At Pavia, fate, but obscurity has its compensations, and instead of being held to ransom he was at once released. When Francis I returned from his exile, Monluc was at the head of a Gascon band of eight hundred men who formed part of Lautrec's Italian army. He led the attack upon Porchianna, a small town near Ascoli, with a determination that added to his fame but nearly cost him his life. (His account of the attack can be read further on).

Suffering from wounds which were but partly healed, and with his arm bound up in a sling, he made his way upon a mule to Naples. He intended to witness the siege merely as a spectator, but the disembarkation of the Prince of Navarre was carried out in so blundering a style that Monluc's professional feeling and eagerness to be in a fight were roused, and he took an active part in the ensuing battle. The result brought little credit to the French arms, though Monluc had the good fortune to overhear a remark about his own conduct which he inserts 'without bragging or vain glory.'

> The gentleman who was with the Marquess de Saluces, when he came to command me to retire, I have forgot his name, said to him (for I heard him very well) "*Monsieur*, I now see that the ancient proverb is true, which says, that one man is worth an hundred, and an hundred are not so good as one: I speak it by this captain who has his arm in a scarf, and leans to the Rampire (for in truth I was quite spent) for it must needs be acknowledged that he is the only cause of our preservation."

This commendation, Monluc tells us, made his heart 'swell with courage,' and he observes that 'these little points of honour serve very much in matters of war, and are the cause that when a man shall again happen to be in the service he fears nothing.'

'It is very true,' he continues, 'that men are sometimes mistaken and gain nothing but blows; but,' he adds philosophically, 'there is no remedy for that, we must give and take.'

The siege of Naples was a succession of disasters for the French. The Prince of Navarre died three weeks after his arrival, Lautrec soon afterwards, and his souldiers were forced to capitulate. They were escorted by the Imperial troops to the frontiers of Naples, and then dismissed to beg their way home. The failure of the expedition was a grave personal misfortune for Monluc. He writes:

> For my part, with that little that was saved, which was almost nothing, I returned the greatest part of my journey on foot, with my arm in a scarf (having above thirty ells of taffeta about me, forasmuch as they had bound my arm and my body together with a cushion between) wishing a thousand times rather to die than to live, for I had lost all my masters and friends who knew and loved me. . . . In this handsome equipage I came home to my father's house, where, poor gentleman, I found him engaged in too many necessities of his own to be in any capacity of much assisting me; forasmuch as his father had sold three parts of four of the estate of the family, and had left the remainder charged with five children by a second venture, besides us of my father's who were no less than ten.
>
> By which anyone may judge in what necessities we who are come out of the family of Montluc have been constrained to follow the fortunes of the world. And yet our house was not so contemptible but that it had near upon five thousand *livres* yearly revenue belonging to it before it was sold. To fit myself in all points I was constrained to stay three years at home, without being able to get any cure for my arm, and after I was cured I was to begin the world again, as I did the first day I came out from a page, and as a person unknown seek my fortune in all sorts of necessities, and with extreme peril of my life.

Once again the wars between Charles V and Francis I called Monluc into active service. On his own initiative he planned and performed the destruction of the mills of Auriol, which helped to victual the Imperial army—an enterprise in which reckless daring and calculation were united. To Monluc's disgust the whole credit for the feat was taken by Barbezieux, his incapable superior. Monluc says:

> Monsieur de Lautrec would not have served me so, neither is it handsome to rob another man of his honour; and there is nothing that does more discourage a brave heart.

During the truce that followed the campaign in Provence, Monluc visited Paris and:

> Tryed (forsooth) to be a courtier, but in vain, for I was never cut out for that employment, I have ever been too free and too open-hearted to live at court; and I succeeded there accordingly.

Nor was the trade of spy, which a little before this he also essayed, more to his taste. The Constable de Montmorency had in 1537 obtained permission for two of his officers to visit Perpignan. Montmorency suggested that Monluc should accompany them in the character of a cook, and obtain information concerning the fortification of the city.

> Now you must know this was only a pretended divertisement of Poyet and Bayart, who durst by no means take the king's engineer in their company, as the connestable would have had them, fearing he might be discovered, and themselves by that means detained prisoners: neither did they fail to relate to him afterwards the fright they were in when a Spanish captain challenged me by my name: but I faced him out of the business, counterfeiting both my country and language, and dissembling better to understand how to handle a larding-pin than a sword, and saying that I was a cook to Monsieur le President Poyet, who himself had not a word to say for the terrible fear he was in lest I should be discovered, but General Bayart laughed the Spanish captain out of his conceit, in private telling him that he was not the first who had been so deceived, but that the man he took me for was one of the best captains the King of France ever had. At all this story the constable did only laugh; but I very seriously told him that he should never make me play the spye again so long as he lived. 'Tis an employment of too great danger, and that I have ever abhorred.

The next extraordinary event in Monluc's life—for he carried on his trade of souldier with an ardour that made battles, wounds, and hair-breadth escapes ordinary events in his existence—was his mission from the Comte d'Anguien to Francis I. The young count was opposed in Piedmont by a powerful force under the Marquis du Guast. Perplexed by the contradictory opinions of his lieutenants, he despatched Monluc to inform the king of the situation and to receive his orders. The scene at the royal council when Monluc's advocacy turned the scales in favour of an immediate battle, is one of the most dramatic in the *Commentaires* and can be read in detail further on. It is enough to say here that though no official document confirms Monluc's account, and though in writing it he seems to have refreshed his memory by consulting Martin du Bellay's *Mémoires*, there is no sufficient reason for doubting his general accuracy. He lost no time in bringing the news to the army, going among the souldiers and:

> Assuring them that we should all be highly recompensed by the king, making the matter something better than it was; for a man must now and then lye a little for his master.

The battle was murderous even for those times. Over ten thousand were killed, and it was said that in Cérisoles and for a quarter of a league around, the horses went up to their knees in blood. Monluc, as usual, did prodigies of valour, but this time he received some of the credit he deserved.

> Thus then we arrived at the camp, where Monsieur d'Anguien was, to whom I went, and making my horse curvet, said to him sportingly these words: "What think you. Sir, am I not as pretty a fellow on horseback as I am on foot?" to which he made answer (though yet very melancholy) "you will always behave yourself very well, both in the one posture and in the other," and bowing his body was pleased to embrace me in his arms, and knighted me upon the place; an honour I shall be proud of so long as I live, both for being performed upon the field of battel, and by the hand of so generous and so great a prince.

We pass on to what was in many respects the culminating event in Monluc's career—his famous defence of Siena in 1554 and 1555. The extracts, (further on), from his own full description of the siege will enable readers to judge of the qualities that made him so brilliant a souldier. Monluc at last held the first place, and was in supreme command of an army, but it was under conditions that would make the stoutest heart quail. Opposed to him was an intelligent and energetic enemy, ably led, well supplied with artillery, and urged on by a well-founded hatred. With him were souldiers of four countries, speaking four different languages, mostly mercenaries devoid of patriotism or loyalty, disheartened by the remembrance of recent defeat, and little disposed to show any desperate courage for a king and a cause concerning which they knew little and for which they cared less. He had to defend a city whose inhabitants were proverbially fickle and difficult to lead, easily roused to enthusiasm but no less easily thrown into despair, one moment full of confidence in their commander, the next anxious to parley with the enemy.

Monluc had to weld all these divergent units into a single coherent body, to inspire them with his own determination to hold out at any sacrifice, and to smooth out the jealousies and suspicions which were always dividing them from one another. He had to keep on the watch night and day, to resist surprises from without, and to guard against treachery within. That he kept the besiegers at bay for as long as he did is a feat not only of endurance, but of generalship and all the qualities necessary to a leader of men, and one which has seldom been equalled. That he described it in the way he has is almost an equal ground for our admiration. All the incidents of the siege are brought before our eyes with a vividness and sense of reality that make the description one of the most memorable ever written. It is true that the narrator has no false shame, and does not shrink from taking full credit for his own achievements. But the credit was well deserved, and among stories of their own deeds told by great men of action, Monluc's description of the defence of Siena will always take a high place.

From Monluc's point of view the siege of Siena had but one defect. It ended in the victory of the besiegers. In April 1555, after incredible privations and a resistance as remarkable for the skill as for the heroism with which it was conducted, the people of Siena told Monluc that it was useless to expect a relieving force, and that it was beyond human endurance to hold out any longer. He recognised the inevitable, but the proud old souldier swore that the name of Monluc would never be written at the foot of any capitulation, and after some negotiations between the Siennese and the Spaniards, he and his French troops marched out with all the honours of war. On their retreat the troops and their commander were driven to feed upon horses and nettles, occasionally moistened by a little oil taken out of the lamps in the churches.

> In this manner then, nothing but skin and bone, and more like ghosts than men we arrived at Montalsin. . . . Now where will you find in any history, that ever man went out of a place without capitulation, if he did not steal away by night, but not after the manner I went out. For everyone will confess that I did

not belong to the Siennese and that consequently they could not capitulate for me. So it was, that by the good will of God, I came out after this manner, and the patent is to be seen in the King's Treasury, as I shall say hereafter.

Monluc had at last achieved the fame for which he lived. On his way back to France he passed through Rome, and the Pope, though 'so ill that he had much ado to speak,' complimented him highly and set him in a chair by his bedside to hear the account of his adventures. Cardinals and ambassadors were equally eulogistic, and though 'the pomps, pleasures, delights, and curiosities' of the city attracted Monluc, he set out for home without delay, 'conceiving I might elsewhere be serviceable to the king my master.'

> One thing I must needs say, though it be in my own commendation, that as I passed along the streets, and going to the Castle of St Angelo, everyone ran to the windows, and to their doors to see the man that had so long defended Sienna. Which only served to enflame my courage the more to acquire honour; and though I had scarce money to carry me home, I fancied myself as rich as the greatest man in France.

Afterwards, at the court of Henry II, he received a welcome which went a long way to satisfy his appetite for glory. The king gave him audience after dinner, an hour usually reserved for ambassadors and personages of importance. Henry II delighted in narratives of war, and required Monluc to give him a minute account of the siege, 'which made the story so long that the captains who were come along with me, and waited without upon the terrass, told me that they heard the clock strike five times whilst I was in the gallery with the king.' Next day Diane de Poitiers told Monluc that 'she had never known any man return from an employment with whom the king was better satisfied,' and a day later he was created a Knight of the Order,' which in those times was so noble a thing, and so much sought for, that the greatest prince in France could not have been satisfied without it, and would rather the king should never confer any honour upon him, than deny him that.' He was also given a rent of three thousand crowns charged upon certain Gascon estates, a pension of three thousand *francs*, and two thousand crowns in cash. In the blaze of this signal triumph he returned to Gascony.

Three weeks later, 'having scarce seen his house and his friends,' he was again summoned to take the field, and thenceforward there were few military expeditions in which he did not play a leading part. His fortune indeed advanced so rapidly that his head was a little turned. He refused to obey Thermes, who replaced Brissac in Piedmont; carried out another campaign in the province of Siena; fought for some time under the Duke of Ferrara, and returned to Paris where a new honour awaited him.

> Two dayes had not past before the king sent for me to come to him to Cressy, without giving me notice what it was about, and I heard the next morning after I departed from thence the king had caused Monsieur d'Andelot to be arrested about some answer he had made him concerning religion. So soon as I was come the king sent for me into his chamber, where he had with him the Cardinal of Lorraine and two or three others, and there the king told me that I must go to Metz to the Duke of Guise, there to command the foot, of which Monsieur d'Andelot was colonel. I most humbly besought His Majesty not to make me to intermeddle with another man's command, which rather than I would do, I would go serve His Majesty under the Duke of Guise in the quality of a private souldier, or else would command his pioneers, rather than take upon me this employment. The king then told me that Monsieur de Guise, so soon as he had heard of Andelot's imprisonment, had himself sent to demand me to exercise the said command.
> Seeing then I could get nothing by excuses, I told His Majesty that I was not yet cured of a dyssentery my disease had left me, and that this was a command which required health and disposition of body to perform it; which were neither of them in me; whereupon His Majesty told me that he should think this command better discharged by me in a litter than by another in perfect health, and that he did not give it me to exercise for another but that he intended I should have it for ever.

This appointment as Colonel-General of Infantry was a signal honour, but the astute Gascon recognised that it was also a dangerous one. It made him one of the principal personages in the kingdom, but it set against him the powerful families of Montmorency and Châtillon. He was stepping into the shoes of the brother of Admiral Coligny and the nephew of the Constable of France. Such a rivalry was not to be lightly undertaken by a provincial nobleman, and after the Treaty of Cateau-Cambrésis he hastened to resign his perilous distinction.

He left the court, where the constable was again in high favour, and once more returned to his Gascon estates. There he heard of the tragic death of Henry II, of the events of his successor's brief reign, and of the turmoil that ushered in the regency of Catherine de Medici.

The wars of religion were about to begin, and a new field was opening for Monluc's zeal and activity, a field in which he admits that he 'was constrained, contrary to his own nature, to use not only severity, but even sometimes to be cruel.' With the close of the Italian wars and the outbreak of the wars of religion, the spirit of Monluc's narrative and our view of his character undergo a change. Hitherto we have been able to admire the souldier, inspired by a burning passion for glory, carving his way to the highest place by the might of his own right arm.

We must now look upon him, still as a souldier, but a souldier whose activities resembled closely those of an executioner, carrying out his task of reducing his country to order, but doing it with a ruthless severity that appalled even his contemporaries. This sinister reputation is all the more to his disgrace because he seems for a moment to have leant an ear to the reformed opinions. The fact was that he cared little for points of theological doctrine, and few men would have given a more whole-hearted support to Nietzsche's *dictum* that '*a good war justifies any cause.*'

By his own confession he was 'rather inclined to violence than to peace, and was more prone to fighting and cutting of throats than to making of speeches.' His title of 'the King's butcher' was well earned, and he recounts his own most barbarous doings with a complacency that approaches cynicism. At the very beginning of the proceedings he procured two hangmen—

> Whom they have since called my *lacquais*, because they were very often at my heels—(and he went to one of the disturbed districts where he executed several of the Huguenots)—without sentence or writing, for in such matters, I have heard, men must begin with execution, and if everyone that had the charge of provinces had done the same they had put out the fire that has since consumed all.

Hardly a day passed without wholesale hangings and burnings, he writes:

> One might see all thereabouts which way I had gone, the trees upon the highways wearing my livery, one man hanged terrified more than an hundred that were killed.

19

When he appeared before Agen, so great was the terror of his name, that he 'wondered the people should be so damnably timorous and did not better defend their religion,' for they 'no sooner heard my name but they fancied the rope about their necks.'

In such warfare, quarter was not to be expected, and Monluc speaks with regret whenever his prisoners had to be ransomed. He records:

> We were so few that we were not enough to kill them all. Had the king paid his companies I should not have suffered ransom to have been in use in this quarrel.

At the taking of Montségur:

> The slaughter continued till ten of the clock or after, because they were fain to ferret them out of the houses, and there was not above fifteen or twenty taken prisoners, whom we presently hung up, and amongst the rest all the king's officers, and the consuls, with their hoods about their necks. There was no talking of ransoms unless for the hangmen.

It would, however, be doing Monluc an injustice not to insist upon the facts that extenuate, though they are far from justifying, the policy that led to this deluge of blood. In the first place it was largely a reprisal, for the excesses of the Protestants were at least as terrible as those of their opponents. They pillaged churches, desecrated tombs, levied taxes on all classes to pay for their troops, and altogether acted with an effrontery that naturally drove the Catholics into extremes. Moreover, they were continually in communication with foreign powers, and the rebellion seemed to men like Monluc a blow at the vitals of France, he comments:

> It is not in this case as in a foreign war, where men fight for love and honour; but in a civil war we must either be master or man, being we live as it were all under a roof; and that's the reason why we must proceed with rigour and cruelty, otherwise the temptation of gain is such that men would rather desire the continuation than the end of the war.

To this must be added the fact that Monluc's reputation for severity rests largely on his own testimony. He boasted that he was cruel, and the world has accepted his statement. Yet, apart from the conditions of civil warfare just mentioned, we shall not be far wrong in assigning some of the darkest shadows in the picture to the wealth of his

Gascon imagination. We are not justified in holding him responsible for the excesses of the ferocious troops he commanded, any more than we can blame Coligny for those of his *reiters* in Agenais, though these latter are attested by the most authentic documents. Monluc carried on war in a barbarous fashion, but he was constrained to do this, partly by the character of the men he had to lead, and partly by that scourge of the mercenary armies of the sixteenth century, the necessity of allowing them to subsist on the enemy and take their pay in pillage. Terrible as Monluc was, he was outspoken in his condemnation of the conduct of the Spanish troops who were sent by Philip II to join him before Agen.

If we turn away from the moral side of the religious wars, and regard Monluc solely as a military commander, the closing years of his life brought him nothing but additional reputation. The importance of his services to the Catholic cause cannot be easily over-estimated. He was everywhere at once, keeping the enemy continually on the watch, harassing them from the most unexpected directions, and carrying on a correspondence of letters and messages with nearly every general in the field. His troops were ill-paid and few in number, but he handled them with consummate mastery and again and again brought them to the strategical position in the nick of time.

His achievements have won for him the title of 'the true creator of the French infantry,' and his conduct of operations in the South before Bordeaux and Toulouse, and in Guyenne, justify his claim to that honour. He was, besides, the life and soul of the various Catholic leagues and combinations, showing a politic wisdom and foresight hardly to be looked for in a man of his impetuous temperament. The end of his active career came when at the siege of the little fortified town of Rabastens, 'a harquebuze-shot clapt into his face,' so that his whole countenance was smashed in, and the cheek bones had to be taken out in splinters.

Thus, the hour of retreat having sounded, the old war-dog retired to Gascony, where, with his face covered by a mask that made his appearance still more formidable, he spent his time riding over his estates, distributing justice among his tenants, dictating his memoirs from time to time, 'crucified with the cholick,' and growling against a government that failed to give their deserts to its best servants. But a final triumph was reserved for him. In 1573 he was summoned to the Catholic camp before Rochelle, where he had the honour of leading the grand assault, though the siege failed because the veteran's advice was not followed. Shortly afterwards he was present at Lyons at the entry of Henry III, the new King of France who, while Duke of Anjou, had known some of Monluc's services.

> Now His Majesty calling to mind the services I had done for the kings his grandfather, father, and brother; some of which he had heard of, and others had himself also seen, he was resolved to honour me with the estate of Mareschal of France, and to make me rich in honour, since he could not do it in matter of wealth and estate. Having therefore caused me to be called for, and being come, to kneel down before him, after I had taken the oath, he put the *mareschal's* staffe into my hand: Which having done, in returning my most humble thanks, I told him, "That I had no other grief in this world, but that I had not ten good years in my belly, wherein to manifest how much I desired to be serviceable to His Majesty and crown in that honourable command." Having received his commands, and those of the queen, I returned into Gascony to make preparation for war, for all things tended that way: but I very well perceived by the tediousness of my journey, that I was rather to think of dying myself, than of killing others.

He made one more brief expedition against the Huguenots, and, returning home, thought for a time of ending his days in a monastery. But he had not yet renounced all warlike projects, for his *Commentaires* end with the words, 'if God lend me life I know not yet what I shall do.'

He died on the 26th of February 1577 at his Château of Estillac, and was buried in the choir of the Cathedral of Condom.

The chief merit of Monluc's *Commentaires* is that they are a record of action written by a man of action. This type of book will always have a special fascination for many readers, and to these the *Commentaires* can be warmly commended. Their author composed them with the two-fold object of doing credit to the house of Monluc, and of giving advice to others who wished to emulate his example. From this latter point of view, the book is full of the wisest practical advice, and there are few souldiers and few men in any capacity whose duty it is to hearten and encourage others who would not benefit by Monluc's counsels. But the *Commentaires* are above all else an autobiography, written, or rather dictated, long after most of the events it narrates.

Monluc is often prolix over episodes personal to himself, and with an old man's love of detail he sets down every incident he remembers. Indeed, this constitutes one of his charms, for out of all the digressions and repetitions there rises in the mind an unforgettable picture of the man, with all his qualities and defects clearly outlined. And if they lose something by lack of method and arrangement, they have the compensation of being perfectly natural and spontaneous. He wrote as a man speaks who is relating his experiences to his friends, and the conversational turn of his sentences adds to the vividness of his narration. He had some hope that the *Commentaires* would be read when he was dead and gone, and he warns his readers what to expect from them, he says:

> I must entreat all those who shall read them not to look upon them as proceeding from the pen of an historian, but of an old souldier and a Gascon, who has writ his own life truly, and in the rough style of a souldier.

This rough style of a souldier, so singularly fitted to its purpose, has been the envy of several men of letters who have written about Monluc.

> It is the style of a man who has had little or no intercourse with books, but who has a natural gift for clear and expressive speech. His thoughts shape themselves in language without any effort. Those who hold the view that the language of literature should be widely differentiated from that of speech had better read Monluc, and then reconsider their position.—Arthur Tilley: *The Literature of the French Renaissance*, Vol. II.

A few words remain to be said about the translator. Charles Cotton, whose memory is grateful to all anglers through his association with Izaak Walton, was a man of varied accomplishments, a brilliant writer, a wit, a poet, and an authority on games of cards. His reputation as a translator rests upon his version of Montaigne, a sound and scholarly piece of work, published eleven years later than his translation of Monluc. Had he had greater prudence, he might have played a distinguished part in his age, but money slipped through his fingers, and he was often hard driven to eke out a living. In his preface to the translation of the *Commentaires*, he tells the reader his reasons for publishing that work.

> A man that has had no better luck in printing books than I, and received from the world so little thanks for his labour, should,

one would have thought, have taken some reasonable warning, and in some moderate time have given over scribbling, but notwithstanding these discouragements, I have hitherto, and do yet continue incorrigible, . . . and seeing I acknowledge this to be a fault, and that every fault requires some excuse, I think fit to give the reader some account why I still persist so obstinate to pester the world with my writings.

He justifies his undertaking on the ground that the work he presents to English readers, 'has been allowed by all to be the best souldier's book, that is the best book for the instruction of a souldier, that ever was writ,' and that such as cannot read Monluc in his own language 'are better with an ill translation than none at all.' The extracts in the present little book provide the reader with some material for judging of Cotton's estimate of his author. But the task of selection is always difficult, for though, like the pious cottar, the editor 'wales a portion with judicious care,' he will nearly always chafe against the limitations of space, and regret that some favourite passage must be excluded. The present writer hopes at some future date to reprint Cotton's translation of Monluc in its entirety and thus make accessible a book which he believes merits the highest encomiums it has received.

Blaise de Monluc

THE AUTHOR'S REASONS FOR WRITING

Being at the age of threescore and fifteen retired home to my own house, there to seek some little repose after the infinite pains and labours I had undergone during the space of above fifty years that I bore arms for the several kings my masters, in which service I past all the degrees and through all the orders of souldier, ensign, lieutenant, captain, camp-master, governor of places, His Majesties lieutenant in the provinces of Tuscany and Guienne, and Mareschal of France: finding myself maimed in almost all my limbs, with harquebuz-shots, cuts and thrusts with pikes and swords, and by that means rendered almost useless and good for nothing, without strength or hope ever to be cured of that great harquebuz-shot in my face, and after having resigned my government of Guienne into His Majesties hands: I thought fit to employ the remainder of my life in a description of the several combats wherein I have been personally engaged in the space of two and fifty years that I had the honour to command: assuring myself that the captains who shall take the pains to read my life will therein meet with passages that may be useful to them in the like occasions, and of which some advantage may be made to the acquiring of honour and renown.

And although I have in the several engagements I have undertaken (and some of them perhaps without great reason on my side to justifie my proceedings) been exceedingly fortunate, and successful beyond all humane aim; I would not yet anyone should conceive that I attribute the success or the glory thereof to any other than to God alone; and indeed whoever shall consider the dangers and difficulties I have gone through and overcome cannot but therein acknowledge his Almighty and immediate Arm. Neither have I ever failed to implore his assistance in all my undertakings, and that with great confidence in his grace and mercy, and assurance of it; wherein His Divine Majesty has been pleased so far to be gratiously assisting to me, that I have never been defeated nor surprised in any exploit of war, where I have been in command; but on the contrary have ever carried away victory and honour. And it is very necessary and fit that all we who bear arms should ever consider and always confess that we, of ourselves, can do nothing without his divine bounty, which inspires us with courage, and supplies us with strength to attempt and execute those great and hazardous enterprises which present themselves to our undertaking.

And because some of those who shall read these *Commentaries* (for it will be very hard to please all, though some will set a just value upon my book) may perhaps think it strange, and accuse me of vain-glory for writing my own actions; and say that I ought in modesty to have transferred that work to another hand: I shall tell such once for all, that in writing the truth, and attributing to God the glory thereof, there will be no harm done: Neither (besides that the testimonies of several men of honour yet living will justifie the truth of what I shall deliver) can anyone give a better account of the designs, enterprises, and executions, and the actions happening thereupon then myself, who was an eyewitness and an actor in them all; and who also design not herein to deprive anyone of his due and particular honour.

The greatest captain that ever lived was Caesar, and he has led me the way, having himself writ his own *Commentaries*, and being careful to record by night the actions he performed by day. I would therefore by his exemple contrive mine, how rude and impolisht soever (as coming from the hand of a souldier, and moreover a Gascon, who has ever been more solicitous to do, than to write or to speak well). Wherein shall be comprehended all the exploits of war in which I have either been personally engaged, or that have been performed by my direction; and these beginning from my greener years, when I first came into the world, to signifie to such as I shall leave behind me how restless I (who am at this day the oldest captain in France) have ever been in the search and acquisition of honour, in performing services for the kings my masters, which was my sole and only end, ever flying all the pleasures and delights which usually divert young men whom God has endowed with any commendable qualities, and who are upon the point of their advancement, from the paths of true virtue and undisputed greatness.

A book not intended however for the learned men of the world, they have historians enough of their own, but for a souldier, and wherein a captain, and perhaps a lieutenant of a province may find something that may be worth his observation. At the least I can affirm that I have written the truth; having my memory as good and entire at this instant as ever, and being as perfect in the names both of men and places, as if all things had past but yesterday, and yet I never committed anything to paper, for I never thought at such an age as this to undertake any thing of this kind: which whether I have well or ill performed, I refer myself to such as shall do me the honour to read my book, which is properly an account of my own life.

To you, therefore (captains my companions) it is that this treatise does principally address itself, to whom peradventure it may in some measure be useful. And you ought to believe that having so many years been in the same command wherein you now are, and having so long discharged the office of a captain of foot, and thrice that of a camp master and colonel, I must needs have reteined something of that condition, and that in a long experience I have seen great honours confered upon some, and great disgraces befall others of that degree. There have been some who in my time have been cashiered and degraded their nobility, others who have lost their lives upon a scaffold, others dishonoured and dismist to their own houses without ever having been more regarded either by the king or any other:

And on the contrary, I have seen others who have trailed a pike at six *francs* pay arrive at great preferments, performing things so brave, and manifesting themselves men of so great capacity, that several who in their original have been no better than the sons of poor labouring men, have raised themselves above many of the nobility by their prowess and virtue. Of all which having myself been an eyewitness, I am able to give a precise and a true account. And although I myself am a gentleman by birth, yet have I notwithstanding been raised to that degree of honour wherein I now stand, as leisurely and as much step by step as any the poorest souldier who has served in this kingdom these many years.

For being born into the world the son of a gentleman, whose father had made sale of all his estate, to only eight hundred or a thousand *livres* yearly revenue, and being the eldest of six brothers that we were, I thought it principally concerned me to illustrate the name of Montluc (which is that of our family) as I have also done with as much peril and as many hazards of my life as souldier or captain ever did; and that without ever having the least reproach from those by whom I was commanded; but on the contrary with as much favour and esteem as ever any captain had who bore arms in the armies wherein I had the honour to serve. Insomuch that whenever there happened any enterprise of importance or danger, the king's lieutenants and collonels would as soon or sooner put me upon it as any other captain of the army; of which the ensuing pages will give you sufficient testimony.

The Action at St Jean de Luz

Having in my greener years been bred up in the family of Anthony Duke of Lorain, and now grown up towards a man, I was presently preferred to an archer's place in the dukes own company, Monsieur Bayard being at that time lieutenant to the same. Not long after being enflamed with the report of the noble feats of arms every day performed in Italy, which in those days was the scene of action, I was possessed with a longing desire to visit that country. To this end making a journey into Gascony, I make shift to procure of my father a little money and a Spanish horse, and without further delay began my journey in order to my design, leaving to fortune the hopes of my future advancement and honour.

About a day's journey from my father's house, and near unto Leitoure, I turned a little out of my way to visit the Sieur de Castelnau, an antient gentleman who had long frequented Italy, of him to inform myself at large of the. This gentleman told me so many things, and related to me so many brave exploits which were there every day performed, that without longer abode, or staying anywhere longer than to refresh myself and my horse, I past over the Alpes, and took my way directly to Milan. Being come to Milan, I there found two uncles of mine by my mother's side, called the Stillatts, both of them men of great reputation and esteem, of which the one served under Monsieur de Lescut, brother to Monsieur de Lautrec (the same who was afterwards Mareschal of France, and then known by the name of the Mareschal de Foix, by whom I was presently put into an archers place in his own company, a place of great repute in those days, there being in those times several lords and great persons who rode in troops, and two or three who were archers in this; but since that discipline is lost and grown degenerate, and all things are turned upside down, without hopes that any man now alive shall ever see them restored to their former estate.

At this time the war betwixt Francis the First and the Emperor Charles the Fifth broke out again with greater fury than before, the later to drive us out of Italy, and we to maintain our footing there, though it was only to make it a place of sepulture to a world of brave and valiant French. God Almighty raised up these two great princes sworn enemies to one another, and emulous of one another's greatness; an emulation that has cost the lives of two hundred thousand persons, and brought a million of families to utter ruin; when after all neither the one nor the other obtained any other advantage by the dispute, than the bare repentance of having been the causes of so many miseries, and of the effusion of so much Christian blood. If God had pleased that these two monarchs might have understood one another, the whole earth had trembled under their arms; and Solyman who was contemporary with them, and who during their contests enlarged his empire on every side, would have had enough to do to defend his own.

The emperour was, 'tis true, a great and a magnanimous prince, yet in nothing superiour to our master, during his life, saving in a little better success, and in that God gave him the grace to bewail his sins in a convent, into which he retired himself two or three years before his death. During the space of two and twenty months that this war continued, I had the good fortune to be an eyewitness of several very brave actions, which were very fit to season a raw souldier; neither did I fail continually to present myself in all places and upon all occasions where I thought honour was to be purchased at what price soever; and it is to be imagined I had my share of fighting, when I had no less than five horses killed under me in the short continuance of that service, and of those two in two days, which Monsieur de Roquelaure, who was cosen germain to my mother, was pleased to give me. For in this beginning of my armes I had the good fortune to gain so far upon the affections of the whole company, that my horses being lost, everyone was willing to help to remount me, and being moreover taken prisoner in battel, I was soon after delivered by the procurement of my friends.

Let such therefore as intend to acquire honour by feats of arms resolve to shut their eyes to all hazards and dangers whatever in the first encounter where they shall happen to be present, for that's the time when everyone has his eyes fixed upon them, to observe their behaviour, and thence to form a judgment of their future hopes. If in the beginning they shall, by any handsom action, signalise their courage and boldness, it sets a good mark upon them for ever, and not only makes them noted and regarded by all but moreover inspires them themselves with mettle and vigour to perform more and greater things. Now you must know that in this war we lost the dutchy of

Millan. Of which (though I do not pretend to be any great clerk) I could write the true history, and should His Majesty command me, I would deliver the truth, and I am able to give as good an account (though I was myself very young at that time) as any man whatever in France, I mean of those passages where I had the fortune to be present, and no other; for I will write nothing by hearsay.

But I intend not to busie myself with a relation of other men's actions, and less of the faults and oversights by them committed, though they are yet as fresh in my memory as at that moment; and seeing that what I myself performed in that country, at that time, was in the quality of a private souldier only, I being not as yet steped into command: I shall no longer insist upon this melancholy subject, which has also been writ before by others: only this I shall make bold to affirm, that Monsieur de Lautrec was by no means to be blamed, he having there performed all the parts of a good, and prudent general, and who indeed was in himself one of the greatest men I ever knew.

Neither shall I trouble myself to give a narration of the Battel of the Bicoque, in which I fought on foot, as also did Monsieur de Montmorency, since Constable of France; A battel that Monsieur de Lautrec was compelled to consent unto, through the obstinacy of the Swisse, quite contrary to his own judgment. A nation whose wilfulness I have seen occasion the loss of several places, and cause great inconveniences in His Majestie's affairs. They are, to speak the truth, a very warlike people, and serve as it were for bullwarks to an army: but then they must never want either money or victuals, for they are not to be paid with words.

After the unfortunate loss of this fair dutchy of Millan, all the forces returned back into France, and with them the company of the said Mareschal de Foix, wherein I then had not only the place of a man at armes but moreover an Assignation of an archer's pay. Sometime after the emperour set another army on foot to recover Fontarabie; whereupon our company and several others were ordered to repair to Bayonne to Monsieur de Lautrec, who was His Majestie's lieutenant in Guienne. The said Sieur de Lautrec, that he might the better make head against the enemy (who made a shew of attempting something upon the frontier), made a suddain leavy of fourteen or fifteen ensigns of foot; which was the occasion that I (who ever had an inclination for foot service) entreated leave of Captain Sayas (who carryed the cornette in the absence of Captain Carbon his brother) for three months only; that I might accept of an ensign offered to me by Captain Clotte;

who at last very unwillingly granted my suite, although he himself had first sent to Captain Carbon to sollicite it in my behalf. Suddainly after this (the enemy being dayly reinforced with fresh supplies) la Clotte was commanded away to Bayonne, and a few days after that Captain Carbon took the companies of Monsieur de Lautrec and the Mareschal his brother, with two companies of foot, to wit, that of Megrin Comenge, and la Clotte to conduct us thorugh the woods straight to St Jean De Luz, where the enemies camp at that time lay.

So soon as we were arrived at the top of a little hill about half a quarter of a league distant from Luz (having already passed a little River by a wooden bridge, another half quarter of a league behind this little hill, at the foot whereof, and before us there ran a rivolet of fifteen or twenty paces broad, and deep to a man's girdle, joyning to which there is also a plain which extends itself in an easie descent down to the said rivolet, from whence one may easily discover St Jean de Luz, one of the finest *burgs* in all France and seated upon the margent of the ocean sea) Captain Carbon who commanded the party, leaving two cornets upon this little hill, the one whereof was carried by Captain Sayas, which was ours, and the other by Captain d'Andouins, which was that of Monsieur de Lautrec (but both of them onely in the absence, the one of Captain Carbon, the other of Captain Artiquiloube), and only twenty horse with each, together with our two companies of foot, took the rest of the *gens-d'armes*, and with them Monsieur Gramont, the same who afterwards dyed in the Kingdom of Naples, and who was at this time lieutenant to the company belonging to Monsieur de Lautrec.

With this party Captain Carbon passed over the little river, and having divided his men into three squadrons (as one might easily discern from the hill where we stood) trotted along the plain directly towards St Jean de Luz. Being come to the middle of the plain, he there made a halt for an hour or more, whilst a trumpet went twice and sounded the fanfare to the enemy, after which being about to retreat, as not believing anyone would stir out of the enemies' camp, the forlorn which he had sent out towards the utmost skirts of the plain returned back upon the spur, to acquaint him that all the enemies' camp began to move; and suddenly after we began to discover three of their squadrons of horse, appearing upon their march one upon the heels of another, and making directly towards Monsieur de Carbon.

Of these the first that came up presently and smartly charged the foremost of ours, where there were many launces broken on both sides; but more of ours than theirs, for as much as in those times the Spaniards carried but few launces, and those very slender, long, and pointed at both ends. During this charge Captain Carbon was leisurely drawing off the other two squadrons towards the place where we were, when the second of the enemies' squadrons coming up, and uniting with the first, beat up our first to our second squadron, commanded by Monsieur Gramont, where the skirmish was very hot, and a great many men thrown to ground both on the one side and the other, amongst whom were the Seigneurs de Gramont, who had his horse killed under him, de Luppe, standard-bearer to Monsieur de Lautrec, de Poigressi, who is since turned Hugonot, de la Fay de Xaintonge, who is yet living, and divers others.

At the same instant we discovered another great party of horse advancing towards us a little on our left hand, at the sight of which the captains who carried our colours came both of them running to me, and saying we are all lost, whereupon I told them, that it were better than so to conclude to hazard fourscore or an hundred foot to bring off our horse who were engaged. To which La Clotte, and Megrin made answer, that that venture would only occasion a greater loss, and that moreover they very much doubted the souldiers would hardly be perswaded to go down, seeing death so manifest before their eyes. Now you must understand there was no one present at this discourse, saving the two forementioned captains and myself, our foot standing drawn up fourteen, or fifteen paces behind; and it was not amiss; for I make a great question had they heard what we said, and seeing the *gens-d'armes* in manifest danger to be lost, whether I should have been so chearfully followed as I was.

And it is a good rule as much as a man can to conceal from the souldier the danger of any enterprise, if you intend to have them go briskly to their work. To this last objection of the two captains, I made answer that I would run the hazard to lead them on, and that lost or not lost it was better to hazard and to lose fourscore or an hundred foot than all our *gens-d'armes*. And thereupon without further deliberation (for long consultations are often the ruine of brave attempts) I returned back to the souldiers and the captains with me (for the business required hast), saying to them only these few words, 'Come on. Come on comrades, let us go, and relieve our *gens-d'armes*,' and was thereupon followed by an hundred foot of our own company, who with very great resolution descended with me to the foot of the hill, where at the head of my men I passed over the brook, and there delivered twenty of my men to be led by the Bastard of Auzan, a gentleman who has nothing blemished the legitimate sons of his race; though all of them men of singular beauty and remarkable valour.

Now you must know that the company I commanded was no other than cross-bows, for at this time the use of the harquebuze had not as yet been introduced amongst us; only three or four days before six Gascon harquebusiers came over to us from the enemy, which I had received into my company, having by good fortune been that day upon the guard at the great gate of the city; and of those six, one was a native of the territory of Montluc. Would to heaven that this accursed engine had never been invented, I had not then received those wounds which I now languish under, neither had so many valiant men been slain for the most part by the most pitiful fellows and the greatest cowards; poltrons that had not dared to look those men in the face at hand, which at distance they laid dead with their confounded bullets: but it was the Devil's invention to make us murther one another.

Being thus past the river, I ordered the Bastard d' Auzan not to suffer his men to shoot, but only to present as if they intended to do it, to the end that he might favour mine, and give them time to discharge and retire again into their order. Now when I was under the foot of the hill, I could not possibly see what our men did; but being advanced a little further into the plain, I saw all the enemies' three squadrons drawn up into one body, and the great party on the left hand, marching upon a good round trot directly towards ours, who were rallied and stood firm without being able either to advance forwards or to retire back by reason of some great stones that lay scattered in their rear. Here it was that Captain Carbon (who had no arms on, having before been wounded in his left arm by an arquebuze shot) seeing me so near him, came up to me and said, 'Oh Montluc, my dear friend, charge up boldly.'

'I will never forsake thee: Captain,' said I, 'take you only care to save yourself and your *gens-d'armes*,' at the same instant crying out. 'Shoot, comrades, at the head of these horse.'

I was not above a dozen paces distant from the enemy when I gave them this volley, by which (as it appeared by the testimony of the prisoners who were taken a few days after) above fifty horses were killed and wounded, and two troopers slain, an execution that a little cooled their courage, and caused their troops to make a halt. In the meantime Captain Carbon had leisure with his party to retire full gallop towards the brook I had passed over to relieve him; where such as had their horses lost, taking hold of the others horse tayls, saved themselves also, and all together passed over the river. Which hast they were necessitated to make, or otherwise the great party of horse on the left hand had charged them in the flank, had they drawn more leisurely off. In the meantime under favour of the twenty cross-bows of d'Auzan, who sustained us, we rallied again and gave another volley. So soon as Captain Carbon had passed the river with his horse, remounted Monsieur de Gramont on another horse, and mounted the rest *en crouppe*, he commanded the said Sieur de Gramont to ride to the top of the hill, and in all hast to draw off the ensigns both of horse and foot at a round trot directly to the other river, where the bridge was that leads towards Bayonne.

Which order being given, he suddenly turned back again towards me, having in his company an Italian called Signior Diomede, and the Sieur de Mainahaut, where he found me retreating towards a ditch upon the edg of a marish, and of which I might be within some twelve or fourteen paces, which not only hindered him from getting up to me, but moreover gave him enough to do to save himself. I notwithstanding in spite of the enemy recovered the ditch of the marish, being still sheltered by d'Auzan, whom I commanded to climb over in great diligence, and there to make head, which he accordingly performed.

The Spaniards in the meantime made a shew as if they meant to charge, but they durst not attempt to break into me; neither were my six harquebusiers idle all this while, but did wonders with their shot, when having at last retreated my men within five or six paces of the ditch, I caused them all in an instant to throw themselves into it, and under favour of d'Auzan, almost as suddainly to mount the ditch bank on the other side, over which we all got safe and sound saving three souldiers who were slain with harquebuze shot for not having been so nimble as the rest; and here it was that, as in a little fort, I made head against the enemy. Now you must know, that that party of the enemy which came up on the left hand, made a halt at the bank of the river when they saw our horse were already got half way up the hill; and those who had fought, and to whom I had given a stop at the ditch bank, were now upon their retreat home, when seeing three squadrons of harquebusiers coming along the plain, and making towards them with all the speed they could, it revived their spirits, and inspired them with new courage to face about again.

I, in the meantime, (having also discovered these fresh succours) began to shift along by the ditch, till being by the return of a corner of it slipt out of their sight, I drew my men into a very narrow meadow from whence at full speed I gained the foot of the hill I had descended before, and having repassed the river, soon recovered the top of the mountain. The danger wherein I saw myself to be, as well of the horse I had pressing upon my rear, as of the battaillon of infantry which I saw fast advancing towards me, did not however make me loose my judgment in a time of so great need; nor hinder me from discerning and taking this opportunity for my retreat, during which I made the little handful of men I had march very close together; and by turnes encouraging and speaking to them, made them often face about and salute the cavalry, who pursued me both with cross-bow and har-quebuze shot; when having gained the top of the hill, I drew into an orchard, making fast the gate on the inside that the horse might not so suddainly enter, and by the favour of that and several others planted with apples, still made on towards the bridge, till I came to a little church called Haitée, from whence I perceived the great road to be all covered over with the enemies' horse.

There being nevertheless a great ditch betwixt them and me, from whence I bestowed upon them some arquebuze and cross-bow shot, which also very seldom failed of their effect, and compelled them (seeing they could not come up to me) some to advance forwards, and others to retire. I then put some of my men into the churchyard, thinking there again to make head; the greatest folly I committed throughout the whole action; for in the meantime a good number of their horse gliding along by the meadow straight towards the bridge, were already advanced so far that I saw myself totally enclosed with-out all manner of hope to escape and to save myself.

Now so soon as Captain Carbon had recovered the bridge, and that the horse and foot were all passed over, he commanded Monsieur Gramont to hast away, not only a trot but a full gallop; for he already discovered the enemies' infantry in the orchards, which I could not do; neither did I ever perceive them till they began to shoot at me; and then I made a sign to my souldiers in the churchyard to come and draw up to me in the great high way. Captain Carbon in the interim, being he saw nothing of me, half concluded us all for killed or taken, and yet seeing all the enemies' troops of horse both on the right hand and on the left, making directly towards the bridge, would leave Cap-tain Campai (an admirable good souldier) at the end of the bridge with five and twenty horse and thirty cross-bows of Captain Megrin's company, to try if there were any possible means to relieve me, were I yet alive, causing the bridg in the meantime to be broken down. Now because that troop of the enemies' horse, which marched on the right hand, made a great deal more hast towards the bridge, than that of the left, I quitted the great high way, and under favour of a hedg made straight towards the river, where I was again to encounter the horse, which notwithstanding I made my way thorow, chopt into the river, and in despite of them all, passed over to the other side, wherein the banks of the river being high, favoured me very much, they being too steep for the horse to get down, neither was our shot of both sorts idle in the meantime.

At last I recovered the end of the bridge, when I found Captain Campai very busie at work to break it, and who so soon as he saw me was very importunate with me to save myself, at the same time presenting me the crupper of his horse to that end: but he had no other answer from me but this, that God had hitherto preserved me, and my souldiers also, whom I was likewise resolved never to abandon till I had first brought them into a place of safety. Whilst we were in this dispute we were aware of the Spanish infantry coming directly towards the bridg, when finding ourselves too weak to stand the shock, Campai with the cross-bows of Captain Megrin took the van in order to a retreat, and I remained in the rear, having gained a ditch that enclosed a little meadow, which was sufficient to defend me from the horse, it being so high that they could not come to charge.

I had now nothing left me but my six harquebusiers, my cross-bows having already spent all their arrows, nevertheless to shew that their hearts were not down I caused them to hold their swords ready drawn in the one hand, and their bows in the other to serve instead of a buckler. Now Captain Campai's men had broken down the greatest part of the bridg before they went away, by reason of which impediment the cavalry could not so soon come up to us, having been constrained to foord the river two harlquebuze shot on the right hand, whilst the foot in the meantime with great difficulty filed it over one by one by the rails of the bridge, a posture wherein it had been a very easie matter to defeat them, had I not foreseen that then the cavalry would have come up to enclose me, and our honour depended upon our retreat.

Wherefore still getting ground, and from ditch to ditch, having gained about half a quarter of a league of way, I made a halt that my men might not be out of breath, when looking back I perceived the enemy had done so too, and saw by his countenance that he grew weary of the pursuit, a thing at which I was very much astonished and not a little glad, for in plain truth we were able to do no more, having taken a little water and cider and some maiz bread out of a few small houses we met upon the way. In the meantime Captain Campai sent out some horse to see what was become of us, believing me to be either dead or taken. And now behold us arrived in a place of safety, with the loss of only three men in the first ditch, and the brave Bastard d'Auzan who by loytering something too long in a little house by the church was unfortunately lost.

In the interim of this bustle which continued pretty long, the alarm was carried to Monsieur de Lautrec to Bayonne, together with the news that we were all totally defeated, at which he was exceedingly troubled, in regard of the ill consequences that usually attend the fleshing and giving an enemy blood in the beginning of a war. However he drew out presently into the field, and was advanced but a very little way when he discovered our ensigns of foot conducted by the Sieur de Gramont, marching upon the road towards him, who so soon as he came up, presently gave him an account of what had happened, and did me the honour to tell him that I was the cause of their preservation: but that withall I was lost in the service. Captain Carbon was not yet arrived, forasmuch as he had made a halt to stay for Captain Campai, from him to learn the issue of the business: but in the end he came up also, to whom Monsieur de Lautrec spoke these words.

> Well, Carbon, was this a time wherein to commit such a piece of folly as this? which I do assure you is not of so little moment, but that you have thereby endangered the making me lose this city of Bayonne, which you know to be a place of so great importance.

To which Carbon made answer.

> Sir, I have committed a very great fault, and the greatest folly that ever I was guilty of in my whole life: to this hour the like disgrace has never befallen me; but seeing it has pleased God to preserve us from being defeated, I shall be wiser for the time to come.

Monsieur de Lautrec then demanded of him, if there was any news of me, to which he made answer, that he thought I was lost: but as they were returning softly towards the city in expectation of further news,

Captain Campai also arrived, who assured them that I was come safely off, relating withal the handsom retreat I had made, in despite and in the very teeth of the enemy, with the loss of four men only, and that it was not possible but that the enemy must have lost a great number of men. I was no sooner come to my quarters, but that a gentleman was sent from Monsieur de Lautrec to bring me to him, who entertained me with as much kindness and respect as he could have done any gentleman in the kingdom, saying to me these words in Gascon;

> Montluc mon amie, you a' oublideray jamai lou service qu' abes fait au roy, et m'en seviera tant que you vivrai.

Which is:

> Montluc, my friend, I will never forget the service you have this day performed for the king; but will be mindful of it so long as I live.'

There is as much honour in a handsom retreat as there is in good fighting, and this was a Lord who was not wont to caress many people; a fault that I have often observed in him; nevertheless he was pleased to express an extraordinary favour to me all the time we sate at supper, which he also continued to me ever after, insomuch that calling me to mind four or five years after, he dispatched an express courrier to me from Paris into Gascony with a commission to raise a company of foot, entreating me to bear him company in his expedition to Naples, and has ever since put a greater value upon me, than I deserved. This was the first action I was ever in in the quality of a commander, and from whence I began to derive my reputation.

THE TAKING OF CAPISTRANO AND THE SUBSEQUENT CONSULTATION BETWEEN TWO DOCTORS AND A SURGEON

Now near unto Ascoly there is a little town called Capistrano, seated upon the top of a mountain, of so difficult access that the ascent is very steep on all sides, saving on those of the two gates, into which a great number of the souldiers of the country had withdrawn, and fortified themselves. The Court Pedro de Navarre, who was our collonel, commanded our Gascon companies to attaque this post, which we accordingly did, and assaulted the place. We caused some *marteletts*, (moving pent-houses under the protection of which souldiers use to approach a wall), to be made wherewith to approach the wall, in which we made two holes of capacity sufficient for a man easily to enter in, about fifty or threescore paces distant the one from the other: whereof I having made the one, I would myself needs be the first to enter at that place. The enemy on the other side had in the meantime pulled up the planks and removed the boards and tables from the roof of a parlour into which this hole was made, and where they had placed a great tub full of stones.

One of the companies of Monsieur de Luppé, our Lieutenant Colonel, and mine prepared to enter at this place, and now God had granted me the thing that I had ever desired, which was to be present at an assault there to enter the first man or to lose my life: I therefore threw myself headlong into the parlour, having on a coat of mail, such as the Germans used in those days, a sword in my hand, a *targuette* upon my arm, and a *morrion* upon my head; but as those who were at my heels were pressing to get in after me, the enemy poured the great tub of stones upon their heads, and trapt them in the hole, by reason whereof they could not possibly follow. I therefore remained all alone within, fighting at a door that went out into the street: but from the roof of the parlour, which was unplanked and laid open for that purpose, they peppered me in the meantime with an infinite number of harquebuze shot, one of which pierced my *targuette*, and shot my arm quite through, within four fingers of my hand, and another so battered the bone at the knitting of my arm and shoulder, that I lost all manner of feeling, so that letting my *targuette* fall.

I was constrained to retire towards my hole, against which I was born over by those who fought at the door of the parlour: but so fortunately nevertheless for me, that my souldiers had, by that means, opportunity to draw me out by the legs, but so leisurely withal that they very courteously made me tumble heels over head from the very top to the bottom of the grasse, wherein rowling over the ruines of the stones, I again broke my already wounded arm in two places. So soon as my men had gathered me up, I told them that I thought I had left my arm behind me in the town, when one of my souldiers lifting it up from whence it hung, as in a scarf, dangling upon my buttocks, and laying it over the other, put me into a little heart; after which, seeing the souldiers of my own company gathered round about me. 'Oh my comrades (said I) have I always used you so kindly, and ever loved you so well, to forsake me in such a time as this?' which I said, not knowing how they had been hindered from following me in.

Upon this my lieutenant, who had almost been stifled to death in the hole, called la Bastide (father to the Savillans now living, and one of the bravest gentlemen in our army) proposed to two Basque captains called Martin and Ramonet, who always quartered near unto my company, that if they would with ladders storm by a canton of the wall hard by, he would undertake, at the same time, to enter by the hole itself, and either force his entry that way, or lose his life in the attempt. To which I also encouraged them, as much as my weakness would permit. The ladders being therefore presently brought, and tyed together, because they proved too short, la Bastide made towards the hole, having sent to the other captains to do as much to the other; but they did no great feats. In the interior la Bastide was fighting within, having already gained the hole, Martin and Ramonet gave a brave scalado to the canton, and with so good success, that they beat the enemy from the wall, and entred the town.

Of this being presently advertised, I sent to la Bastide to conjure him to save me as many women and maids as he possibly could, that they might not be violated (having that in devotion for a vow I had made to our Lady of Loretta, hoping that God, for this good act, would please to be assisting to me) which he did; bringing fifteen or twenty, which were also all that were saved; the souldiers being so animated to revenge the wounds I had received, and to express their affection to me, that they killed all before them, so much as to the very children, and moreover set the town on fire. And although the Bishop of Ascoly (this being a member of his diocess) was very importunate with Monsieur de Lautrec in behalf of the town, the souldiers could notwithstanding never be made to leave it till they saw it reduced to ashes.

The next day I was carried to Ascoly, where Monsieur de Lautrec sent Messieurs de Gramont and de Montpezat to see how I did, with whom he moreover sent two chirurgeons the king had given him at his departure, the one called Master Alesme, and the other Master George; who, after they had seen how miserably my arm was mangled and shattered, positively pronounced, that there was no other way to save my life but to cut it off, the execution whereof was deferred till the next morning. Monsieur de Lautrec thereupon commanded the said Sieurs de Montpezat and de Gramont to be present at the work, which they promised they would, but not without some difficulty, out of the friendship they both had for me, especially the Sieur de Gramont. Now you must understand that my souldiers had, a few days before, taken prisoner a young man, a chirurgeon, who had formerly belonged to Monsieur de Bourbon.

This young fellow having understood the determination to cut off my arm (for I had entertained him into my service) never ceased to importune me, by no means to endure it, representing to me that I was not as yet arrived to the one half of my age, and that I would wish myself dead an hundred times a day when I should come to be sensible of the want of an arm. The morning being come, the forementioned lords and the two chirurgeons and physicians came into my chamber with all their instruments and plaisters, without more ceremony, or giving me so much as leisure to repent, to cut off my arm, having in command from Monsieur de Lautrec to tell me that I should not consider the loss of an arm to save my life; nor despair of my fortune; for although His Majesty should not regard my service, nor take it into consideration to settle a subsistence for me, yet that nevertheless his wife and himself had forty thousand *livres* a year revenue wherewith to recompence my valour and to provide that I should never want, only ne wished me to have patience, and to manifest my courage upon this occasion.

Everything being now ready, and my arm going to be opened to be cut off, the young chirurgeon, standing behind my bed's head, never desisted preaching to me by no means to suffer it, insomuch that (as God would have it) though I was prepared and resolved to let them do what they would with me, he made me to alter my determination; whereupon, without doing anything more, both the lords and the chirurgeons returned back to Monsieur de Lautrec to give him an account of the business, who (as they have all of them several times since assured me) said these words.

I am glad to hear he is so resolved, and should also myself have repented the causing of it to be done; for had he dyed, I should ever have suspected myself to have been the occasion of his death; and had he lived without an arm, I should never have looked upon him but with exceeding great trouble, to see him in such a condition; let God therefore work his will.

Immediately after the two forenamed chirurgeons came to examine mine, whether or no he was sufficient to undertake the cure; for otherwise it was ordered that one of them should remain with me; but they found him capable enough, to which they also added some instructions what was to be done upon such accidents as might happen. The next day, which was the fourth after my hurt. Monsieur de Lautrec caused me to be carried after him to Termes de Breffe, where

41

he left me in his own quarters, to the care of the man of the house, who was a gentleman, and for the further assurance of my person carryed hostages with him two of the most considerable men of the town, whereof one was brother to the gentleman of the house, assuring them that if any the least foul play was offered to me those two men should infallibly be hanged. In this place I remained two months and a half, lying continually upon my reins, insomuch that my very back bone pierced through my skin, which is doubtless the greatest torment that anyone in the world can possibly endure; and although I have written in this narrative of my life that I have been one of the most fortunate men that have born arms these many years, in that I have ever been victorious wherever I commanded; yet have I not been exempt from great wounds and dangerous sicknesses, of which I have had as many and as great as any man ever had who outlived them.

God being still pleased to curb my pride, that I might know myself, and acknowledg all good and evil to depend upon his pleasure: but all this notwithstanding a scurvy, sour, morose, and cholerick nature of my own (which savours a little and too much of my native soil) has evermore made me play one trick or another of a Gascon, which also I have no great reason to repent. So soon as my arm was come to a perfect suppuration, they began to raise me out of bed, having a little cushion under my arm, and both that and my arm swathed up close to my body. In this posture I continued a few days longer, until mounting a little mule that I had, I caused myself to be carried before Naples, where our camp was already sate down, having first sent away a gentleman of mine on foot to our Lady of Loretta to accomplish my vow, I myself being in no condition to perform it.

The pain I had suffered was neither so insupportable nor so great as the affliction I had not to have been present at the taking of Malphe and other places; nor at the defeating of the Prince of Orange, who after the death of Monsieur de Bourbon, (slain at the Sack of Rome) commanded the Imperial Army. Had not this valiant prince (of deplorable memory for the foulness of his revolt from his lord and master) dyed in the very height of his victories, I do believe he had sent us back the Popes into Avignon once again.

At my arrival at the camp, Monsieur de Lautrec and all the other great persons of the army received me with great demonstrations of kindness and esteem, and particularly Count Pedro de Navarre, who caused a confiscation to be settled upon me of the value of twelve hundred *duckets* yearly revenue called la Tour de la Nunciade, one of the fairest castles in all the territory of Labour, and the first Barony of Naples, belonging to a rich Spaniard called Don Ferdino. I then thought myself the greatest lord in all the army: but I found myself the poorest rogue in the end, as you shall see by the continuation of this discourse. I could here dilate at full how the Kingdom of Naples was lost, after it was almost wholly conquered, a story that has been writ by many: but it is great pity they would not or durst not relate the truth, being that kings and princes might have been taught to be so wary by this exemple as not to suffer themselves to be imposed upon and abused, as they very often are: but nobody would have the great ones learn to be too wise, for then they could not play their own games with them so well, as they commonly do.

I shall therefore let it alone, both for that I do not pretend to record the faults of other men, as also because I had no hand in these transactions, and shall only write my own fortunes to serve for instruction to such as shall follow after, that the little Montlucs my sons have left me may look with some kind of Glory into the life of their grandfather, and aim at honourable things by his exemple.

The Skirmish of the Maddalena

But to return to the landing of the Prince of Navarre, because there was something of action there performed wherein I had a share, I shall give an account of that business. Captain Artiguelaube (who was colonel of five Gascon Ensigns which were wont to be under Monsieur de Luppée, and of five others commanded by the Baron de Beam) was commanded, as also was Captain de Buch, eldest son of the family of Candale, to draw down to that place, and I also (poor wretch as I was) was one of the number. So soon as we were got down to the shore, the *marquess* left all our pikes behind a great rampire, which the Count Pedro de Navarre had caused to be cast up, and that extended on the right hand and on the left for about half a mile in length. Close adjoyning to this was a great portal of stone, through which ten or twelve men might march a breast, and that I do believe had been a gate in former times, for the arch and other marks thereof were still remaining; to the cheeks of which portal, our rampire was brought up, both on the one side and the other.

Our battaillon was drawn up about an hundred paces distant from this portal, the black regiments some three hundred paces behind ours, and the greatest part of the horse yet further behind them. Monsieur le Marquis, Monsieur le Captau, the Count Hugues, Captain

Artiguelaube, and almost all the captains, as well Italians as Gascons along with them, went down as well to facilitate as to be present at the Princes Landing; which said Seigneur Captau had six ensigns, three of Piedmontoise and three of Gascons. They were so long about their landing that they were staid three long hours; for they made the prince to stay and dine aboard before he came out of the galley: a little delay sometimes occasions a great mischief, and it had been better that both he and all the company with him had made a good sober fast; but the vanity of the world is such that they think themselves undervalued if they do not move in all the formalities of State, and in so doing commit very often very great errors. It were more convenient to move in the equipage of a simple gentleman only, and not to prince it at that rate, but to do well, than to stand upon such frivolous punctillios and be the cause of any misadventure or disorder.

Captain Artiguelaube in the meantime had placed me with three-score or fourscore harquebusiers upon the cross of a high way very near to the Magdaleine, which is a great church some hundred or two hundred paces distant from the gates of Naples; and upon another cross of the highway, on the left hand of me, where there stood a little oratory, two or three hundred harquebusiers of the black regiments, with an ensign of pikes; in the same place also, and a little on the one side, was placed the company of Seigneur de Candale, consisting of two or three hundred harquebusiers, about two hundred paces distant from and just over against the place where I stood. Being thus upon my guard I saw both horse and foot issuing out of Naples, and coming full drive to gain the Magdaleine; whereupon mounting a little mule that I had, I galloped straight down to the water side.

All the lords and gentlemen were as yet on board, caressing and complementing one another, to whom by certain skippers that were plying too and again betwixt the gallies and the shoar I caused it to be cryed out that the enemy was sallying out of the town by whole troops to intercept them and to recover the blind of the Magdaleine, and that they should think of fighting, if they so pleased; an intelligence at which some were basely down in the mouth, for everyone that sets a good face on the matter has no great stomach to fight. I presently returned back to my men, and went up straight to the Magdaleine, from whence I discovered the enemies' horse sallying out dismounted, with the bridles in the one hand and their launces in the other, stooping as much as they could to avoid being seen, as also did the foot, who crept on all four behind the walls that enclosed the backside of the church: I then presently gave my mule to a souldier, bidding him ride in all hast to acquaint Monsieur de Candale and Captain Artiguelaube therewith, whom he found already got on shore, and who upon my first advertisement had caused a galley to put out to sea, from whence they discovered all that I had told them, which being in the port they could not possibly do.

This galley upon the fight presently began to let fly whole broadsides of canon at us, one whereof killed two men of my company close by me, and so near that the brains both of the one and the other flew into my face. There was very great danger in that place, for all the bullets as well of this galley as of the others which did the same played directly into the place where I was, insomuch that seeing them still to continue their shot (for those of the gallies took us for the enemy) I was constrained to draw off my men into the ditches to secure them.

In the meantime they mounted the prince in all hast on horseback and made him to save himself full speed towards the camp, all his gentlemen running after on foot. They had no great leisure to stay with us, for I believe being so lately come they had no mind to dye. Their hast was so great that they had no time to land either the princes baggage or his bed, and there were some who were wise enough to keep themselves aboard the gallies. But the Seigneur de Candale and Count Hugues were men of another sort of mettle, and staid upon the cross high way where their men had been placed before; and Captain Artiguelaube went to the battaillon that was drawn up behind the rampire. The game began with me, and I do not know whether it be my good or my evil fortune but so it is that in all places where I have been that I have evermore found myself in the thickest of the blows and there where the business ever first began.

Now a band of harquebusiers came directly towards me, running: and that because I had placed one part of my harquebusiers behind a ditch bank that borders all along upon the highway, and the rest on the right and left hand in the ditches in file (which I did more for fear of the artillery that plaid from our own gallies than for any apprehension of the enemy) and came within twenty paces of us, where we entertained them with a smart volley of all our shot, by which five or six of their men fell dead upon the ground, and the rest took their heels and fled, we following after as far as the Magdaleine. There they rallyed, and withdrew from the highway on their right hand and on that side where Monsieur de Lavall of Dauphiné stood with his company of *gens-d'armes,* he was nephew to Monsieur de Bayard and

45

father to Madame de Gordes, who is at this time living and a very valiant gentleman.

Monsieur de Candalle, who had seen my charge, and saw that the enemy now all discovered themselves, and that both horse and foot drew into a great meadow where Monsieur de Lavall stood; fearing they might charge me again, he sent me a supply of fifty harquebusiers, just at the time when a battaillon of German foot presented themselves within twenty paces on my right hand. The Spanish harquebusiers in the meantime fired with great fury upon our *gens-d'armes,* who began to draw off at a good round trot towards the high way possessed by Monsieur de Candalle, where there was a great oversight committed, which I will also give an account of, that such as shall read it may take use of the exemple when the chance of war (as at one time or another it may) shall perhaps reduce them to the same condition.

Count Hugues and Monsieur de Candalle had drawn up their pikes upon the great road without leaving room for the cavalry to retire, and there was a necessity that Monsieur de Lavall must, in spite of his heart, pass that way, for betwixt Monsieur de Candalle and me there was a great ditch that horse could not possibly get over. Had they left the road open, and drawn themselves up in battalia behind the ditch, they might have given a stop to the enemies' fury, and by that means Monsieur de Lavall might at great ease have got off along by the high way and have made an honourable retreat.

So soon as the enemy saw that Monsieur de Lavall was forced to his trot they presently charged him both in flank and rear, with both horse and foot at once, when having thrown himself into the road to get clear of this storm, he encountered these pikes upon his way, where he was constrained against his will to force his way thorough, and in so doing bore down and trampled underfoot all that stood before him; for our pikes were drawn up so close that they had no room to open.

This put all into confusion, and I was ready to run mad to see so great an absurdity committed, yet is not the blame justly to be laid upon Monsieur de Candalle, he being very young, and having never been upon such a service before; but Count Hugues is highly to be condemned, who was an old souldier and understood the discipline of war; yet I will not say but that he behaved himself with very great bravery in his own person: but it is not enough to be bold and hardy, a man must also be wise and foresee all that can happen, forasmuch as oversights are irreparable in matters of arms, and small faults are oftentimes the occasion of very great losses, as it happened here to him, who had not provided against all adventures: For he was himself taken prisoner, as also Monsieur de Candalle, being wounded in his arm with a harquebuze shot. Three days after, the enemy seeing he was not likely to live, sent him back to Monsieur de Lautrec, who was his kinsman, and the next day he died and was buried at Bresse.

He was a brave, and a worthy young man as ever came out of the house of Foix, and would in time doubtless have been a great souldier, had he lived to hold on as he had begun. I never knew man so industrious and desirous to learn the practice of arms of the old captains as this lord was. To which effect he rendred himself as obsequious to the Court Pedro de Navarre as the meanest of his servants. He was inquisitive into the reasons of things, and informed himself of all, without fooling away his time about trifles that other young men covet and love: and was more frequent at the quarters of the Court Pedro de Navarre than at those of Monsieur de Lautrec; insomuch that the count would always say he was there training up a great captain. And in truth when he was brought back into the camp, the said count kissed him with tears in his eyes. It was a very great loss to him. All who were at the same post were either killed or taken, some excepted who saved themselves by the ditches, leaping from ditch to ditch, but these were very few, for the enemy pursued their victory on that side very well.

I on my side began to march along by the side of a hedge, with my face still towards the German foot, the lesser evil of the two, and by good fortune both for me and my company, the enemy in my rear pursued us coldly enough. At my coming to the portal I spoke of before, I there found a great troop of the enemies' horse, commanded by Don Ferdinando de Gonzaga (for it was he who gave the charge) so that to recover the portal I must of necessity fight with a resolution either to pass thorough or die. I made my men therefore to give them a volly of harquebuze shot, for I for my part had nothing wherewith to fight but my voice; upon which volly they made me way, so that having passed the portal, I faced about and stood firm.

At which time their harquebusiers also came up, who at once altogether charged upon us with all their united power both of horse and foot; when seeing this torrent coming upon me, I recovered the back side of the trench, with my harquebusiers only, who had saved themselves from the first encounter; which the *marquess* seeing, he was in so great a perplexity that he gave us all over for lost. I there disputed the portal a long half hour from the back side of the trench, for it remained free as well on their side as on ours; they durst not attempt to pass, neither did we dare to approach it. If ever souldiers plaid the men, these did it at this time; for all that I had with me could not arise to above an hundred and fifty men. The *marquess* then came up to Captain Arteguelaube, to make him rise, they being all couched upon one knee, for had they stood upright the Spanish foot had had them in their aim, and cryed to him:

> Captain Arteguelaube, I beseech you rise, and charge, for we must of necessity pass the Portal.

But he returned him answer that he could not do it without losing the best of our men, as it was very true, for all the Spanish foot were then come up. I was close by the portal, and heard all; but the *marquess*, not satisfied with this answer, spurred up to the black regiments, commanding them to march up towards the portal, which they accordingly did. I knew by the manner of their motion what command they had received, which was the reason that I stept out and cried to Captain Arteguelaube;

> Comrade, you are about to be disgraced for ever, for here are the black regiments, that, upon my life, are making towards the portal, to carry away the honour of the service.

At which words he started up (for the man wanted no courage) and ran full drive towards the portal, when seeing him come, I suddenly threw myself before the portal, and passed with all those who followed me, marching straight towards the enemy, who were not above a hundred paces distant from us; we were immediately followed by the foot, sent by the *marquess*: but as we were half passed thorough, the *marquess* gave the word from hand to hand, to make a halt, and to advance no further. The enemy seeing us come on with such resolution, and the cavalry following in our rear, thought it the wisest course to retire. I was by this time advanced where we were plying one another with good round vollies of shot at fifty paces distance, and we had a good mind to fall on to the sword, when the *marquess* and another gentleman with him came himself on horseback to stay me. I think he did ill in it; for had we all passed thorough, we had certainly pursued them fighting up to the very gates of Naples. There was in this place very many on both sides beaten to the ground, that never rose again, and I admire how I escaped, but my hour was not come.

That which occasioned the *marquess* to retire was the fear he had of tempting fortune a second time; he was contented with what he had already lost, without being willing to hazard anymore, so that tired out and over spent, we returned to repass the portal that had been so long disputed, where a great many good men lay dead upon the place. There it was that the gentleman who was with the *marquess*, when he came to command me to retire, I have forgot his name, said to him (for I heard him very well);

> *Monsieur*, I now see that the antient proverb is true, which says that *one man is worth an hundred, and an hundred are not so good as one*: I speak it by this captain who has his arm in a scarf, and leans to the rampire (for in truth I was quite spent), for it must needs be acknowledged, that he is the only cause of our preservation.

I heard likewise well enough, though I took no notice of it, the *marquess* make him this answer. 'That man will always do well wherever he is.' A passage that although it be to my honour and my own commendation I would however insert it here, without bragging nevertheless, or vain glory I have acquired honour enough besides: but this may perhaps serve to excite the other captains, who shall read my life, to do the same upon the like occasion. And I must needs confess that I was then better pleased with this character that this gentleman and the said *marquess* were pleased to give of me, than if he had given me the best *mannor* in his possession, though I was at that time very poor.

This commendation made my heart to swell with courage, and yet more when I was told that someone had entertained Monsieur de Lautrec and the prince with the same discourse all the time they sate at supper. These little points of honour serve very much in matters of war, and are the cause that when a man shall again happen to be in the like service, he fears nothing: it is very true that men are sometimes mistaken, and gain nothing but blows: but there is no remedy for that, we must give and take.

You captains, and lords who lead men on to death (for war is nothing else) when you shall see a brave act performed by any of your fellows, commend him in publick, and moreover relate it to others who were not present at the service: if his heart sit in a right place, he will value such a testimony more than all the treasure of the world, and upon the next occasion will strive to do still better. But if (as too many do) you shall not deign to regard or to take notice of the bravest exploit can by man be performed, and look upon all things with an eye of disdain, you will find that you must recompense them by effects, since you would not vouchsafe to do it by word of mouth. I have ever treated the captains so who have been under my command, and even the meanest of my souldiers; by which they thought themselves so obliged that I could have made them run their heads against a wall, and have stood firm in the most dangerous post in the world as (for exemple) I did here.

The Affair of the Mills of Auriolle

Whilst the emperor lay very long at Aix, in expectation of his great canon, wherewith to come and batter the walls of Marselles, his provisions did every day more and more wast and diminish. In which point of time the king arrived at Avignon, where His Majesty was advertised that if means could be made to destroy some mills the emperor had seized into his hands towards Aries, and especially one within four leagues of Aix, called the mill of Auriolle, the enemies' camp would soon suffer for want of bread. Upon which advice the king committed the execution of the burning of those mills about Aries to the Baron de la Garde, who had a company of foot, to Captain Thorines standard-bearer to the Count de Tandes, and some others, who accordingly executed the design. Which notwithstanding the spies still brought word to the king that he must also burn those of Auriolle; forasmuch as they alone ordinarily nourished not the emperor's whole household only, but moreover the six thousand old Spanish foot which he always kept about his own person. His Majesty sent therefore several times to Messieurs de Barbezieux, and de Montpezat to hazard a regiment of men to go and burn the said Mills of Auriolle.

The first to whom they recommended the execution thereof, was to the foresaid Christophle le Goast, who positively refused to undertake it, alledging that it was five leagues to the aforesaid mills, where they were to fight threescore guards that were within it, and an entire company that were quartered in the town, so that he should have five leagues to go, and as many to return, by means whereof he should going or coming be infallibly defeated upon the way, for the emperor could not fail of intelligence, it being no more than four leagues only from the said Auriolle to Aix; and on the other side the souldiers would never be able to travel ten long leagues without baiting by the way. This answer was sent back to the king, who notwithstanding would not take it for currant pay; but on the contrary sent another more positive order than the former that it should be proposed to some others, and that though a thousand men should be lost in the enterprise, yet let them not concern themselves, for the benefit that would accrue by burning the mills would countervail the loss (such easie markets princes make of the lives of men).

Whereupon it was offered to Monsieur de Fonterailles, who was once in mind to undertake it: but some of his friends representing to him his certain ruine in the attempt, he passed backwards, and would by no means touch. All which being sent word of to His Majesty (who continually had the manifest advantage the destroying of the other mills had brought to His Majesties affaires reminded to him) he still persisted to press the aforesaid lords to send someone or another to demolish these.

Now one day, after I had heard how discontented the king was, and the excuses that had been alledged by those to whom it had hitherto been recommended (which in truth were very rational, and just), I began to meditate with myself which way I might execute this design, and to consider that if God would give me the grace to bring it about, it would be a means to bring me to the knowledg of the king, and to restore me to the same reputation and acquaintance I had formerly acquired; and that now by three years idleness, and the length of my cure, was as good as vanished and lost: for it is nothing to get a good repute if a man do not uphold and improve it.

Having therefore taken with myself a resolution to execute this design, or to die in the attempt: I enformed myself at full of my landlord of the scituation and condition of the place where these mills were; who told me that Auriolle was a little town enclosed with high walls, where there was a castle well-fortified, and a *bourg* composed of many houses, with a fair street thorough the middle of it, and at the end of the said *bourg*, which led from the town towards the mill, was a little on the left hand the mill itself. That at the gate of the said town there was a tower which looked directly down the great street towards the mill, before which no man could stand without running great hazard of being either slain, or wounded; and that beyond the mill was a little church at the distance of about thirty or forty paces. He told me, moreover, that I was to go to Ambaigne, two leagues from Marselles, and that from thence to Auriolle, it was three more if we went by the mountains, which the horse could not possibly do, but must be constrained to go near upon a league about, where they were moreover to pass a river that was deep to the saddle skirts, by reason that the bridges had been broken down.

My landlord having told me all this, I considered that if I should undertake this affair with a great party I should be defeated; for the place being only four leagues distant from the emperor's camp he would have present intelligence, and would send out his horse to intercept me in my return, as it also fell out; for immediately upon our coming to the mill, the captain of the castle dispatched away in all hast to the emperor. So that I conceived it much better for me to undertake it with a small number of men, and those light and active fellows; to the end that if I did the work I went for, I might either have means to retire by one way or another; or at the worst if I should throw myself away, and those who were with me, yet they being but a few, the city of Marselles would by that miscarriage be in no manner of danger to be lost, which was the thing most disputed in the council; whereas by losing a thousand or twelve hundred men, which were thought a necessary proportion for such an enterprise, the said city might be exposed to some danger, especially in a time when they expected a siege.

I then desired my landlord to provide me three fellows, who were expert in the ways, to guide me by night to the said Auriolle, and so that, as near as could be guessed, they should bring me to the mills two hours before day; which he accordingly did, when after having some time consulted with them, I found the men were fearful and loath to go: but at last mine Host so encouraged them that they were all resolved; whereupon I gave to each of them a brace of crowns, and caused them to be kept up in my lodging which was about noon; and having computed with my landlord how many hours the nights were then long, we found that, provided I should set out about the twilight, I should have time enough to do my business.

All this being done, that my design might not be known, I went myself first to Monsieur de Montpezat to acquaint him with what I intended to do; and moreover that I was resolved to take with me no more than six score men only, which I would choose out of the *seneschall's* regiment, to which I was lieutenant colonel. In all places wherever I have been I have still made it my study to discern betwixt the good men and the bad, and to judg what they were able to do; for all men are not proper for all uses.

The said Sieur de Montpezat thought my resolution very strange, and out of friendship advised me not to do so ridiculous a thing as to hazard myself with so few men; telling me that I might as well have five hundred if I would. To which I made answer that I would never demand five hundred men for the execution of an enterprise that I could better perform with six score, and tormented him so that in the end he was constrained to go along with me to Monsieur de Barbezieux who yet thought it more strange than the other, and would needs know of me my reasons and by what means I would execute this design with so few people. To whom I made answer that I would not declare to anyone living which way I intended to proceed: but that nevertheless (if they so pleased) I would undertake it. Whereupon Monsieur de Montpezat said to him, 'let him go; for though he should be lost, and all those with him, the city will not for that be in the more danger to be lost, and it will give His Majesty content.'

Monsieur de Villebon who was present at the deliberation, laughed and jeered at me, saying to Monsieur de Barbezieux, 'let him go, he will infallibly take the emperor, and we shall all be ashamed, when we see him bring him into the city tomorrow morning.'

Now this man did not love me for some words that had passed betwixt us at the Port Royal; neither could I forbear to tell him that he was like a dog in a manger, that would neither eat himself nor suffer others. All was passed over in jest, though in plain truth I was half angry, for a little spurring would serve to make me start. The Seneschal de Tholouse, my colonel, adheared to my opinion, whereupon I had immediate leave granted me to go choose out my six score men and no more, which I did, taking only one centenier, and a corporal, the rest were all gentlemen and so brave a company that they were better than five hundred others.

It is not all to have a great number of men, they sometimes do more hurt than good, which made me entreat Monsieur de Barbezieux to cause the gate of the city to be shut, being well assured that otherwise I should have had more company that I desired; which he also did, and it hapned well for another reason, for in less than an hour my design was spread all over the whole city.

Just at sunset, I, with my six score men, repaired to the gate, the wicket whereof was only open: but the street was so full of souldiers ready to go out with me, that I had much ado to distinguish my own, and was therefore constrained to make them all take hands, for I very well knew them everyone. As I was going out of the gate, Monsieur de Tavannes (who was since Mareschal of France, and at this time standard-bearer to the Grand Escuyer Galliot) came to me with fifteen or twenty gentlemen of their own company, telling me that he with those friends of his were come to offer themselves, resolved to run all hazards with me in the execution of my design.

I used all the arguments I could to divert him from that resolution: but it was time and labour lost; for both he and those with him were all positively resolved. Messieurs de Barbezieux, de Montpezat, de Boitieres, de Villebon, and the Seneschal de Tholouse, were all without the gate and before the wicket, drawing us out one by one, when Monsieur de Tavannes, offering to pass Monsieur de Barbezieux would not permit him, telling him that he should be none of the party, and there some words and a little anger passed, both on one side and the other: but Monsieur de Tavannes overcame at last, and passed the wicket; for which cause they detained from me fifteen or twenty men of those I had chosen: but I lost nothing by the exchange, only these disputes deferred the time so long that the night was shut up before we began to march.

Monsieur de Castelpers, lieutenant to Monsieur de Montpezat (who was my very particular friend) having heard how I had been railled and jeered amongst them, determined to get to horse, with some fifteen or twenty men at arms of the said company, being all very well mounted, and to that end had spoken to Monsieur de Montpezat at his going out of the gate, to entreat him that he would not be displeased if he made one in the enterprise; telling him that I was a Gascon, and that if I failed in the attempt, it would beget matter of sport for the French, and they would laugh us to scorn. Monsieur de Montpezat was at first unwilling to it, but seeing him begin to grow into a little heat, at last consented, whereupon he presently ran to mount to horse, and there might be nineteen or twenty of the party.

Now to give a full account of this enterprise (which although it was not the conquest of Millan, may nevertheless be of some use to such as will make their advantage of it), so soon as we came to the Plan St Michel, I gave to Captain Belsoleil (centenier to our company) threescore men; and threescore I kept for myself (Monsieur de Tavannes and his followers being comprised in that number) to whom I also delivered a good guide, telling him withal that he was not to come near me by a hundred paces, and that we would continually march at a good round rate.

Which order being given, and Monsieur de Tavannes and I beginning to set forward, up comes Monsieur de Castelpers, of whose deliberation we till then knew nothing, forasmuch as it had been resolved upon at the very moment of our going out at the wicket, which hindred us another long half hour: but in the end we agreed, that he should go the horse way, and gave him another of my guides, which he mounted behind one of his men; so that we had three parties, and to every party a guide.

At our parting I gave him instructions that so soon as he should arrive at the end of the *bourg*, he should draw up behind the church, for should they enter into the street the company quartered in the town would either kill them or their horses; and that therefore he was not to appear till first he heard us engaged. We now began to set forward, and marched all night, where as far as Aubaigne we found the way to be exceeding good: but from thence to Auriolle we were fain to crawl over the sides of mountains, where, I believe, never anything but goats had gone before: by which abominable way having got within half a quarter of a league of Auriolle, I made a halt, bidding Monsieur de Tavannes to stay there for me, for I must go speak with Belsoleil.

I therefore went back, and met him within a hundred paces of us, or less; where speaking to him and his guide, I told him that when he should arrive at the *bourg* he was by no means to follow me, but to march directly to the gate of the town, betwixt the *bourg* and the said town, and there make a stand at the gate, it being necessary that he should gain two houses next adjoyning to the said gate, which he must suddainly break into, to keep the enemy from sallying out to disturb us; and that there he was to stay and fight, without taking any care to relieve us at all; after which order given to him, I moreover past the word from hand to hand to all the souldiers, that no one was to abandon the fight at the gate to come to us to the mill; but that they were punctually to observe whatever Captain Belsoleil should command them.

Returning then back to Monsieur de Tavannes, we again began to march, when being come near to the castle, under which and close by the walls of the town we were of necessity to pass, their centinels twice called out to us, Who goes there? to which we made no answer at all, but still went on our way, till coming close to the *bourg*, we left the way that Captain Belsoleil was to take, and slipt behind the houses of the said *bourg*, when being come to the further end where the mill stood, we were to descend two or three stone steps to enter into the street, where we found a centinel, that never discovered us, till we were within a pike's length of him, and then he cryed out 'Qui vive?' to which I would answer in Spanish 'Espagne,' (wherein I was mistaken, for the word was not *Espagne* but *Impery*) whereupon without more ceremony he gave fire; but hit nothing.

The alarm being by this means given, Monsieur de Tavannes and I threw ourselves desperately into the street, and were bravely followed, where we found three or four of the enemy without the door of the mill: but they immediately ran in. The door of this mill was made with two folding leaves, both of which were to be bolted fast with a great iron bar on the inside; one of these had a great chest behind it, and the other the foresaid bar held more than half shut, and had these fellows behind it. The mill was full of men, both above stairs and below (for there was threescore men in it, with the captain, who had no dependence upon the governor of the town, each of them having his command apart), and we were one by one to enter this place.

Monsieur de Tavannes would very fain first have entered, and pressed forward with that intent; but I pulling him back by the arm, withheld him, and pushed in a souldier that was behind me: the enemy made but two harquebuze shot, having leisure to do no more, being all fast asleep, excepting these three or four who had been placed as centinels before the mill door in the street. So soon as the souldier was got in, I said to Monsieur de Tavannes, now enter if you will; which he presently did, and I after him, where we began to lay about us to some purpose, there being no more but one light only to fight by within.

In this bustle, the enemy, by a pair of stone stairs of indifferent wideness, recovered the upper room, where they stoutly defended the said stairs from the floor above, whilst I in the meantime sent a souldier to tell the rest that were without that they should get up upon the outside of the mill, and uncovering the roof, shoot down upon their heads, which was immediately performed; so that the enemy, perceiving our men to be got upon the roof, and that they already let fly amongst them, they began to throw themselves into the water out of a window on the backside of the mill: but we nevertheless mounted the stairs and killed all those that remained, the captain excepted, who with two wounds, and seven others all wounded, were taken prisoners. Hereupon I presently sent one away to Captain Belsoleil, to bid him take courage and stoutly to dispute the gate of the town, for the mill was our own.

The alarm in the meantime in the town was very great, and those within three times attempted to sally: but our men held them so short that they durst never open their gates. I sent Captain Belsoleil moreover most of my men to assist him, and in the meantime, with the rest, fell to burning the mill, taking away all the iron work, especially the spindles and rinds, that it might not be repaired again, never leaving it till it was entirely burnt down to the ground, and the mill-stones rowled into the river. Now you must know that Captain Tavannes took it a little to heart that I had pulled him back by the arm, and asked me afterwards upon our returne why I would not permit him to enter the first, suspecting I had more mind to give the honour of it to the souldiers: to whom I made answer that I knew he was not yet so crafty to save himself as those old souldiers were; and that, moreover, that was not a place considerable enough for a man of his worth and condition to dye in; but that he was to reserve himself for a noble breach, and not to lose his life in a paltry mill.

Whilst these things were in doing, Monsieur de Castelpers arrived, and leaving his party behind the church, came up to us on foot, and upon this the day began to appear: wherefore I entreated Monsieur de Tavannes and de Castelpers to retire behind the church (for the shot flew very thick in the street where they could see anyone pass) telling them that I would go draw off Belsoleil; whereupon they both accordingly retired, and as I was drawing off, our men one after another running down on both sides the street, Monsieur de Castelpers presented himself with his twenty horse at the end of the street by the church, wherein he did us very great service, for the enemy might otherwise have sallyed out upon us.

I had only seven or eight men hurt, who nevertheless were all able to march, one gentleman only excepted, called Vigaux, whom we set upon an ass of those we had found in the mill, and presently began to retire towards the top of a mountain, which was almost the same way by which Monsieur de Castelpers had come, when the enemy discovering us to be so few, they all sallyed out in our rear; but we had already gained the top of the hill when they arrived but at the foot of it, and before they recovered the height we were got into the valley on the other side, ready to climb another (there being many little hills in that place), and yet we never marched faster than a foot pace; and so went straight on to Aubaigne.

I had given order to the souldiers that went along with us, that everyone should take with him a loaf of bread, which they eat by the way, and I also had caused some few to be brought, which I divided amongst the *gens-d'armes* of Monsieur de Tavannes, and we ourselves eat as we went; which I here set down to the end that when any captain shall go upon an enterprise, where he is to have a long march, he may take exemple to cause something to be brought along to eat, wherewith to refresh the souldiers, that they may be the better able to hold out; for men are not made of iron.

So soon as we were come to Aubaigne, two leagues from Marselles, where we had thought to have halted, and to have taken some refreshment, we heard the artillery of the gallies and of the town, which at that distance seemed to be volleys of harquebuzeshot; an alarm that constrained us without further delay or taking away other refreshment than what we had brought along with us, to march forwards, and to enter into consultation amongst ourselves what course we were best to take; we already took it for granted that the emperor was arrived before the town, and that he would certainly sit down before it; and thence concluded it impossible for us to get in again, which made us often repent, and curse the enterprise that had shut us out, the misfortune whereof was wholly laid to my charge, as the author of all. In this uncertainty what course to steer, Monsieur de Castelpers was once resolved to go charge desperately through the enemy's camp, to get into the city.

But when he came to acquaint us with his determination, we remonstrated to him that that would be to throw himself away out of an humour, and that since we had together performed so brave a service, and with which the king would be so highly pleased, we ought likewise together either to perish, or to save ourselves. Captain Trebous, guidon to the company of Monsieur de Montpezat, told him the same, so that we concluded in the end to leave the great high way, and crossing the mountains on the left hand, to fall down behind Nostre Dame de la Garde, making account that in case we could not enter into the city the captain of the said cittadel would receive us in there.

So we turned out of the way, and it was well for us that we did so, for Vignaux and les Bleres keeping on the great road straight to Marselles had not gone on five hundred paces, but they met with four or five hundred horse, which the emperor (having had intelligence from those of Auriolle of what had been done) had sent out to meet and fight us upon the way; and had not the emperor parted from Aix by night to go before Marselles, so that the messengers of a long time could meet with no body to whom to deliver their errand, I do believe we had certainly been defeated: but the emperor knew nothing of it till break of day, whereupon he presently sent out those four or five hundred horse upon the road to Aubaigne, who did no other harm to Vignaux and those who were with him, but only took away their arms.

In this manner we travailed all day from mountain to mountain in the excessive heat, without finding one drop of water, insomuch that we were are all ready to dye for thirst; always within sight of the emperor's camp, and ever within hearing of the skirmishes that were made before the town, Monsieur de Castelpers and his *gens-d' armes* marching all the way on foot, as we did, and leading their horses in their hands, till coming near to Nostre Dame de la Garde, the captain of the castle, taking us for the enemy, let fly three or four pieces of canon at us, which forced us to shift behind the rocks. From thence we made signs with our hats; but for all that he ceased not to shoot, till in the end, having sent out a souldier to make a sign, so soon as he understood who we were, he gave over shooting; and as we came before Nostre Dame de la Garde, we saw the emperor, who was retiring by the way he came, and Christophle Goast, who had all day maintained the skimish, beginning also to retreat towards the city.

We then began to descend the mountain, when so soon as Monsieur de Barbezieux, and Monsieur de Montpezat (who, with some other captains, were standing without the gates of the city) had discovered us, they would have gone in again, taking us for the enemy; but somebody saying that then those of the castle would have shot at us, the said Sieur de Montpezat presently knew Monsieur de Castelpers; and we thereupon arrived at the gate of the city, where we were mightily caressed, especially when they heard of the good success of our enterprise, and they talked with the captain of the mill, who was wounded in the arm and in the head, and after everyone retired to his own quarters.

I made no manner of question, but that Monsieur de Barbezieux, so soon as the king should come to Marselles, would have presented me to His Majesty, and have told him that I was the man who had performed this exploit, that His Majesty might have taken notice of me: but he was so far from doing me that friendship, that on the contrary he attributed all the honour to himself, saying that it was he who had laid the design of this enterprise, and had only delivered it to us to execute; and Monsieur de Montpezat was by ill fortune at that time very sick, and could say nothing in my behalf, so that I remained as much a stranger to the king as ever. I came to know all this by the means of Henry, King of Navarre, who told me that he himself had seen the letters which the said Sieur de Barbezieux had writ to the king to that effect, wherein he attributed to himself the whole honour of that action.

Monsieur de Lautrec would not have served me so; neither is it handsom to rob another man of his honour; and there is nothing that does more discourage a brave heart: but Monsieur de Tavannes, who is now living, can testfie the truth. So it is, that the destroying of the mills, both the one and the other, especially those of Auriolle, reduced the emperor's camp to so great necessity that they were fain to eat the corn pounded in a mortar, after the manner of the Turks, and the grapes they ate put their camp into so great a disorder and brought so great a mortality amongst them, especially the Germans, that I verily believe there never returned a thousand of them into their own country, and this was the issue of this mighty preparation.

The captains who shall read this relation, may perhaps observe that in this enterprise there was more of fortune than of reason, and that I went upon it as it were in the dark, though it was happily brought about: but I do not suspect, however, that anyone will conclude it to be wholly an effect of my good fortune, but will also take notice that I forgot nothing of what was necessary to make the design succeed; and on the other side they may observe, that my principal security was that the enemy within the town by the rule of war, ought not to sally out of their garrison till they should first discover what our forces were, a thing in the obscurity of the night which they could very hardly do, all which notwithstanding, I did not yet so much rely upon their discretion but that I moreover put a bridle in their mouths, which was Belsoleil and his company. A man must often hazzard something, for no one can be certain of the event. I concluded the conquest of the mill for certain: but I ever thought it would be a matter of great difficulty and danger to retreat.

A Notable Enterprise Carried on by a Merchant and its Results

Sometime after Monsieur de Termes carryed on an enterprise that was never discovered to any but to Monsieur Boitieres and myself, not so much as to Monsieur de Tais, though he was our colonel; and it was thus. There was a merchant of Barges, a great friend and servant to Monsieur de Termes, and a good Frenchman, called Granuchin, who, coming from Barges to Savillan, was taken by some light horse belonging to Count Pedro d'Apporte, governor of Fossan, and being a prisoner was sometimes threatened to be hanged; and sometimes promised to be put to ransom, with so great uncertainty that the poor man for seven or eight days together was in despair of his life: but in the end he bethought himself to send word to the count that if he would be pleased to give him leave to talk with him he would propound things that should be both for his advantage and his honour. The count thereupon sent for him, where, being come, Granuchin told him that it should only stick at himself if he were not lord of Barges, for that it was in his power to deliver up the castle into his hands, the city not being strong at all.

The count greedy to listen to this enterprise, presently closed with him about it, agreeing and concluding, that Granuchin should deliver up his wife and his son in hostage; and the said Granuchin proposed the manner of it to be thus; saying that he was very intimate with the captain of the castle, and that the provisions that were put into it ever passed through his hands, and that moreover he had a share in some little traffick they had betwixt them, to wit, betwixt the said captain of the castle, called la Mothe, and himself; and that the Scotchman who kept the keys of the castle was his very intimate friend, whom he also evermore had caused to get something amongst them, and whom he was certain he could make firm to his purpose; not the Captain de la Mothe nevertheless; but that he was sick of a quartan ague that held him fifteen or twenty hours together; so that he almost continually kept his bed.

And that so soon as he should be at liberty he would go and complain to Monsieur de Termes of two men that were reputed Imperialists, who had told him, and given the enemy intelligence of his journey, and that after having left his wife and his son in hostage he would go and demand justice of Monsieur de Boitieres, by the mediation of Monsieur de Termes. And then would go to Barges to the castle, and that upon a Sunday morning he would cause fifteen or twenty souldiers that la Mothe had there, to go out (leaving only the Scotchman, the butler, and the cook within) to take those who had told him, as they should be at the first Mass in the morning, and in the meantime the count should cause forty souldiers to march, who before day should place themselves in ambush in a little copse about an harquebuze shot distant from the postern gate, and that so soon as it should be time for them to come, he would set a white flag over the said postern.

Now there was a priest of Barges, who being banished thence, lived at Fossan, that was a great friend to Granuchin, and had laboured very much for his deliverance, and he also was called into the council, where amongst them it was concluded, that the said priest on a night appointed should come to a little wood the half way betwixt Barges and Fossan, where he was to whistle, to give notice that he was there, and that if he had corrupted the Scot, he should bring him along with him, to resolve amongst themselves how the business should be further carried on.

Things being thus concluded, Granuchin writ a letter to Monsieur de Termes, wherein he entreated him to procure for him a safe-conduct from Monsieur de Boitieres that his wife and his son might come to Fossan, there to remain pledges for him, for he had prevailed so far by the intercession of certain of his friends, that the count was at last content to dismiss him upon a ransom of six hundred crowns; but that if he was not abroad, and at liberty, no man would buy his goods, out of which he was to raise that sum; which safe-conduct if he should obtain in his behalf, he desired he would please to deliver it to a friend of his he named in Savillan, to whom he also had writ to desire him to make what hast he could to send his wife and son to the said Fossan.

All this being accordingly procured and done, and the said Granuchin set at liberty, he forthwith came to Savillan to find out Monsieur de Termes, to whom he gave an account of the whole business. Whereupon Monsieur de Termes (who already began to feel himself falling sick of a disease that commonly held him fourteen or fifteen days at a time) sent for me, to whom he communicated the enterprise, where it was by us all three concluded that Granuchin should go talk with Monsieur de Boitieres and inform him at large of the whole design. To which purpose Monsieur de Termes gave him a letter to Monsieur de Boitieres, who, having received and read it, made no great matter of the business, only writing back to Monsieur de Termes that if he knew Granuchin to be a man fit to be trusted he might do as he thought fit.

By which slight answer Monsieur de Termes entered into an opinion that Monsieur de Boitieres would be glad he should receive some baffle or affront, (and indeed he did not much love him) which made him once in mind to break off the design and to meddle no more in it: but seeing the said Granuchin almost in despair to think that the business should not go forward, and I being more concerned than he that such an opportunity of trapping the enemy should be lost, earnestly entreated Monsieur de Termes to leave the whole business to my care; which he made great difficulty to grant, ever fearing that should anything happen amiss. Monsieur de Boitieres would do him a courtesie to the king, as the custom is: for when any one bears a man a grudge he is glad when he commits any oversight, that the master may have occasion to be offended and to remove him from his command; condemning him for that he would not be governed by the wise: but in the end, with much importunity, he was content to refer the management of the business wholly to my discretion.

The said Granuchin departed then to go to Barges, where he made discovery of all to Captain la Mothe and the Scotchman, to whom Monsieur de Termes writ also, and the night appointed being come, they both went out, and alone (for Granuchin was very well acquainted with the way) and came to the wood, where they found the priest; with whom they agreed, first that that the said count should acquit Granuchin of his ransom, giving him as much as the souldiers that took him had taken from him, and moreover appoint him an apartment in the castle with the captain he should put into it, with a certain pension for his support; and secondly that he should marry the Scotchman to an inheritrix there was in Barges, and also find out some handsom employment for him, forasmuch as he was never after to return either into Scotland, or into France. All which was agreed and concluded betwixt them, and moreover that the priest should bring all these articles signed and sealed with the arms of the said count to a summer house in the fields belonging to the brother of the said priest, to which he sometimes repaired at nights; and that the Sunday following the business should be put in execution.

Having accordingly received all these obligations, Granuchin returned again to Savillan, where he gave us an account of all, and shewed us the bond. Now there was only three days to Sunday, wherefore we made him presently to return, having first agreed that he should bring along with him two guides of the very best he could find out; not that he should however discover anything to them of the business, but only shew them some counterfeit letters, wherein mention should be made of some wine he had bought for me.

The guides came accordingly by Saturday noon to Savillan, when, seeing them come, I took Captain Favas my lieutenant apart, and privately in my chamber communicated to him the whole design, telling him withal that I had made choice of him for the execution of it; which he made no scruple to undertake (for he had mettle enough) and it was agreed that he should tye the guides together, and that they were by no means to enter into any highway or road, but to march cross the fields. We had much ado to persuade the guides to this, forasmuch as they were to pass three or four rivers, and there was snow and ice all along, so that we were above three hours disputing this way:

but in the end the two guides were content, to each of which I gave ten crowns and moreover a very good supper.

We were of advice that we should not take many men that less notice might be taken; and at that time we were making a rampire at that gate towards Fossan, where, in order to that work, we had broken down a little part of the wall and made a bridge over the grasse, over which to bring in earth from without. By this breach I put out Captain Favas, and with him four an thirty more only, and so soon as we were without, we tyed the guides for being lost, and so he set forwards. Now the enemies' assignation and ours was at the same hour; so that Granuchin had directed them the way on the right hand to come to this copse, and ours he had ordered to march on the left hand, near to the walls of the city; who, so soon as they were come to the postern, there found Granuchin and the Scot ready to receive them, it being the hour that the Scotchman used to stand centinel over the said postern, so that they were never discovered, and he disposed them into a cellar of the castle, where he had prepared a charcoal fire, with some bread and wine.

In the meantime the day began to break, and as the bell rung to low Mass in the town, the Scot and Granuchin commanded all the souldiers in the castle to go take these two men (that Granuchin had accused to have betrayed him) at Mass, so that there remained no more in the castle but only la Mothe himself, his *valet de chambre*, who also trayled a pike, the butler, the cook, the Scotchman, and Granuchin.

The Scot then pulled up the bridge, and called out Captain Favas, making him to skulk behind certain bavins in the base court, kneeling upon one knee, which being done, they went to set up the white flag upon the postern; soon after the priest arrived, and with him about forty souldiers, who were no sooner entered in, but the Scotchman shut the gate, and at the same instant Captain Favas and his company flew upon them, who made some little resistance, insomuch that seven or eight of them were slain; but Granuchin saved the priest, and would not endure he should have the least injury offered to him.

In the meantime a country fellow, as he was coming from a little house below the castle, saw the Spanish souldiers with their red crosses enter in at the postern gate, and thereupon ran down into the town to give the alarm, and to tell them that the castle was betrayed; at which news, the souldiers who had been sent out to take the two men at Mass would have returned into the castle; but ours shot at them, though so high as not to hit them, taking upon them to be enemies, and crying out *'Imperi, Imperi, Savoy, Savoy,'* which was the reason that the souldiers fled away to Pignerol carrying news to Monsieur de Boitieres, that Granuchin had betrayed the castle and that the enemy was within it.

Monsieur de Boitieres thereupon in a very great fury, dispatched away a courrier to Monsieur de Termes, who lay sick in his bed, and almost distracted at the disaster, often crying out, 'Ah Monsieur Montluc you have ruined me, would to God I had never hearkened to you': and in this error we continued till the Wednesday following. In the meantime the souldiers who had entered were claped up in the cellar, my souldiers taking the red crosses, and moreover setting up a white flag with a red cross upon a tower of the castle, and crying out nothing but *'Imperi, Imperi.'*

Things being in this posture, Granuchin immediately made the priest to subscribe a letter, wherein he had writ to the count that he should come and take possession of the town and castle, for that Granuchin had kept his word with him, and then sent for a labourer, who was tenant to the brother of the said priest, to whom he caused the letter to be given by the priest himself, saying and swearing to him, that if he made any kind of sign, either in giving the letter or otherwise, that he would presently kill him; making him moreover deliver several things to the messenger by word of mouth.

The fellow went away, and upon a mare of his own made all the haste he could to Fossan, it being but twelve miles only, immediately upon whose coming the count resolved that night to send away a corporal of his called Janin, with five and twenty of the bravest men of all his company, who about break of day arrived at Barges.

So soon as he came to the castle, Granuchin, the priest, and the Scot were ready to let him in at the foresaid postern, whilst Captain Favas went to plant himself behind the bavins as before, although Granuchin was something long in opening the gate, both because he would clearly see and observe whether the priest made any sign, and also for that he had a mind those of the city should see him enter; when so soon as it was broad day, he opened the postern, telling them that the souldiers who came in with the priest were laid to sleep, being tired out with the long labour they had susteined the day before, and so soon as they were all in, the Scot suddainly claped to the gate, and as suddainly Captain Favas start up, and fell upon them without giving them time, saving a very few, to give fire to their harquebuzes, as ours did who had them all ready; nevertheless they defended themselves with their swords, so that six of mine were hurt, and fifteen or sixteen of this company were slain upon the place, of which Corporal Janin was one (which was a very great misfortune to us) together with a brother of his, the rest were led into the cellar tyed two and two together, for there were already more prisoners in the castle than souldiers of our own.

Now this fight continuing longer than the former, the enemy in fighting still cryed out '*Imperi*' and ours '*France*'; insomuch that their cries reached down into the city, and especially the rattle of the harquebuze shot, so that to avoid being so soon discovered, their design being to train the count thither (for to that end tended all the farce) they all got upon the walls of the castle and from thence cryed out '*Imperi*' and '*Savoy*,' having on their red crosses as I said before.

Now the country fellow that had been sent with the letter to the count did not return with those men up to the castle but staid at his master's country house by the way, wherefore he was again suddainly sent for, and another letter delivered to him by the hands of the priest to carry to the said count to Fossan, wherein he gave him to understand that Corporal Janin was so weary he could not write but that he had given him in charge to render him an account of all, and that he was laid down to sleep.

So soon as the count had read this letter he put on a resolution to go, not the next day which was Tuesday, but the Wednesday following (when God intends to punish us he deprives us of our understandings, as it happened here in the case of this gentleman). The count in the first place was reputed one of the most circumspect (and as wise as valiant) leaders they had in their whole army, which notwithstanding he suffered himself to be gulled by two letters from this priest, especially the last which he ought by no means to have relyed upon; nor to have given credit to anything, without having first seen something under his corporal's own hand, and should have considered whether or no it were a plausible excuse to say that the said corporal was laid down to sleep. But we are all blind when we have once set our hearts upon anything of moment. Believe me, gentlemen, you that are great undertakers of enterprises, you ought maturely to consider all things, and weigh every the least circumstance, for if you be subtle, your enemy may be as crafty as you.

A trompeur trompeur et demy, says the Proverb, *Harm watch harm catch.* And *The cunninget snap may meet with his match.* But that which most of all deceived the count was that the Tuesday those of the town who thought themselves to be become Imperialists, and yet in some doubt by reason of the various cries they had heard during the fight, had sent five or six women to the castle under cover of selling cakes, apples, and chesnuts, to see if they could discover anything of treason (for all those that remained in the town had already taken the red cross); whom so soon as our people saw coming up the hill, they presently suspected their business, and resolving to set a good face on the matter, went to let down the little draw bridge to let them in.

My souldiers then fell to walking up and down the base court with their red crosses, all saving three or four that spake very good Spanish, who fell to talk with the women, and bought some of their wares, taking upon them to be Spaniards, insomuch that they afterwards returning to the town, assured the inhabitants that there was no deceit in the business: and moreover brought a letter which la Mothe writ to a friend in the town, wherein he entreated him to go to Monsieur de Boitieres, and to tell him that he had never consented to Granuchin's treachery; which letter he delivered to one of the women, knowing very well that the party to whom it was directed was not there to be found; but would be one of the first to run away, as being a very good French man: but their design was that the letter should fall into the hands of those of the Imperial party, as according it did.

As the count was coming on Wednesday morning, our people in the castle discovered him marching along the plain, and the people of the town went to meet him without the gate, where being come, he asked them if it were certainly true that the castle was in his hands, to which they made answer, that they believed it so to be: but that at the entrance of his men the first time, there were a great many harquebuzes shot off within, and a very great noise was made: and that on the Monday morning, when the others entered, they likewise heard a very great noise that continued longer than the former, and that they once thought they heard them cry one while 'France', and another 'Imperi' and 'Duco': but that notwithstanding they had yesterday sent their wives into the castle with fruit, bunns, and chesnuts, whom they had permitted to enter, where they saw all the souldiers with red crosses.

The count hearing this, commanded his lieutenant to alight, and to refresh his horses and men, bidding those of the town speedily get something ready for him to eat; for so soon as he had taken order in the castle, he would come down to dinner, after which he would take their Oath of Fidelity, and so return back again to Fossan. Now you must know it is a very steep and uneasy ascent from the town to the

67

castle, by reason whereof the count alighted, and walked up on foot, accompanied with a nephew of his, another gentleman, and his trumpet, so soon as he came to the end of the bridge, which was let down, and the gate shut, but the wicket left open, so that a man might easily pass, and lead his horse after him.

Granuchin and the priest being above in the window, saluting him, desired him to enter; to which nevertheless he made answer that he would advance no further till he had first spoken with Corporal Janin; seeing then that he refused to enter, Granuchin in his hearing said to the priest (to get him from thence) 'Pray Father go down, and tell Corporal Janin that my lord is at the gate, where he stays to speak with him,' and at the same time himself also departed from the window, pretending to go down; whereupon Captain Favas and his souldiers ran to open the gate, which was only bolted, and all on a suddain leaped upon the bridge.

Seeing this, the count who was one of the most active men of all Italy, and who held his horse by the bridle (the best one of them that ever that country bred and which I afterwards gave to Monsieur de Tais) vaulted over a little wall which was near to the bridge, drawing his horse after him, with intent to have leaped into the saddle (for their was no horse so tall (provided he could lay his hand upon the pummel) but he could armed at all pieces, vault into the seat) but he was prevented by the Bastard of Bazordan, called Janot (yet living and then of my company) who by misfortune being he either could not or would not get over the wall to lay hands upon him, let fly at him an harquebuze.

Which taking the default of his arms, went into his belly, piercing thorough his bowels almost to the other side, of which shot he sunk down to the ground. Captain Favas took his nephew, and another the trumpet, but the other gentleman escaped down the hill, crying out that the count was either killed or taken; whereupon the lieutenant and all his company skutled to horse in so great a fright that they never looked behind them till they came to Fossan. Had it so fallen out that Janin at the second entry had not been slain, they had not only snaped the count, and by degrees all his whole troop (for they might have compelled him to have spoke to them, with a dagger at his reins ready to stab him should he make a sign), but moreover might perhaps from hence have spun out some contrivance against Fossan itself; for one enterprise draws on another.

These things being done, they in the evening dispatched away Captain Milhas (a gentleman of my company) to bring me the news, and to relate to me from point to point how all things had passed; together with a letter from the said count, wherein he entreated me, seeing he was my prisoner, and that greater advantage was to be made of his life than of his death, to do him the courtesie as to send him with all speed a physician, a chirurgeon, and an apothecary. Captain Milhas arrived just at the time that they opened the gates of the city, so that he found me putting on my cloaths, and there related to me the whole business, thereby delivering me from the great anxiety, and trouble wherein from Sunday till Wednesday I had continually remained; for though I was really concerned for the place, yet was I much more afflicted for the loss of my lieutenant and my souldiers, who were most of them gentlemen and all very brave men. Immediately upon the news, I ran to Monsieur de Termes his lodgings, whom I found sick a bed: but I dare say that neither he nor I were ever so overjoyed; for we both very well knew that had it fallen out otherwise there were rods in piss.

So soon as I departed from him, I presently sent away a phisician, a chirurgeon, and an apothecary, whom I mounted upon three horses of my own for the more speed; neither did they either stop or stay until they came thither: but it was impossible to save him, for he died about midnight, and was brought to Savillan, whom everyone had a desire to see, even Monsieur de Termes himself as sick as he was, and he was very much lamented by all.

The next day I sent the body to Fossan, but deteined the nephew and trumpet with the rest that were taken prisoners at Barges, until they should send me back the wife and son of the said Granuchin, which the next day they did, and I also delivered up all the prisoners.

I beseech you, captains, you who shall see and hear this relation, to consider whether or no this was a stratagem for a merchant; believe me, the oldest captain would have been puzzled, and have had enough to do to carry it on with so much dexterity and resolution as he did; wherein although Captain Favas was the performer of it when it came to execution, nevertheless the merchant was not only the original contriver, but also a principal actor throughout the whole business, having the heart, in order to his revenge, to expose his wife and son to the extreamest danger.

In reading of which (fellows in arms) you may learn diligence with temper, and take notice what sleights and policies were used and continued for the space of four days together, such as no man either of theirs (or which is more, of our own) could possibly discover, both parties being held equally suspended. The count, for a prudent cavalier, behaved himself herein with very great levity, especially upon the second letter; but he repaired his fault when he refused to enter the castle without first seeing his man; though that caution signified nothing as it fell out.

Whenever therefore you design an enterprise, weigh everything, and never go handover head; and without precipitating yourselves, or being too easie of beliefe upon light foundations, judge and consider whether there be any appearance or likelyhood in the thing; for I have seen more deceived than otherwise, and whatever assurance is given you, or whatever promises may be made, be sure to raise your counter-battery, and never rely so wholly upon him who is to carry on the work but that you have still a reserve to secure your venture, should his faith or conduct fail. It is not, I confess, well done to condemn him who has the management of an affair if it do not succeed; for men should always be attempting however they speed, and hit or miss 'tis all one provided there be neither treason nor absurdity in the case.

Men must try, and fail, for being we are to confide in men, no one can see into their hearts: but however go warily to work. I have ever been of opinion (and do think that every good captain ought to have the same) that it is better to assault a place upon a surprise, where no one is privy to the design, than to have perhaps some traytor for your guide; for as much as you are certain there can be no counter-treason against you; and though you fail, you retire with the less danger, for your enemy can have laid no ambuscados to entrap you.

Caesar de Naples being this day at Carmagnolle, had there news brought to him of the count's disaster and death, at which he was extremely afflicted; and to secure Fossan, would send thither three companies of Italians, which had formerly been in garrison there, to wit, that of Blaise de Somme, a Neapolitan, that of Baptista, a Millanese, and that of Raussanne, a Piedmontois, who nevertheless refused suddainly to depart (fearing we would fight them by the way) and would not stir till they might have a good and strong convoy; and the Germans he had with him would not be perswaded to go, by which means he was constrained to send to Reconis to the four Spanish companies which were in garrison there; that is to say, that of Don Juan de Guebara, camp-master, of Louys de Quichadou, Aquilbert, and Mendoza, which made it two days before they durst set out to march. In the meantime Monsieur de Termes was advertised by his spy that the said Italian companies were to set forth the next morning, to go put themselves into Fossan, and that they were to have two troops of horse to conduct them: but he had heard nothing that the Spaniards were to go.

The said *seigneur* was at this time but newly recovered of his sickness, who the same morning communicated the affair to me, and at the very instant we concluded to draw four hundred foot out of all our companies, all picked and choice men, to wit, two hundred harquebusiers and as many pikes wearing corslets. Captain Tilladet (who had lost but two or three of all his launces) was not yet returned to Savillan, which was the reason that Monsieur de Termes his company was not so strong; and on the other side Monsieur de Bellegarde, his lieutenant, was gone to his own house, and had taken some few with him, by which means Captain Mons could make but fourscore horse in all; and the spy told us that the Italian companies were to take the same way by which their army had marched when they went to Carignan, which was by the plain, where we before had fought the Italians.

We therefore concluded to take the way of Marennes, and to be there before them; when as we were going out of the town, Monsieur de Cental arrived, who came from cental, having with him fifteen launces of Seigneur Maure, and twenty harquebusiers on horseback, which hindred us a little, forasmuch as he entreated Monsieur de Termes to give him a little time to bait his horses, for he was also of necessity to pass the same way we were designed to march, to go to his Government of Cairas. To whom we made answer that we would go but very softly before, and stay for him at Marennes: but that he should make haste; for in case we should hear the enemy was passing by, we could not stay for him. Monsieur de Termes had once a great mind to have gone along with us himself; but we entreated him not to do it, both because he had been so lately sick, and also that the town being left in a manner naked, should any misfortune happen to us it would be in great danger to be lost.

Being come to Marennes we there made a halt, staying for Monsieur Cental, where we ordered our battail in this manner, to wit, that the captains Gabarret and Baron should lead the two hundred corslets, and I the two hundred harquebusiers, with whom I presently took the vanne, the corslets following after me, and so marched out of the village. Captain Mons also divided his horse into troops: but to whom he gave the first I am not able to say, they being all comrades, but I do believe it was either to Masses, Moussene, Ydrou, or the younger Tilladet; and when we had marched a little way, before we would discover ourselves to the valley thorough which the enemy was to pass, we made a stand. I then took a gentleman along with me called la Garde (he being on horseback) and advanced a little forward to discover the valley, where presently on the other side in the plain of Babe (a castle belonging to the Castellano of Savoy) I discovered the three Italian companies, and the cavalry marching directly towards Fossan.

At which I was ready to run mad, cursing Monsieur de Cental, and the hour that ever he came, thinking there had been no more than those I saw on the other side, who were already got a great way before us; when being about to return to tell the rest that they were already passed, and looking down into the valley (for before I had only looked into the plain on the other side) I discovered the Spanish foot shewing them to la Garde (who before saw them no more than I) having almost all of them yellow breeches; and moreover saw their arms glitter against the sun, by which we knew they were corslets. We never dreamed of meeting any more than the three Italian companies only, so that had we not by accident made some stay in expectation of Monsieur Cental, we had met the Spaniards and the Italians together, and do verily believe had been defeated, considering what defence the Spaniards made alone.

I presently then went and gave the rest of the captains an account of what I had seen, advising them withal by no means as yet to discover themselves; for the Spaniards had made a halt and stood still. I also began to lose sight of the Italians, who marched directly to Fossan: it was a very great oversight in them to separate themselves at so great a distance from one another; la Garde then returned, and told me that Monsieur Cental was coming hard by, bringing a trooper along with him, whom I made to stay above, keeping always his eye on the Italians, whilst I, with la Garde, went down to number their men, who let fly some harquebuze shot at me: but I notwithstanding went so near that I made shift to count them, to betwixt four and five hundred men at the most, and presently returned to the top of the hill, where I saw their cavalry returning towards them, having left the Italians who were already a great way off and clean out of sight. I then sent the souldier to my companions to bid them presently march, for the Spaniards began to beat their drums to return.

The troops of horse they had were those of the Count de Saint Martin d' Est, Kinsman to the Duke of Ferrara; who himself was not there, but his lieutenant only, and of Rozalles, a Spaniard. Their companies of foot were those of Don Juan de Guibara, Aguillere, and

Mendoza, with one half of that of Louys de Guichadou, he with the other half having put himself into the castle of Reconis. Here Monsieur de Cental and Captain Mons came up to me, they two only, and saw as well as I that the said Spaniards put themselves into file, which we judged to be eleven or thirteen in file, and in the meantime their cavalry came up to them.

Now they had already discovered us, although they had hitherto seen no more than five; and I for my part was particularly known, when I went down to discover, by the sergeant of Mendoza, who had been taken at the defeat of the Italians, and delivered three days after; whereupon they placed all their cavalry before, and only twenty or five and twenty harquebusiers at the head of them, a great company at the head of their pikes, and the remainder in the rear; in which order with drums beating they began to march.

I took my harquebusiers which I divided into three squadrons, the first whereof I gave to Captain Lienard, the second to le Pallu, Lieutenant to Monsieur de Carces, who had his two companies at Savillan, and I myself lead the third in the rear of them, the corslets following after; where, at the first coming up, I had la Garde killed by my side.

The enemy still held on their march without making any shew of breaking, firing upon us all the way with very great fury, and we also upon them, so that I was constrained to call Captain Lienard to come and join with me, forasmuch as a squadron of harquebusiers was drawn off from their front to reinforce their rear. I likewise called up le Pallu, and after this manner they marched on till they came within sight of the castle of St Pre, which was three miles or more, continually plying us with their harquebuze shot.

I had once almost put them to rout, at the passing over a great ditch, near to a house where was a base court, where we pursued them so close that we came to the sword, whereupon twenty or five and twenty of them leaped into the base court, and there some of ours falling in pell-mell amongst them, they were all cut to pieces, whilst in the interim of that execution the rest got over the ditch.

Our cavalry had thought to have charged them but did not, being kept off by the harquebuze shot, by which many of their horses were slain, and as for Captain Gabarret and Baron, they committed on error, who, seeing us in the ditch all shuffled pell-mell together, forsook their horses and took their pikes, yet could they not come up in time, which if they had, and that the corslets could have marched at the rate the harquebusiers did, they had there been infallibly defeated; but it was not possible, being hindred by the weight of their arms, so that the enemy marched on, still ridding ground, till being come near to a little bridge of brick, I left our harquebusiers still fighting, and galloped to our cavalry that was in three bodies.

Monsieur de Cental leading his own, which still keeping at distance out of the reach of the shot, marched sometimes before and sometimes a little on one side, to whom, coming up to him, I said, 'Ah Monsieur de Cental will you not charge? do you not see that the enemy will escape us if they once get over that bridge, and immediately recover the wood of St Fré? which if they do, we are never more worthy to bear arms, and for my part I will from this hour forswear them.'

Who in great fury made answer that it stuck not at him but that I was to speak to Captain Mons, which I also did, saying to him these words. 'Hah Camrade! must we this day receive so great a disgrace, and lose so fair an opportunity, because your horse will not charge?'

Who thereupon answered, 'What would you have us do, your corslets cannot come up to the fight, would you have us fight alone?'

To which I made answer, swearing for rage, that I had no need of corslets, wishing they were all at Savillan, since they could not come up to fight; he then said to me, go speak to the foremost troop, and in the meantime I will advance; I then spurred to them, where I began to remonstrate to Monsieur de Termes his gentlemen, that it was not above nine or ten days since we had fought with the Italians and beaten them, and now that we should fight with the Spaniards to obtain greater honour, must they escape from us? Who thereupon with one voice all cryed out, 'It does not stick at us, It does not stick at us.'

I then asked them if they would promise me to charge so soon as I should have made the harquebusiers betake themselves to their swords, to run in upon them, which they did assure me they would upon pain of their lives. There was at that time amongst them a nephew of mine called Serillac (who after was lieutenant to Monsieur de Cypierre at Parma, and there taken prisoner with him, and since slain at Montepullsianne, and, in truth, amongst these thirty launces there were the best men that Monsieur de Termes had in all his troop) to whom I said; 'Serillac, thou art my nephew, but if thou dost not charge in the first man amongst them, I henceforth disclaim thee, and thou shalt no more be any kinsman of mine'; who immediately returned me answer, 'You shall presently see, uncle, whether I will or no.'

Which said he claped down his beaver, as also did all the rest, to charge. I then cryed out to them to stay a little, till I first got up to my men, and thereupon ran to my harquebusiers, where being come, I told them that it was now no longer time to shoot, but that we must fall onto the sword.

'Captains, my comrades, whenever you shall happen to be at such a feast as this, press your followers, speak first to one and then to another, bestir yourselves, and doubt not but by this means you will render them valiant throughout if they were but half so before.'

They all on a suddain claped hands to their swords, when so soon as Captain Mons who was a little before, and Monsieur de Cental who was on one side, saw the first troop shut down their beavers, and saw me run to the harquebusiers, and in an instant their swords in their hands, they knew very well that I had met with lads of mettle, and began to draw near.

I for my part lighted from my horse, taking a halbert in my hand (which was my usual weapon in fight) and all of us ran headlong to throw ourselves in amongst the enemy. Serillac was as good as his word, for he charged in the first, as they all confessed, where his horse was killed at the head of the enemies' harquebusiers, and our own horse with seven harquebuze shot.

Tilladet, Lavit, Ydrou, Montselier, les Maurens, and les Massae, all Gascon gentlemen of the same troop, and companions of the said Serillac, charged the horse thorough and thorough, whom they overturned upon the head of their own foot. Monsieur de Cental also charged in the flank, quite thorough both horse and foot, Captain Mons charged likewise on the other side, so that they were all overthrown, and routed both horse and foot. And there we began to lay about us, above fourscore or an hundred men being left dead upon the place. Rozalles, captain to one of the two troops of light horse, with four others, got away, as also did Don Juan de Guibara upon a Turk with his page only, who happened to be on horseback, being shot thorough the hand, of which he ever after remained lame, and I do believe is yet living.

This is the true relation of this fight, as it passed, their being several at this day alive, who were present at it, and I desire no other testimony to prove whether I have failed in one tittle of the truth.

THE BRIDGE OF CARIGNAN

Three or four days after came Ludovico de Birague, who proposed an enterprise to Monsieur de Boitieres, which was that in case he would leave Monsieur de Tais about Boulongne (where he was governor) with seven or eight companies of foot, that then he would engage to take Cassantin, St Germain, and St Jago; a thing that, because Monsieur de Boitieres was upon the design of breaking the bridge at Carignan, he made very great difficulty to consent unto, until the said bridge should first be broken down: but Monsieur de Termes being come with his own company and the two companies of the Baron de Nicolai, it was concluded amongst them that Monsieur de Tais might be spared to go with Signior Londiné, with seven ensigns, being that still there would remain five or six, the three companies of Monsieur de Dros, which he had again recruited, and seven or eight others of Italians.

I do not well remember whether Monsieur de Strozzi was himself yet arrived or no, for the last named were his men: but it may suffice, that we made up, what French and Italians, eighteen ensigns besides the Swisse. It was therefore concluded in the Council that before they should take in hand the breaking of the bridge they should first see how the enterprise of the said Signior Ludovico should succeed, which should it miscarry and that they were defeated, all Piedmont would be in very great danger. But in a few days after news was brought to Monsieur de Boitieres that they had taken St Germans and St Jago, with four or five other little enclosed towns.

Neither must I forget that Monsieur de Tais stiffly insisted to have had me along with him, insomuch that there arose some dispute about it: But Monsieur de Boitieres protested he would not undertake to break the bridge unless I was there: Monsieur de Termes, Monsieur d'Aussun, the President Birague, and Signior Francisco Bernardin stood very high on Monsieur Boitieres's side, so that I was constrained to stay, very much against my will, I having a very great desire to have gone along with Monsieur de Tais, both because he loved me and had as great confidence in me as in any captain of the regiment, as also that he was a man of exceeding great mettle and would seek all occasions of fighting: however the forementioned news being brought, the breaking of the bridge was concluded, and after this manner.

It was ordered that I with five or six companies of Gascons should go fight the hundred Germans and hundred Spaniards that had every night kept guard at the end of the bridge ever since our army had been at Pingues. To which I made answer that I would not have so many: for being to pass through narrow ways so great a number of men would make so very long a file that the sixth part of them could never come up to fight: and in short, that I would only have an hundred harquebusiers and an hundred corslets, to be equal to the enemy; not doubting but before the game was done, to make it appear that our nation were as good as either German or Spaniard: but withal that Boguldemar, la Pallu, and another captain (whose name I have forgot) should bring all the rest of the men after, at the distance of three hundred paces, to assist me in case the enemy should sally out of Carignan to relieve their own people. Which accordingly was left to my discretion.

There was a house on the left hand the bridge which it was ordered the Italians (who might be between twelve and fourteen ensigns) should possess themselves of to favour me should the enemy make a sally; that Monsieur de Boitieres should advance with all the cavalry and the Swisse within half a mile; that Captain Labarbac with his company should advance on the other side of the river with two pieces of canon to make some shot at a little house which was on the bridge end on our side, where the enemy kept their guard, and that Monsieur de Salcede (who but a little before was come over to us) with three or fourscore country fellows (everyone bringing a hatchet along with him) should attempt to break the bridge. For whom also seven or eight boats were prepared wherein to convey themselves under the said bridge, where they were to cut the posts, not quite thorough but to the thickness of a man's leg, and that being done, to cut the long beams that supported the bridge above, which dividing from one another the pillars would totter and break of themselves; they had moreover certain fireworks delivered to them, which they were made to believe, being applyed to the pillars, would in a short time burn them down to the water.

Everyone then going to execute the orders they had received, I with my two hundred men, chosen out of all the companies, went full drive directly towards the bridge, where I could not however so soon arrive but that the canon had already made one shot at the little house, had broken into it, and killed a German, whom at my coming I found there not quite dead. And although it was night, yet the moon shone out so clear that we might easily see from the one end to the other, saving that by intervals there fell a mist, which continued sometimes half-an-hour, and sometimes less, during which we could not see a yards distance from us.

Now either frighted at the report of the canon, or at the noise I made at the house (it being not above an hundred paces distant from the bridge) the enemy took their heels, and fled towards Carignan, after whom I sent some harquebuze shot: but followed no further than the end of the bridge. At the same time also Monsieur de Salcede, with his Boors and his boats, arrived underneath, who at his first coming presently fastened his artificial fires to the pillars; but it was only so much time thrown away, and he must of force make the fellows fall to't with their axes, who having tyed their boats fast to the said pillars, began to lay on at the end where the Swisse were, cutting on straight towards me, who kept the other end of the bridge towards the enemy.

This fury of the clowns lasted for four long hours, continually laying on upon the pillars, insomuch that though they were ranked four and four together, and of a very great thickness, yet before we had any disturbance, they were all cut to the very place where I was. Monsieur de Salcede ever caused our company to rest themselves upon the bank of the river, where he had caused a little fire to be made, and from hour to hour made them to relieve one another; during which employment the enemy sent out thirty or forty harquebusiers to discover what we were doing, just at a time when the fog fell, whom I could neither see nor hear for the noise of the axes till they were got within four pikes' length of me and let fly amongst us, which having done they immediately retired: yet could they not see us by reason of the mist. Messieurs de Termes then and de Moniens with three or four horse came up to us to know the meaning of those harquebuze shots; and sent back to Monsieur de Boitieres to tell him that it was nothing, and that for them we nothing desisted from the work, themselves alone still remaining with me.

They had not staid an hour but that the mist again began to fall, and the enemy as soon returned upon us, that is to say, six hundred Spaniards chosen men, and six hundred German pikes, Pedro de Colonne (as I have since understood) having ordered the business thus: That two hundred harquebusiers, again chosen out of the six hundred, should charge full drive directly upon us, the other four hundred to march at an hundred paces distance in the rear of them, and the six hundred Germans two hundred paces after all. Now I had placed the captains who led the ensigns after me against a great ditch bank some two hundred paces behind me, and sometimes Captain Favas, my lieutenant, and sometimes Boguedemar came to me to see what we did, and again returned back to their place.

On that side of the bridge towards the Swisse we peradventure had broken down some twenty paces, having begun to cut the beams above, and found that, as the bridge divided, it fell down for fifteen or twenty paces together, which gave us hope that we should make an end of the work. In the meantime Monsieur de Salcede still made the pillars to be cut over again, yet not quite thorough; but only a little more than before, which was the reason that he had divided his work-men into three parts, whereof one was in the boats, the other upon the bridge cutting the traverse beams, and ten or twelve by the fire side. As God is pleased sometimes to be assisting to men, he this night wrought a real miracle; for in the first place, the two hundred harque-busiers came up to me, finding me in such a posture that scarce one souldier had his match cocked, for they went by turns ten or a dozen at a time to the country mens' fire to warm their hands, having two centinels out a hundred paces from me upon the way towards the city, and not doubting but the Italians on their side would also have the same, for they were a little nearer than I; but it was a little on one side.

How they ordered their business I cannot tell, for I had no more than my two centinels, who came running in to me, and as they came in with the alarm, the Spaniards also arrived crying out 'Spain, Spain,' all the two hundred harquebusiers firing upon us together. Where-upon Messieurs de Termes and de Moneins, being on horseback and alone, ran unto Monsieur de Boitieres, who had already seen the be-ginning of the disorder; and note that almost all the two hundred men I had at the end of the bridge ran away straight to the ensigns, and on a suddain the ensigns also fled, and in like manner at the same time the Italians who were on our left hand did the same, neither once looking behind them till they came to the head of the cavalry, where Monsieur de Boitieres himself stood. Our word was St Pierre, but that did me no good; seeing which, I began to cry out, 'Montluc, Montluc, you cursed cowardly whelps, will you forsake me thus?'

By good fortune I had with me thirty or forty young gentlemen, who had never a hair on their faces, the handsomest and the bravest youth that ever was seen in one little company, who thought I had ran away with the rest; but hearing my voice, returned immediately towards me; with whom, without staying for any more, I charged straight to the place from whence the shot came whizzing by our ears: but to see one another was impossible for the mist that fell, together with the thick smoak that was mixt with it, and in running up to them my men discharged all together, crying out 'France,' as they cryed out 'Spain'; and I dare affirm that we fired at less than three pikes' distance, by which charge their two hundred harquebusiers were overturned upon the our hundred, and all of them upon the six hundred Germans; so that all in a rout and confusion, they fled full speed towards the city, for they could not discover what we were.

I pursued them about two hundred paces; but my pursuit was interrupted by the great noise in our camp (I never heard the like), you would have sworn they had been all stark staring mad, calling and bawling upon one another; yet these great bawlers are none of the greatest fighters. There are a sort of men who bustle up and down, call, command, and keep a great clutter, and in the meantime for one step they advance, retire two paces backwards; but this hideous noise was the reason that I could never discover the enemies disorder; neither could they discover ours by reason of the great outcry they made at their entrance into the city, which was no other than a postern near to the castle, into which three or four men only could march a-breast. Thus then I returned to the end of the bridge, where I found Monsieur de Salcede all alone, with ten or a dozen of the country fellows whose turn it was to rest; for the others that were in the boats cut the ropes, and fled away with the current of the river straight to Montcallier, those on the top that were cutting the traverse beams on that side towards the Swisse, leaving their axes and hatchets upon the bridge, cast themselves into the water which was there no more than wast deep, they being not yet come to the depth of the river.

The Swisse, likewise, who heard this dismal noise, fell to running towards Carmagnolle, having an opinion that both we and all our camp were in a rout, and taking the two cannons along with them made all the hast they possibly could to recover Carmagnolle. I sent one of my souldiers after the run-aways to enquire news of my Lieutenant Captain Favas, whom he met (having rallyed thirty or forty of his men) returning towards the bridge, to see what was become of me, believing me to be slain; who presently dispatched away to Boguedemar, la Pallu, and some other captains who had made a halt, rallying some part of their men whom he caused in all hast to march directly towards the bridge, telling them that I had beaten back the enemy, who thereupon came at a good rate to seek me.

Captain Favas was the first that came, all torn and tattered like a skare-crow; forasmuch as the souldiers in a crowd all run over his belly as he thought to have rallyed, who found Monsieur de Salcede and me at the end of the bridge, consulting what we were best to do. So soon as he came he gave us an account of his fortune, and that of the rest of his companions, when seeing him so accoutred, we turned all into laughter; but the hubub in our camp continued above a long hour after.

The other captains being come up to us, we concluded to make an end of breaking down the bridge, or there to lose our lives; whereupon I presently took fifty or threescore souldiers, and Monsieur de Salcede the ten or twelve country fellows he had left, giving order to Captain Favas, Boguedemar, and la Pallu to remain at the end of the bridge and to set out centenels almost as far as the gates of the city. I believed that the Italians, notwithstanding the hurly-burly in our camp, were yet at their post, and therefore commanded Captain Favas himself to go and see if they were there or no; who at his return found that I had caused fifteen or twenty souldiers to take up the axes the peasants had left upon the bridge, who, together with the ten or twelve country fellows, were cutting the cross beams above; where he told us that he had been at the house, but that he had found nobody there. This news put us a little to a stand what we were best to do; but nevertheless we stopt not to execute our former resolution; and so soon as the tumult was a little over came Messieurs de Termes and de Moneins, who brought me a command from Mr de Boitieres immediately to retire.

The said Sieur de Moneins alighted from his horse, for Monsieur de Termes could not for his gout, and came to me on foot, where he found that since the disorder we had at two cuttings made above thirty paces of the bridge to fall, and were falling upon the third, each of them being fifteen or twenty paces long; who thereupon returned to Monsieur de Boitieres to acquaint him how all things had passed, Monsieur de Salcede having lost almost all his peasants; but that our souldiers had taken their axes, with which they did wonders in cutting, and that all the captains and souldiers Monsieur de Salcede and I were resolved to die rather than depart from thence, till first the bridge was totally broken down. Monsieur de Boitieres thereupon sent him back to protest against me for any loss that might happen contrary to his command, which the said Sieur de Moneins did, telling us moreover that the said Sieur de Boitieres was already upon his march to return, though he halted within a mile of us; which I conceive he did to the end that by that means he might draw me off; for he wanted no courage, but he was always in fear to lose.

Whoever is of that humour may perhaps make a shift to save himself, but shall never achieve any great conquests. Monsieur de Termes had made a stop at the end of the bridge, so soon as he had heard Monsieur de Boitieres to be upon his march, and returned no more back with Monsieur de Moneins to carry my answer; but presently sent orders to his company not to stir from the place where he had left them, and so we cut on all the remainder of the night 'till within an hour of day, that we marched towards the little house upon the hill. Monsieur de Moneins returned again to us, just at the instant when the last blow was given, and Monsieur de Termes ran to his company, to cause them to advance a little towards us that they might favour our retreat, and Monsieur de Moneins ran towards Monsieur de Boitieres, whom he found expecting his return; so that having deprived the enemy of a great convenience, we retired without any manner of impediment at all. I was willing to commit this to writing, not to magnifie myself for any great valour in this action; but to manifest to all the world how God has ever been pleased to conduct my fortune. I was neither so great a fop nor so fool hardy but that could I have seen the enemy, I should have retired and perhaps have run away as fast as the rest, and it had been madness and not valour to have staid. Neither is there any shame attends a rational fear when there is great occasion; and I should never have been so senseless as with thirty or forty foot only to have stood the fight.

Captains by this may take exemple, never to run away, or (to put it into a better phrase) to make a hasty retreat, without first discovering who there is to pursue them, and moreover having seen them, to attempt all ways of opposition till they shall see there is no good to be done. For after all the means that God has given to men have been employed and to no purpose, then flight is neither shameful nor unworthy: but believe me (gentlemen) if you do not employ it all, everyone will be ready to say (nay, even those who have run away with you) it he had done this, or if he had done that, the mischief had been prevented and things had fallen out better than they did; and such a one vapours most and speaks highest, who perhaps was himself the first that ran away.

Thus shall the reputation of a man of honour (let him be as brave as he will) be brought into dispute with all the world. When there is no more to be done a man ought not to be obstinate, but to give way to fortune, which does not always smile. A man is no less worthy of blame for wilfully losing himself when he may retire, and sees himself at the last extremity, than he who shamefully runs away at the first encounter: Yet the one is more dirty than the other; and this difference there is betwixt them, that the one will make you reputed rash and hair-brained, and the other a poltroon and a coward. Both extreams are to be avoided. You are never to enter into these ridiculous and senseless resolutions but when you see yourselves fallen into the hands of a barbarous and merciless enemy; and there indeed you are to fight it to the last gasp, and sell your skin as dear as you can.

One desperate man is worth ten others. But to fly, as they did here, without seeing who pursues you, is infamous and unworthy of the courage of a man. It's true that the Frenchman is accused for one thing, that is, that he runs and fights for company: and so do others as well as they. There are ill workmen of all trades. Now after the place was surrendered, I will tell you how I came to know the enemies' disorder. It was by the people of Carignan themselves, and from Signior Pedro de Colonna's own mouth, who related it to Susanne, in the presence of Captain Renovard, who conducted him to the king by the command of Monsieur d'Anguien, according to his capitulation after the Battle of Serizolles, which you shall have an account of in its proper place.

MONLUC IS SENT ON AN EMBASSY, AND PERSUADES THE KING TO ALLOW A BATTLE TO BE FOUGHT

At the arrival of this brave and generous prince, which promised great successes under his conduct, he being endued with an infinite number of shining qualities, as being gentle, affable, valiant, wise, and liberal; all the French and all those who bore arms in our favour, did very much rejoyce, and particularly I, because he had a kindness for me, and was pleased to set a higher esteem upon me than I could any way deserve. After he had taken a view of all the forces, magazines, and places that we held, and that he had taken order for all things after the best manner he could, about the beginning of March he dispatched me away to the king, to give His Majesty an account how affairs stood, and withal to acquaint him that the Marquis de Guast was raising a very great army, to whom new succours of Germans were also sent, and moreover that the Prince of Salerna was also coming from Naples with six or seven thousand Italians under his command.

It was at the time when the emperor and the King of England were agreed and combined together jointly to invade the Kingdom of France, which they had also divided betwixt them. I had waited at court near upon three weeks for my dispatch, having already acquitted myself of my commission, which was in sum only to demand some succours of the king and to obtain leave to fight a battel. And about the end of the said month came letters also to the king from Monsieur d'Anguien, wherein he gave him notice that seven thousand Germans were already arrived at Millan, of the best of those the emperor had had before Landreci, where there were seven regiments of them; but being he could not at that time fight with the king, he commanded the seven colonels to choose each a thousand out of their respective regiments ordering them to leave their lieutenants to get their regiments ready, and so sent them into Italy to joyn with the Marquis de Guast.

Wherefore the said Monsieur d'Anguien humbly besought His Majesty to send me speedily away to him, and also requested him that he would please to do something for me, as a reward for my former services, and an encouragement to more for the time to come. Upon which letter His Majesty was pleased to confer upon me the office of a gentleman waiter (which in those times was no ordinary favour; nor so cheap as now a days) and made me to wait upon him at dinner, commanding me in the afternoon to make myself ready to return into Piedmont, which I accordingly did.

About two of the clock Monsieur de Annebaut sent for me to come to the king, who was already entred into the council, where there was assisting Monsieur de St Pol, the admiral, Monsieur le Grand Escuyer, Galliot, Monsieur de Boissy (since grand *escuyer*), and two or three others whom I have forgot, together with the *dauphin* who stood behind the king's chair; and none of them were set, but the king himself, Monsieur de St Pol, who sate hard by him, and the admiral on the other side of the table over against the said Sieur de St Pol.

So soon as I came into the chamber, the king said to me, 'Montluc, I would have you return into Piedmont to carry my determination and that of my Council to Monsieur d'Anguien, and will that you hear the difficulties we make of giving him leave to fight a battel according to his desire,' and thereupon commanded Monsieur de St Pol to speak.

The said Monsieur de St Pol then began to lay open the enterprise of the emperor and the King of England, who within six or seven weeks were determined to enter into the kingdom, the one on the one side and the other on the other; so that should Monsieur d'Anguien lose the battel, the whole kingdom would be in danger to be lost: for as much as all the king's hopes (for what concerned his foot) resided in the regiments he had in Piedmont, for that in France there were no other but what were new legionary souldiers, and that therefore it was much better and more safe to preserve the kingdom

84

than Piedmont, concerning which they were to be on the defensive part, and by no means to hazzard a battel, the loss whereof would not only lose Piedmont but moreover give the enemy footing on that side of the kingdom.

The admiral said the same, and all the rest, everyone arguing according to his own fancy. I twittered to speak, and offering to interrupt Monsieur de Galliot as he was delivering his opinion, Monsieur de St Pol made a sign to me with his hand, saying 'not too fast, not too fast,' which made me hold my peace, and I saw the king laugh. *Monsieur le Dauphin* said nothing, I believe it is not the custom, though the king would have him present that he might learn; for before princes there are evermore very eloquent debates, but not always the soundest determinations; for they never speak but by halves, and always sooth their masters' humour, for which reason I should make a very scurvy courtier; for I must ever speak as I think. The king then said these words to me, 'Montluc, have you heard the reasons for which I cannot give Monsieur d'Anguien leave to fight?' to which I made answer that I had both heard and weighed them very well; but that if His Majesty would please to give me leave to deliver my opinion I would very gladly do it: not that nevertheless for that His Majesty should any ways alter what had already been determined in his council.

His Majesty then told me that he would permit me to do so, and that I might freely say whatsoever I would. Whereupon I began after this manner. I remember it as well as it had been but three days ago; God has given me a very great memory in these kind of things, for which I render him hearty thanks; for it is a great contentment to me, now that I have nothing else to do, to recollect my former fortunes, and to call to mind the former passages of my life, to set them truly down without any manner of addition; for be they good or bad you shall have them as they are.

Sir,—I think myself exceedingly happy as well that you are pleased I shall deliver my poor opinion upon a subject that has already been debated in your Majestie's Council, as also that I am to speak to a warlike king; for both before your Majesty was called to this great charge, which God has conferred upon you, and also since, you have as much tempted the fortune of war as any king that ever ruled in France, and that without sparing your own royal person any more than the meanest gentleman of your kingdom; wherefore I need not fear freely to deliver my opinion, being to speak both to a king and a souldier.

(Here the *dauphin*, who stood behind the king's chair, and just over against me, gave me a nod with his head, by which I guessed he would have me to speak boldly, and that gave me the greater assurance, though, in plain truth, I had ever confidence enough, and fear never stoped my mouth.) I said:

Sir, we are betwixt five and six thousand Gascons upon the list, for your Majesty knows that the companies are never fully compleat; neither can all ever be at the battel; but I make account we shall be five thousand and five or six hundred Gascons compleat, that I dare make good to your Majesty upon my honour: Of these every captain and souldier will present you with a list of all their names, and the places from whence we come, and will engage our heads to you, all of us to fight in the day of battel, if your Majesty will please to grant it, and give us leave to fight. 'Tis the only thing we have so long expected and desired, without sneaking thus up and down from place to place and hiding our heads in corners. Believe me, Sir, the world has not more resolute souldiers than these are, they desire nothing more than once to come to the decision of arms.

To these there are thirteen ensigns of Swisse: Of which the six of St Julien I know much better than those of le Baron, which Fourly commands, yet I have seen them all mustered, and there may be as many of them as of ours. These will make you the same promise we do, who are your natural subjects, and deliver in the names of all to be sent to their cantons, to the end that if any man fail in his duty, he may be cashiered, and degraded from all practice of arms for ever. A condition to which they are all ready to submit, as they assured me at my departure. And being of the same nation, I make no doubt but those of le Baron will do the same. Your Majesty may have taken notice of them all before Landrecy.

Here then, Sir, are nine thousand men or more, on which you may depend and assure yourself that they will fight to the last gasp of their lives. As for the Italians and Provençals which are under Monsieur des Cros, and also the Fribourgers that came to us before Ivreé, I shall not take upon me to become security for them, but I hope they will all do as well as we, especially when they shall see how we lay about us (at which I lifted up my arm (in the earnestness of speaking) as if I were going to strike, whereat the king smiled.)

You should also, Sir, have four hundred men at arms in Piedmont, of which there may well be three hundred, and as many archers, as well disposed as we. You have four captains of light horse, which are Messieurs de Termes, d'Aussun, Francisco Bernardin, and Maure, each of which ought to have two hundred light horse, and amongst them all they will furnish you with five or six hundred horse, all which are ambitious to manifest the zeal they have to your service. I know what they are and what they will do very well.

The king then began to be a little angry to hear that the companies of the *gens d'armes* were not all compleat: but I told him that it was impossible; forasmuch as some of them had obtained leave of their captains to go home to their own houses to refresh themselves, and others were sick; but that if His Majesty would please to give leave to those gentlemen who would beg it of him to be present at the battel, they would very well supply that default. Said I, (continuing my discourse):

Since then, Sir, that I am so happy as to speak before a souldier king, who would you have to kill ten thousand foot, and a thousand or twelve hundred horse, all resolute to overcome or dye? Such men as these, and so resolved, are not so easily defeated: neither are they novices in war. We have several times attaqued the enemy upon equal terms, and for the most part beaten them. And I dare boldly say that had we all of us one arm tyed behind us, it would not be in the power of the enemy to kill us all in a whole day's time, without losing the greatest part of their army, and the choicest of their men. Imagine then when we have both our arms at liberty, and our weapons in our hands, how easie it will be to beat us. Truly, Sir, I have heard great captains discourse, and say that an army of twelve or fifteen thousand men is sufficient to confront an army of thirty thousand; for 'tis not the crowd but the courage that overcomes, and in a battel the one half of them never comes to fight. We desire no more than we have, let us deal it out.'

(The *dauphin* all this while stood laughing behind the king's chair, and still made signs to me, for by my behaviour I seemed already to be in battel.)

No, No, Sir, these are not men to be beaten, and if these Lords who have spoken had once seen them at their work, they would alter their opinion, and so would your Majesty too. These are not men to lye dozing in a garrison, they require an enemy, and have a mind to shew their valour; they beg leave of you to fight, and if you deny them, you take away their spirits, and give it to your enemies, who will be puffed with vanity to see themselves feared, whilst your own army shall moulder away to nothing. By what I have heard, Sir, all that these lords stumble at, who have delivered their opinions before you, is the apprehension of losing the battel, and that makes them always cry, if we lose, if we lose; but I have not heard one of them tell you, if we win it, what great advantages will thereby accrue. For God's sake. Sir, fear not to grant our request, and let me not return with such a shame upon me that men shall say you durst not trust the hazard of a battel in our hands, who so voluntarily and chearfully make a tender of our lives to do you service.

The king who had very attentively hearkened to me, and that was delighted at my gestures and impatience, turned his eyes towards Monsieur de St Pol, who thereupon said to him:

Sir, will you alter your determination at the importunity of this coxcomb, that cares for nothing but fighting, and has no sense of the misfortune nor the inconveniences that the loss of a battel would bring upon you? Believe me. Sir, 'tis a thing of too great importance to be referred to the discretion of a young hair-brained Gascon.

To whom I made answer in these very words.

My Lord, assure yourself I am neither a *bragadochio* nor so arrant a coxcomb as you take me for; neither do I say this out of bravado, and if you will please to call to mind all the intelligences His Majesty has received since we returned from Perpignan into Piedmont, you will find that whenever we encountered the enemy, whether on horseback or on foot, we have always beaten them, excepting when Monsieur d'Aussun was defeated; who also miscarried through no other default than for attempting to retreat at the head of an army, which a prudent captain never ought to do. It is not yet three months (I am sure you have heard it, for it is known to all the world) since the two brave combats we fought both on foot and on horseback in the plain over against St Fré, first against the Italians, and since against the Spaniards, and both in ten days' time; and Monsieur d'Aussun fifteen days before he was taken fought and defeated an entire regiment of Germans. Consider then we that are in heart, and they in fear; we that are conquerours, and they beaten; we who despise them, whilst they tremble at us; what difference there is betwixt us. When should it be that the king should give us leave to fight, if not now that we are in this condition in Piedmont? It must not be when we have been beaten that His Majesty ought to do it; but now that we are in breath and fleshed with conquest. Neither is there any thought to be taken, save only to take good heed that we assault them not in a fortress as we did at the Bicoque: but Monsieur d'Anguien has too many good and experienced captains about him to commit such an error; and there will be no other question if not how to tempt them into the open field where there shall be neither hedge nor ditch to hinder us from coming to grapple with them, and then. Sir, you shall hear news of one of the most furious battels that ever was fought and I most humbly beseech your Majesty to expect no other news but that of a great and glorious victory, which if God give us the grace to obtain (as I hold myself assured we shall) you will so stop the emperor and the King of England in the midst of their carreer, that they shall not know which way to turn them.

The *dauphin* still continued laughing more than before, and still making signs, which gave me still the greater assurance to speak. All the rest of them then spoke everyone in his turn, and said that His Majesty ought by no means to rely upon my words: only the admiral said nothing, but smiled; and I believe he perceived the signs the *dauphin* made me, they being almost opposite to one another; but Monsieur de St Pol replyed again, saying to the king: 'What, Sir, it seems you have a mind to alter your determination, and to be led away at the persuasion of this frantick fool.

To which the king made answer, 'By my Faith, Cozen, he has given me so great reasons, and so well represented to me the courage of my souldiers, that I know not what to say.'

To which Monsieur de St Pol replyed, 'Nay, Sir, I see you are already changed'; (now he could not see the signs the *dauphin* made me, as the admiral could, for he had his back towards him) whereupon the king directing his speech to the admiral, asked him what he thought of the business, who again smiling returned His Majesty this answer:

Sir, will you confess the truth? You have a great mind to give them leave to fight, which if they do, I dare not assure you either of victory or disgrace; for God alone only knows what the issue will be: but I dare pawn my life and reputation that all those he has named to you will fight like men of honour; for I know their bravery very well, as having had the honour to command them. Do only one thing. Sir, (for we see you are already half overcome, and that you rather incline to a battel than otherwise) address yourself to Almighty God, and humbly beg of him, in this perplexity, to assist you with his counsel, what you were best to do.

Which having said, the king, throwing his bonnet upon the table, lift up his eyes towards heaven, and, joining his hands, said:

My God, I beseech thee, that thou wilt be pleased to direct me this day what I ought to do for the preservation of my kingdom, and let all be to thy honour and glory.'

Which having said, the admiral asked him, 'I beseech you. Sir, what opinion are you now of?'

When the king, after a little pause, turning towards me, with great vehemency cryed out, 'Let them fight, let them fight.'

'Why then,' says the admiral, 'there is no more to be said, if you lose the battel, you alone are the cause, and if you overcome the same, and alone shall enjoy the satisfaction, having alone consented to it.'

This being said, the king and all the rest arose, and I was ready to leap out of my skin for joy. The king then fell to talking with the admiral about my dispatch, and to take order for our pay which was a great deal in arrear. Monsieur de St Pol in the meantime drew near unto me, and smiling said, 'thou mad Devil, thou wilt be the cause either of the greatest good or the greatest mischief that can possibly befall the king,' (now you must know that the said Sieur de St Pol had not spoken anything for any ill will that he bore me, for he loved me as well as any captain in France, and of old, having known me at the time when I served under the Mareschal de Foix) and moreover told me that it was very necessary I should speak to all the captains and souldiers, and tell them that the confidence His Majesty reposed in our worth and valour had made him condescend to permit us to fight, and not reason, considering the condition he was then in. To whom I replyed:

My Lord, I most humbly beseech you not to fear, or so much as doubt but that we shall win the battel, and assure yourself that the first news you will hear will be that we have made them all into a *fricasse*, and may eat them if we will.

The king then came to me and laid his hand upon my shoulder, saying:

Montluc, recommend me to my cozen d'Anguien and to all the captains in those parts, of what nation soever, and tell them that the great confidence I have in their fidelity and valour has made me condescend that they shall fight, entreating them to serve me very well upon this occasion, for I never think to be in so much need again as at this present, that now therefore is the time wherein they are to manifest the kindness they have for me, and that I will suddainly send them the money they desire.

To which I made answer, 'Sir, I shall obey your commands, and this will be a cordial to chear them and a spur to the good disposition they already have to fight, and I most humbly beseech your Majesty, not to remain in doubt concerning the issue of our fight, for that will only discompose your spirit; but chear up yourself in expectation of the good news you will shortly hear of us; for my mind presages well, and it never yet deceived me'; and thereupon, kissing his hand, I took my leave of His Majesty.

The admiral then bid me go and stay for him in the wardrobe, and whether it was Monsieur de Marchemont or Monsieur Bayart that went down with me, I cannot tell: but going out, I found at the door Messieurs de Dampierre, de St Andre, and d'Assier, with three or four others who demanded of me if I carried leave to Monsieur d'Anguien to fight, to whom I made answer in Gascon, '*hares y harem aux pics, and patacs*'; go in presently, if you have any stomach to the entertainment, before the admiral depart from the king, which they accordingly did, and there was some dispute about their leave: but in the end His Majesty consented they should go; which nothing impaired the feast; for after them came above a hundred gentlemen post-haste to be present at the battel.

Amongst others the Sieurs de Jarnac and de Chatillon, since admiral, the son of the Admiral d'Annebaut, the Vidame of Chartres, and several others; of which not one was slain in the battel, save only Monsieur d'Assier, whom I loved more than my own heart, and Chamans who was wounded when I fought the Spaniards in the plain of Perpignan; some others there were that were hurt, but none that dyed. There is not a prince in the world who has so frank a gentry as ours has, the least smile of their king will enflame the coldest constitution, without any thought of fear, to convert mills and vineyards into horses and arms, and they go volunteers to dye in that bed which we souldiers call the bed of honour.

Being arrived soon after at the camp, I acquitted myself of my charge towards Monsieur d' Anguien, and presented him my letters from the king, who was infinitely overjoyed, and embracing me in his arms, said these very words: 'I knew very well that thou wouldst not bring us peace,' and turning to the gentlemen about him, 'Well, my masters,' said he, 'the king is pleased to gratifie our desire, we must go to 't.' I then gave him an account of the difficulty I had met with in obtaining that leave, and that the king himself was the only cause of it, which ought the more to encourage us to behave ourselves bravely in the battel.

He was moreover very glad when I told him that the forementioned lords were coming after me, being certain that several others would also follow after them, as they did. Bidding me by all means go discharge myself of His Majestie's commands to all the colonels, captains of the *gens d'armes*, light horse, and foot; which I did, not observing one that did not mightily rejoyce, when I gave them to understand what assurance I had given the king of the victory. Neither did I satisfie myself with speaking to the officers only; but moreover went amongst the souldiers, assuring them that we should all be highly recompenced by the king, making the matter something better than it was; for a man must now and then lye a little for his master.

THE DAY OF CÉRISOLES

Now being we had the day before left the enemy in the plain betwixt Sommerive and Cerizolles, Monsieur d'Anguien did not very well know whether they might be at Sommerive or at Cerizolles, notwithstanding that the governor of Sommerive had sent him word that the camp intended to quarter there. Signior Francisco Berdardin therefore sent out three or four of his light horse towards the said Cerizolles, who went so near that they discovered their camp, which was already in arms, and the drums beginning to beat. That which had made them return to Cerizolles, was to stay for the Spanish foot, who were gone for the two pieces of canon, as has been said before. Monsieur de Termes likewise sent out again three or four of his people also, and in the meantime we marched underneath toward Sommerive; but so soon as the light horse returned with the same intelligence, we turned on the left hand, and come up into the plain, where the whole army was, and there made a halt.

And there Monsieur d'Anguien and Monsieur de Tais gave me all the harquebusiers to lead, for which honour I returned him my most humble thanks, telling him that I hoped, by Gods assistance, to acquit myself so well of my charge that he should remain satisfied with my service, and said as much to Monsieur de Tais, who was my colonel, and who came and commanded all the captains and lieutenants that I would take to obey me equally with himself.

I then took four lieutenants, namely le Brûeil (whom I have mentioned before) le Gasquet, Captain Lienard, and Captain Favas, who was my own lieutenant. To Favas and Lienard I gave the right wing, and myself with the two other took the left, leading towards the little house that was afterwards so much disputed; and it was ordered that the Swisse which were commanded by Monsieur de Boitieres (who a little before the rumour of the battel had been recalled from his own house) and we should fight together in the vantguard; the battel was to be conducted by Monsieur d'Anguien, having under his cornet all the young lords that came from court, and the rear-guard was commanded by Monsieur d'Ampierre, wherein were four thousand Fribourgers, and three thousand Italians, led by the Sieur de Dros and des Cros, together with all the guidons and archers of companies.

Now there was a little eminence that dipt towards Cerizolles and Sommerive, which was all on a little copse, but not very thick; the first of the enemy that we saw enter into the plain to come towards us were the seven thousand Italians conducted by the Prince of Salerna, and in the flank of them three hundred launciers, commanded by Rodolpho Baglione, who belonged to the great Duke of Florence.

The skirmish began by this little hill, on the descent whereof the enemy had made a halt just over against us, and as soon as the skirmish was begun, I gave one squadron to Captain Brûeil, being that which was nearest to me, and the hindmost to Captain Gasquet, about two hundred paces distant the one from the other, and of my own I gave forty or fifty harquebusiers to a serjeant of mine called Arnaut de St

Clair, a valiant man and one that very well understood his business, and I myself stood for a reserve.

Being at the foresaid little house, I discovered three or four companies of Spanish harquebusiers, who came full drive to possess themselves of the house, and in the meantime Favas and Lienard fought the Italians in the valley on the right hand. The skirmish grew hot on both sides, the enemy one while beating me up to the house, and I again other whiles driving them back to their own party; for they had another that was come up to second the first, and it seemed as if we had been playing at base, but in the end I was constrained to call Captain Brûeil up to me, for I saw all their foot embody together, with a troop of horse to flank them. Now I had not so much as one horse with me, notwithstanding that I had advertised Monsieur d'Anguien that their cavalry was also with the harquebusiers that came up to me. Let it suffice, that of a long time nobody came, insomuch that I was constrained to quit the house; but not without a great dispute, which continued for a very great space. I then sent back Captain Brûeil to his place, the skirmish continued for almost four hours without intermission, and never did men acquit themselves better.

Monsieur d'Anguien then sent Monsieur d'Aussun unto me, commanding me to repossess myself of the house, which was neither of advantage nor disadvantage to me; to whom I made answer 'Go and tell Monsieur d'Anguien that he must then send me some horse, to fight these horse that flank their harquebusiers (which he also saw as well as I) for I am not to fight horse and foot together in the open field.'

He then said to me: 'It is enough for me that I have told you,' and so returned to carry back my answer to Monsieur d'Anguien; who thereupon sent Monsieur de Moneins to tell me that one way or another he would that I should regain it, with whom also came the Seigneur Cabry, brother to Seigneur Maure, bringing with him three-score horse, all launciers, and Monsieur de Moneins might have about some five and twenty, he being then but beginning to raise his troop. To whom I returned the same answer I had given before to Monsieur d'Aussun, and that I would not because of the loss of the battel: but that if they would go charge those horse that flanked the harquebusiers, I would quickly regain the house. They then answered that I had reason, and that they were ready to do it.

Whereupon I presently sent to Captain Brûeil to come up to me, and to Captain Gasquet to advance to his place, and immediately

Captain Brûeil coming up on the right hand, and the horse in the middle, we marched at a good round trot directly up to them; for we were not above three hundred paces distant from one another. All this while the skirmish never ceased, and as we drew within a hundred or six score paces off them, we began to fire, upon which the cavalry faced about, and their foot also, and I saw their launciers turn their backs, retreating to their troops. Monsieur de Moneins, and Seigneur Cabry went immediately hereupon to Monsieur d'Anguien, to tell him what they had seen their cavalry do, and that if he did not send me up horse to second me, I could not choose but be routed. I sent back Captain Brûeil and Gasquet into their places.

Now there was a little marish near unto Cerizolles, and a great hollow way, which hindred the enemy that they could not come up to us drawn up in battalia: and the Marquis de Guast had caused six pieces of artillery to pass over this marish, and they were already advanced a good way on this side, when seeing their people driven back they were afraid that the whole army followed the pursuit, and that they should lose their canon. Wherefore they presently made the Germans to pass over this marish, and thorough the said hollow way, who, so soon as they came into the plain, drew up again into battalia; for it was not possible for them to pass, but in great disorder, and in the meantime the cavalry and Spanish harquebusiers came up to me as before; insomuch that having no horse with me, I was necessitated to quit them the place, and to retire to the place from whence I came.

Now I had discovered their German foot and their artillery, and as I was retiring. Monsieur de Termes and Signior Francisco Bernardin came, and placed themselves on the right hand of our battaillon, and upon the skirt of the hill (which was very straight) and over against the battaillon of the Italians; for their launciers were exactly opposite to our pikes. Monsieur de Boitieres with his company and that of the Count de Tande advanced on the left hand of our battail, and the Swisse were three or four score paces behind us, and a little on the one side.

In the meantime our harquebusiers that were conducted by Lienard and Captain Favas sometimes beat back the enemy as far as their main battalia and sometimes the enemy repelled them up to ours. I saw then that I must of necessity disarm our battaillon of the harquebusiers that made our flank on that side where Monsieur de Boitieres stood, and give them to them, wherewith to make a charge, which they did, and with great fury beat them up to their battail: and it was high time; for their harquebusiers had almost gained the flank of our horse. I therefore ran up to them, and we began a furious skirmish, which was great, and obstinately fought, for all our squadrons were closed up together, and it continued a long hour or more.

Now the enemy had placed their canon by the side of the little house, which played directly into our battaillon; Monsieur de Mailly then advanced with ours and placing himself close by us, began to shoot at those of the enemy by the little house; for there where we maintained the skirmish he could not do it without killing our own men; when, looking towards our own battail, I saw Monsieur de Tais, who began to march with his pikes, charged directly towards the Italians, whereupon I ran up to him, saying, 'Whither do you go. Sir, whither do you go, you will lose the battel; for here are all the Germans coming to fight you, and will charge into your flank.'

The captains were the occasion of this, who ceased not to cry out to him, 'Sir, lead us on to fight; for it is better for us to dye hand to hand, than stand still here to be killed with the canon.'

'Tis that which terrifies the most of anything, and oftentimes begets more fear than it does harm: but however so it was that he was pleased to be ruled by me, and I entreated him to make his men kneel on one knee, with their pikes down; for I saw the Swisse behind laid at their full length squatt to the ground, so as hardly to be seen; and from him I ran to the harquebusiers. The enemies' harquebuziers by this time were beginning to retire behind the house, when, as I was going up to charge straight up to them, I discovered the front of the Germans battaillon, and suddainly commanded the Captains Brûeil and Gasquet to retire by degrees towards the artillery, for we were to make room for the pikes to come up to the fight, and I went to our battel, where being come, I said to my men these words.

Oh my fellow souldiers let us now fight bravely, and if we win the battel we get a greater renown than any of our nation ever did; It was never yet read in history that ever the Gauls fought the Germans pike to pike but that the Germans defeated them, and to set this honourable mark upon ourselves that we are better men than our ancestors, this glory ought to inspire us with a double courage to fight so as to overcome or dye, and make our enemies know what kind of men we are. Remember, *camerades*, the message the king sent to us, and what a glory it will be to present ourselves before him after the victory.

'Now, Sir,' said I to Monsieur de Tais, 'it is time to rise,' which he suddenly did, and I began to cry out aloud:

Gentlemen, it may be there are not many here who have ever been in a battel before, and therefore let me tell you that if we take our pikes by the hinder end, and fight at the length of the pike, we shall be defeated; for the Germans are more dextrous at this kind of fight than we are: but you must take your pikes by the middle as the Swisse do, and run head-long to force and penetrate into the midst of them, and you shall see how confounded they will be.

Monsieur de Tais then cryed out to me to go along the battail, and make them all handle their pikes after this manner, which I accordingly did, and now we are all ready for the encounter.

The Germans marched at a great rate directly towards us, and I ran to put myself before the battail, where I alighted from my horse; for I ever had a lacquey at the head of the battaillon ready with my pike; and as Monsieur de Tais and the rest of the captains saw me on foot, they all cryed out at once, 'Get up. Captain Montluc, get up again, and you shall lead us on to the fight.'

To whom I made answer that if it was my fate to dye that day, I could not dye in a more honourable place than in their company, with my pike in my hand. I then called to Captain la Burre, who was serjeant major, that he should always be stirring about the battaillon when we came to grapple, and that he and the serjeants behind and on the sides should never cease crying, 'put home, soldiers, put home, to the end,' that they might push on one another.

The Germans came up to us at a very round rate, insomuch that their battail being very great, they could not possibly follow; so that we saw great windows in their body, and several ensigns a good way behind, and all on a suddain rushed in among them, a good many of us at least, for as well on their side as ours all the first ranks, either with push of pikes or the shock at the encounter, were overturned; neither is it possible amongst foot to see a greater fury: the second rank and the third were the cause of our victory; for the last so pushed them on that they fell in upon the heels of one another, and as ours pressed in, the enemy was still driven back: I was never in my life so active and light as that day, and it stood me upon so to be; for above three times I was beaten down to my knees.

The Swisse were very sly and cunning; for till they saw us within ten or a dozen Pikes' length of one another, they never rose: but then like savage boars they rushed into their flank, and Monsieur de Boitieres broke in at a canton, (corner), Monsieur de Termes and Signior Francisco in the meantime charged Rodolpho Baglione, whom they overthrew and put his cavalry to route. The Italians, who saw their cavalry broken, and the Lansquenets and Germans overthrown and routed, began to take the descent of the valley, and as fast as they could to make directly towards the wood. Monsieur de Termes had his horse killed under him at the first encounter, and by ill fortune his leg was so far engaged under him in the fall that it was not possible for him to rise, so that he was there by the Italians taken and carried away prisoner, and, to say the truth, his legs were none of the best.

Now you are to take notice that the Marquis de Guast had composed a battaillon of five thousand pikes, namely two thousand Spaniards and three thousand Germans, out of the number of six thousand, being the same that Count Laudron had brought into Spain, where he had remained ten years or more, and who all spoke as good Spanish as natural Spaniards. He had formed this battaillon only to clear away the Gascons; for he said that he feared our battaillon more than any of the other, and had an opinion that his Germans (being all chosen men) would beat our Swisse. He had placed three hundred harquebusiers only in the nature of a forlorn hope at the head of this battaillon, which he reserved to the forenamed effect, and all the rest maintained the skirmish. Now as he was by the little house on the same side with the Germans, he saw the Fribourgers, who were all armed in white, and took them for the Gascons, and thereupon said to his men, 'Hermanos, hermanos, a qui estant todos Gascones, sarrais à ellos.' They were not gone two hundred paces from him but that he perceived our battail, which start up, and saw his error when it was too late to help it, for we all wore black arms.

This battaillon of five thousand pikes marched then at a good round rate directly upon the Fribourgers, and they were of necessity to pass hard by Monsieur d'Anguien, who by somebody or other was very ill advised; for as they passed by he charged with his *gens d'armes* quite thorough their battallion in the flank, and there were slain and wounded a great many brave and worthy men, and some of very considerable quality, as Monsieur d'Assier, le Sieur de la Rochechouard, with several others, and yet more at the second charge.

There were some who passed and repassed quite thorough and thorough; but still they closed up again, and in that manner came up to the Fribourgers battalia, who were soon overthrown without so much as standing one push of pike, and there died all their captains and lieutenants who were in the first rank and the rest fled straight to Messieur des Cros: but this battaillion of Spaniards and Germans still at a very great rate pursued their victory, and overthrew the said Sieur des Cros, who there dyed and all his captains with him; neither could Monsieur d'Anguien any way relieve him, forasmuch as all the horses almost of his cavalry in these two furious but inconsiderate charges were wounded and walked fair and softly over the field towards the enemy.

He was then in the height of despair, and curst the hour that ever he was born, seeing the overthrow of his foot, and that he himself had scarce an hundred horse left to sustein the shock, insomuch that Monsieur des Pignan of Montpellier (a gentleman of his) assured me that he twice turned the point of his sword into his gorget, to have offered violence to himself, and himself told me at his return that he was then in such a condition he should have been glad anyone would have run him thorough. The Romans might have done so; but I do not think it becomes a Christian. Everyone at that time passed his censure upon it according to his own fancy. For our parts we were as well as heart could wish, and as much pleased as the enemy was afflicted; but let us return to the blows, for there were yet both to give and to take.

The cowardice of the Fribourgers occasioned a great loss on that side of the field; in my life I never saw such great lubbers as those were, unworthy ever to bear arms, if they have not learnt more courage since. They are indeed neighbours to the Swisse, but there is no more comparison betwixt them than betwixt a Spanish horse and an asse. It is not all to have a great number of men upon the list; but to have those that are true bred; for a hundred of them are worth a thousand of the other. And a brave and valiant captain with a thousand men that he knows he may trust to will pass over the bellies of four thousand.

Siena

As the defence of Siena was one of the most striking episodes in Monluc's career, and its description occupies a great deal of space in the *Commentaires*, it has been thought best, even at the sacrifice of passages from other portions of the book, that the extracts from this section should be as full as possible.

Monsieur de Strozzy then sent to the king to acquaint him that it was not possible for him both to keep the field and to govern in

Sienna also, and that therefore he most humbly besought His Majesty to make choice of some person in whom he might safely confide to command in the town, so long as he should continue in the field. The king having received this despatch, called for the constable, Monsieur de Guise, and the Mareschal de St Andre, where he acquainted them with Monsieur de Strozzy's request, desiring them to name each of them one for this employment; for all things past through the hands of these three, and nothing was determined without them. All our kings have ever had this trick, to suffer themselves to be governed by some particular men, and perhaps too much, so that it looks sometimes as if they stood in awe of their own subjects.

Of these the constable stood in the highest degree of favour, and was even more beloved by the king than any other; he therefore first named his man, Monsieur de Guise another, and the *mareschal* a third. Which having done, the king said to them, 'You have none of you named Montluc,' to which Monsieur de Guise made answer that it was out of his head, and the *mareschal* said the same. Monsieur de Guise moreover adding, 'if you name Montluc I have done, and shall speak no more of him I nominated before'; 'nor I,' said the *mareschal*, who has since related to me the whole debate.

The constable then stood up and said that I was by no means proper for this employment, as being too humorous, peevish, and passionate, to which the king made answer that he had ever observed and known me to be peevish and passionate upon the account of his service only, when I saw him not served so well as he ought to be, and that he had never heard I ever had a quarrel with anyone upon my own particular account. Monsieur de Guise and the *mareschal* said also the same, adding moreover that I had already been governor both of Montcallier and Alba, without so much as any one man's opening his mouth to complain of my administration; and that also had I been a person of that temper the Mareschal de Brissac would never have loved and favoured me at the rate he did, nor have reposed so great a confidence in me as he had ever done.

The constable hereupon answered very roundly again, and made good his former objection with great vehemency, and would by all means that the person he had nominated should stand: for he was impatient of being controverted, and more of being over-ruled; neither indeed did he ever much love me, nor any of his. The Cardinal of Lorrain was there present, who may better remember than I who it was that the constable named: but (if I be not deceived) it was Boccal, who is since turned Hugonot: however in the end the king would carry it, having Monsieur de Guise and the Mareschal de St Andre on his side, and dispatched away a courier to the Mareschal de Brissac to send me into Avignon, where accordingly I staid expecting a gentleman His Majesty sent to me, who brought my despatch to go presently away to Sienna.

Now the *mareschal* had some dayes before given me leave to retire to my own house, by reason of a sickness I was fallen into, as I have said elsewhere; who had no mind to do it, as he himself confest to me since; and has done me the honour to tell me that had he known of what importance the loss of me would have been to him he would not have so commended me to the king as he had done, and that in his life he never repented anything so much as the letting me depart from him, telling me of a great many things wherein he had not been so well served after my departure out of Piedmont. Monsieur de Cossé, President Birague, and several others can witness how oft they have heard him lament my absence, especially when matters did not succeed according to his desire. And if anyone will take the pains to consider what I performed while I was there under his command, he will find that what I say is very true, and that he had some reason to regret me. I was alwayes at his feet and at his head. I will not say, nevertheless, that anything would have been better done for my being there: but however I must needs speak the truth, and there are those who can say more if they please.

He then writ a letter to the king, and another to the constable, wherein he sent His Majesty word that he had made a very ill choice of me to command in Sienna, for that I was one of the most cross-grained chollerick fellows in the whole world, and such a one as that for half the time I had been with him he had been necessitated to suffer much from me, knowing my imperfections. That indeed I was very good for the maintaining of discipline and justice in an army to command in the field, and to make the souldiers to fight, but that the humour of the Siennois considered, it would be fire to fire, which would be the only means to lose their State, which was to be preserved by gentleness and moderation.

He moreover entreated the constable to remonstrate as much to the king, and in the meantime dispatch a courier to me, who found me very sick, by whom he sent me word, that the king would send me to Sienna; but, that as a friend of mine, he advised me not to accept of that employment, entreating me not to forsake him, to go serve elsewhere under another, and assuring me withal, that if any command happned to be vacant in Piedmont, that I had more mind to than what I already had, I should have it; which were all artifices to detein me.

Oh that a wise lieutenant of a province ought to have an eye, and to take heed of losing a man in whom he may absolutely confide, and whom he knows to be a man of valour, and ought to spare nothing that he may keep him; for oftentimes one man alone can do much. You must eat a great deal of salt with a man before you can rightly know him; and in the meantime you are deprived of him with whom you were thoroughly acquainted, in whom you reposed your trust, and of whose fidelity you have already had sufficient proof. The said *mareschal* had moreover sent word to the king, that I was in Gascony very sick, and in the morning as the letters were read, the constable, who was mighty well pleased with the contents, said to the king, 'Did not I tell your Majesty as much, you find the *mareschal* to be of the same opinion, and no man living can know Montluc better than he who has so often seen him at work.'

To which the king, (who naturally loved me, and had ever done so, after he had seen my behaviour at the Camisado of Bullen) replyed that although all those of the council should speak against me, yet should they prevail nothing by it: for it was his nature to love me, and that he would not alter his election let them all say what they would. Monsieur de Guise then spoke and said,:

Here is a letter very full of contradictions: for in the first place the Mareschal de Brissac says that Montluc is cross-grained and cholerick, and that he will never suit with the Siennois, but will ruine your service if you send him thither; and on the other side commends him for qualities that are required in a man of command, to whom the trust of great things is to be committed: for he speaks him to be a man of an exact discipline and great justice and fit to make the souldiers fight in great enterprises and executions; and who ever saw a man embued with all these good qualities that had not a mixture of choller amongst them? Such as are indifferent whether things go well or ill may indeed be without passion, and as to the rest, since, Sir, your Majesty has yourself made the election, I humbly conceive you ought not revoke it.'

The Mareschal de St Andre spoke next, and said:

Sir, what the Mareschal de Brissac complains of, you may easily correct by writing to Montluc that yourself having made choice of his person above all others for this employment, he must for your sake as much as he can govern his passion, having to do with such a fickle-headed people as those of Sienna.

To which the king made answer that he did not fear but that after he had writ me a letter I would do as he should command me; and immediately thereupon dispatcht away a courrier to me to my own house, by whom he sent me word that although I should be sick I must nevertheless put myself upon my way to go directly to Marseilles where I should meet my dispatch, and should there embark myself with the Germans that the *Rhinceroc* brought, and ten companies of French foot, to which place he would also send me money for my journey, and that I must for a while leave my passion behind me in Gascony, and a little accomodate myself to the humour of that people.

The courrier found me at Agen very sick, and under the physician's hands, notwithstanding which I told him that in eight days I would begin my journey, which I did, and verily thought I should have dyed at Tholouse, from whence by the advice of the physicians I was to return back again, which I could not do: but caused myself to be halled along as far as Montpellier, where I was again advised by the physicians to go no further, they assuring me that if I ventured to proceed on my journey I should never come alive to Marseilles: but whatever they could say, I was resolved to go on so long as life lasted, come on't what would, when just as I was going away there came another courrier from the king to hasten me, and from day to day I recovered my health in travelling; so that when I came to Marseilles I was without comparison much better that when I parted from my own house.

In plain truth the king my good master had reason to defend my cause, for my choler was never prejudicial to his service, it has indeed been sometimes prejudicial to myself and some others who would not avoid nor comply with my humour. I never lost place, battail, nor rencounter, nor ever was the occasion of losing any one of his subjects; my choler never so far transported me as to do anything prejudicial to his service, and if it be violent and prompt, it is the sooner gone: I have ever observed that such people are better to be employed than any other, for they have no malice in them, nor no dangerous reservations, and if they be more suddain they are also more valiant than those who by their moderation would appear to be more wise.

★★★★★★

The *mareschal* then lodged his camp betwixt Porto Novo and Porto Tuffo, in the beautiful suburbs that are there, and not only there, for I dare boldly say that if the suburbs of Sienna had stood altogether they would have been bigger than the city; for in the suburb were more goodly palaces and fine churches and monasteries than there were in the body of the town. The next morning Monsieur de Strozzy carried us up to that part of the wall looking towards the enemies' camp, where we fell into consultations whether or no it were good to hazzard a battail; and there the opinions were various, some thinking it the best, and others conceiving it not convenient so to do. Those who were of opinion that we ought not to fight objected that we could not go to the palace of Dian without passing close by a little fort the *marquis* had made betwixt the little observance and the aforesaid palace, where there was three or four pieces of great artillery (as it was true), and that leaving that behind, we should also leave our own fort of Camolia naked of defence.

I then propounded that for any harm the artillery of the little fort could do us, we could pass by a little before day, and might leave an ensign or two to bridle the little fort from daring to sally out, and as for the fort of Camolia, we could leave three or four companies of the city to keep them likewise in aw, that I on my part with the rest of the forces of the city would go out by Porto Fontebrando, and should by break of day be got to the top of a little mountain, ready to present myself in the plain at so opportune a time, that just as our camp should appear near to theirs I should at the same instant be got so near them that they must of necessity enter into some apprehension to see us come the one on the one side and the other on the other.

The Siennois made account that they could draw four thousand good men out of the town. There were some who approved of my proposal, and of the Siennois also, which was to fight; and others were of a contrary opinion. The game could not be plaid without being lustily disputed, for the *marquis* had three *tertias* of Spaniards, namely that of Sicily, that of Naples, and that of Corsica, (which we call regiments) the two first composed of old souldiers, and that of Corsica of new raised men (wherein nevertheless there were very good souldiers), together with two regiments of Germans, each of them containing twelve ensigns, and four or five Italians. As to the cavalry I think ours would have beaten theirs, for we had very good officers and very brave light-horse; and for the rest, our army consisted of ten ensigns of Germans, ten of Grisons, fourteen of French, and betwixt five and six thousand Italians.

Of all this day Monsieur de Strozzy could not resolve what to do, by reason of the diversity of opinions, nevertheless I think he was resolved the next day to have fought them; for the Sennois were stark mad of fighting, and I do believe fighting for their liberty would have played the devils: But the *marquis* either had some knowledge of his intent, or else his design was not to stay any longer there; for he departed an hour before day in the morning; so that had God inspired Monsieur de Strozzy that he had this day gone out to fight, we had in the morning found them all dislodged, and had fought them upon their retreat and in disorder; but I must repeat what I said before, 'Fa me endeving, e is ti daro denari.'

The *marquis* took the way towards Mauchant, where the *mareschal* had left four ensigns, or else the *marquis* held it, who went to another place hard by, and Monsieur de Strozzy directly to Mauchant, I do not certainly remember whether: but so it was that their camps lay eight or nine days within seven or eight miles of one another, the one going to take some place and the other following after to relieve it. Nevertheless the *marquis* at last arrived before Mauchant, and began to batter either to take or retake it. I was not there, for I staid behind at Sienna, according to the king's intention, and in relation to my command; yet had it not been for a sickness that I began to fall into, I do believe Monsieur de Strozzy would have taken me along with him, and have left Monsieur de Lansac governor, as before; but in the end, as Monsieur de Strozzy marched away.

Monsieur de Lansac took his way towards Rome, to acquit himself of his commission of ambassador. So soon as the *marquis* was sensible of Monsieur de Strozzy's coming, he gave place, and drawing off his artillery, placed himself a little on the right hand, at the distance of a hundred and fifty or two hundred paces from the town, where he made his advantage of two or three little mountains, under which he entrencht himself on that side by the fountains. Monsieur de Strozzy then came and encampt his army all along a hollow way that there was betwixt the *marquis* and the town.

Now Monsieur de Strozzy placed himself so near in design to fight the *marquis*, if he could once tempt him out of his trenches, and there they lay seven or eight days to see which should first dislodge. The *marquis* knew very well that in case he should first move. Monsieur de Strozzy would infallibly fight him: and therefore would by no means be drawn to do it, being expressly forbid to put anything to hazard, as we were after told by Don Juan de Luna himself, who was present with the *marquis* at that time, and in his own person, a very brave Spaniard.

Now betwixt the two camps there was no more than the breadth of one little field, and that not above fifty paces over, wherein there daily hapned skirmishes betwixt the foot of both armies, and so disadvantageous to us that we always came off with the worse, by reason of the artillery the *marquis* had planted upon the three forementioned little mountains, so that Monsieur de Strozzy lost more men by their canon than by their smaller shot. The said Sieur de Strozzy was possest of one fountain only, upon which the artillery from one of the mountainets continually played, and killed a great many men; so that they were constraint to fetch all their water by night; neither could he ever draw up his cavalry into battalia, but that the great shot did great execution upon them; and I was told that in three or four dayes time he had above six score men and horses killed, insomuch that our cavalry was infinitely discouraged, and the foot also very much baffled and out of heart.

Notwithstanding all which Monsieur de Strozzy persisted obstinate not to remove his quarters, and that both out of the hope he had that the *marquis* would first dislodge, and give him an opportunity to fight him, as also out of punctilio, that he would not give him that advantage, as the first to forsake his ground. Both the one and the other of these generals had mettle enough, and both of them had glory in their prospect: but it is better to do one's master's business than to stand upon nicities of honour; I mean if there be no manifest shame in the case.

Monsieur de Strozzy every day sent an account of all he did, both to me and to the Senat, as we also met every day in council to debate upon what he writ to us, and I every hour advised and entreated him not to consume his forces with continuel loss, which would encourage the enemies' souldiers and dishearten his own; the lords of the Senate likewise counseled him the same; but he had so passionate a desire to fight with the *marquis* that that longing alone blinded his judgment and deprived him of the knowledge of his daily loss. I dyed with desire to go to him, but the Senate would by no means consent unto it: at last he writ me word that within two dayes he would retire in the face of the enemy, directly to Lusignano.

Whereupon I immediately dispatcht away a gentlemen to him,

who was present when the letter came, called the Sieur de Lescussan, by him entreating and conjuring him not to make his retreat by day, since the loss in the skirmishes had hapened on his side (for by ill fortune our people had lost more the two last dayes, than of all the time before), and that whoever might advise him to the contrary, I begged of him to be ruled by me, and to retire by night, for it was no more than two miles to Lusignano; beseeching him withall to remember that King Francis had retreated from before Landrecy after this manner, and was so far from being condemned for so doing, that on the contrary he was highly applauded for it, and it was lookt upon by all the princes and potentates of Christendome for the most prudent thing he ever did; yet had he sustained no loss by skirmishes.

I gave him moreover to understand, that hitherto I had never seen a good retreat made after this manner, neither by friend nor enemy, if they who made it were closely pursued. I further represented to him the retreat that Messieurs de Montage and de Boissy would make at Brignolles, who would not be perswaded to retire without seeing the enemy, for all the captains who were present with them could do or say, which was the cause they were defeated within less than half a mile of their quarters. I also sat before him the exemple of Monsieur d'Annebaut, at that time Mareschal of France, at Theroanne, of Monsieur d'Aussun at Carignan, and several others: and that since so great a prince and so great a souldier as King Francis was, had by all the world been commended for that discreet way of proceeding, he ought to take him for his president, considering also that so many valiant leaders had lost themselves in retreating at the head of an army; and that by such a loss (if it should so unhappily fall out) he might guess what would become of the city of Sienna.

In short, Monsieur de Lescusson brought me word that once Monsieur de Strozzy was resolved to do it after this sort, and had it not been for one unlucky fellow called Thomas d'Albene he had with him, he had retreated after the manner I advised: but as there are some men in the world whom God has appointed to be good so has he created others to do mischief, as he did this Thomas; for he represented to Monsieur de Strozzy so many things, and so preacht what a dishonour it would be to him to steal away by night, that in the end he made him to alter his determination; who thereupon sent me word that he was resolved to make his retreat in the face of the enemy: Whereas before, to let me see that he was resolved to follow my advice, he had at one of the clock in the night sent away two pieces of canon he had with him straight to Lusignano; at which place I do believe they were already arrived (for it was but two little miles) before he altered his resolution.

It was four of the clock in the morning before Monsieur de Lescussan parted from him, who brought me his determination, and arrived at seven of the clock in the morning, à *la mode de France*. This hapned to be in August, and presently I sent to the Senate, desiring them all to meet me at the palace, for that I had something of importance to deliver them, which they did.

Now my sickness was still more and more encreast upon me, and was at last turned into a continued feavor and a flix, notwithstanding which about nine of the clock I came to the palace, where I began a speech to them in Italian, which I spoke better then than I can write it now, which is one reason why I have here set it down in French, as also to the end that the gentlemen of Gascony, who few of them understand that language, and shall read my book, as I am confident they will, may not be put to the trouble to have it interpreted to them. I very well remember what I said, and I do truly believe I do not miss ten words, for my discourse was only what was dictated to me by nature without any help of art.

> Gentlemen, I have requested you to this assembly that I might remonstrate to you four things, which I conceive to be very important to your conservation, and have been moved so to do, by reason that Monsieur de Strozzy has this night sent me word by Monsieur de L'Escussan of the resolution he has taken this morning to retreat in open day to Lusignano, in the very face of his enemy. You all know very well what perswasions and entreaties we have used, that he would take heed of retreating after this manner, and particularly what arguments and exemples I laid before him by the said Seiur de L'Escussan, which he relisht very well at first, and was once resolved to do as King Francis did before Landrecy; nevertheless, by I know not what misfortune, he suffers himself to be carried away by a man he has with him, one Thomas d'Albene, who has made him alter his determination by making him believe that to retreat by night would be dishonourable to him: God grant the ill counsel of this man do not prove dishonourable and ruinous both to him and to you also.
>
> Now gentlemen, whilst we are in expectation what will be the

issue of this battail, I have four things to remonstrate to you. The first, and which most nearly concerns you, is that you will please to call to mind that you are soveraigns in your own republick, that your predecessors from father to son have left you this honourable title: that this war aims at nothing but the mine of that soveraignty; for if the enemy remain victorious, you are to hope for no other than from soveraigns to be converted into subjects and slaves; and that therefore it is much better for you to die with your arms in your hands in the defence of this honourable title than tamely to part with your birth-right and to outlive the loss of your priviledges and liberty with shame and infamy.

The second is that you will consider the friendship the king my master has towards you, who pretends to no other advantage from you than that your amity be reciprocal to his, and that since he has generously taken you into his protection, you will have this confidence in him that he will never forsake you: for should you go less in your resolution for one little blow of fortune, consider with what contempt the whole world will look upon you; there is not a prince upon the earth that will aid and assist you should they once discover you to be a mutable and irresolute people.

For all these considerations therefore I beseech you to continue firm and constant, and approve yourselves magnanimious and faithful in adversity, when you shall hear news of the loss of the battail, which I very much fear you will soon do, considering the resolution Monsieur de Strozzy has taken, though God of his goodness divert the misfortune. The third is that you will consider in what a height of reputation your forefathers lived and dyed, which also they have left you to inherit, that you may for ever carry the name of the most valiant and warlike people of all Italy, and have moreover left behind them honourable memory of the battails they have won of those of their own nation. You also derive yourselves from the antient warlike Romans, and pretend to be their true legitimate sons, giving their antient arms, which is the wolf with Romulus and Remus, founders of their proud city, the metropolis of the world.

I therefore most earnestly beseech you gentlemen, that you will call to mind who you are and what your projenitors have ever been; which title of honour should you once lose, what a shame and infamy would it be to your famous ancestors, and what cause will your children have to curse the hour that ever they were descended of such fathers, who have abandoned their liberty to submit their necks to the yoke of servitude and subjection.

The fourth thing I have to trouble you withal is to remonstrate to you that as I have an entire confidence you will manifest your valour and verture upon this occasion, you in order thereunto will suddainly think of making provision of all things necessary to the conservation of your city; for the battail I already give you for lost, not that it will nevertheless proceed from any default in Monsieur de Strozzy, but from the losses we have susteined in the several skirmishes that have been fought before Mauchaut, it being impossible by reason thereof but that our people must be mightily crestfallen and dejected, and those of the enemy in greater heart and courage. 'Tis an effect of victory to be exalted, and fear is the issue of misfortune and disgrace; neither do the little losses in skirmishes, which are the usual forerunners of a battail, ever portend anything but disaster and ruine.

On the other side also those who retire must of necessity show their backs to the enemy: where, although they often face about, yet must they still make forward, where it will be impossible but they must meet with some hedge or ditch over which they must of necessity pass in disorder; for upon a retreat everyone will strive to be foremost, because fear and terror are the ordinary concomitants of those who would retire; and for never so little disorderly haste they shall make, all will be lost if the enemy have but half the courage that men should have. Remember (gentlemen) the battail that Hannibal gained of the Romains at Cannee near to Rome. The Romans who were at home in the city never suspected it possible that their people should be beaten, and therefore made no kind of provision, nor took any order in their affairs; so that when news came of the defeat they were strook into so great a terror that the gates of Rome remained for three days and three nights wide open, not a man so much as daring to go shut them; so that had Hannibal pursued his victory, he might without any opposition have entered the city; as Titus Livie reports in his *History*.

Therefore (gentlemen) give present order for the securing of your gates, and appoint men to guard them, which you must also choose out of those of best repute for the bravest and most faithful amongst you: In the next place cause proclamation to be made throughout the city that all those who have corn or meal at the mills shall make haste to get their corn ground, and bring it all into the city. Cause also all those who have grain or any other sorts of provision in the villages immediately to fetch it into the town, upon penalty of having it burnt or put to sack if by tomorrow night it be not all brought within the walls; and all this to the end that we may have wherewith to support ourselves and maintain the siege till the succours the king will send us shall arrive; for he is not so inconsiderable a prince but that as he has had the power to send you those aids that are already come, he is yet able to send you more; and moreover command your three standard-bearers to have all their companies in a readiness at the beat of drum.

My fever pressing upon me, I am constrained to retire to my lodging, in expectation of such news as God shall please to send us, and you I hope in the meantime will take present order about such things as I have put you in mind of, in which assurance, for the service of the king my master and particularly your own, I make you a tender not only of the little experience God has given me, but moreover of my life for the defence of your city and the ancient priviledges thereof.

Thus then I departed from them, who immediately resolved to have patience in what fortune soever God should be pleased to send them, and to eat to their very children before they would for any misfortune that should befall them depart from the amity and protection of the King of France. I perceived both by their countenance and their speeches that they were a people very well resolved to defend their liberty and to preserve inviolate the friendship they had promised and sworn to me. A resolution at which indeed I was mightily well pleased. They immediately then caused proclamation to be made, upon which everyone ran to the field to fetch in what they had, and about five a'clock in the evening arrived Captain Cambas, camp-master to the French infantry, who came to bring me news that the battail was lost and Monsieur de Strozzy wounded to death, whom they had laid upon poles to carry him to Montalsin, and that that very night all those of the army who had escaped the battail would be at the gates of Sienna.

I leave anyone to judge what a condition I was in, being sick of a fever and a dissentery, seeing our general dead, or what was as bad, it being not above fourteen or fifteen dayes since I arrived in this republick, not having any acquaintance with any one person in the city, and consequently not knowing who were good Frenchmen and who were not. Time is required to the knowledge of men. Monsieur de Strozzy had left me but five Italian companies, of which I did not know so much as one captain, and those he had left in the citadel and the fort of Camolia, which were the keys of the city. I then sent Captain Cambas to carry the news to the Senate, who were nothing dismaied at it, but told him that three or four dayes before I had remonstrated to them that this retreat would be dangerous; and that although by what I had said to them they had given the battail for lost, they would nevertheless nothing alter the good inclination they had for the king, nor despair of being relieved by him.

Do not think it strange (fellow captains) if foreseeing the loss of a battail, I also foretold it to the Siennois, which I did not to dishearten but to assure them, to the end that the sudden news thereof might not strike a general astonishment throughout the whole city; 'twas this made them resolve, this made them take counsel to prepare themselves; and in opinion men do better in expecting the worst than in being over confident of their fortune. Upon what I had said to them every one put on a resolution to die in the defence of their walls, and everything was presently brought into the city.

Now the *marquis* lodged the *Tertia* of Corsica at the little observance, the *Tertia* of Sicily at the *chartreux*, where he entrencht them so well that we could by no means come to them, and himself with the residue of his camp remained at Arbeirotte, and part of his cavalry were quartered at Bonconvent. He trusted to the garrison he had in the Fort St Mark every night to go to the *patrouille*, and to scoure the road on that side towards Fontebrando, that no provision should enter into Sienna; yet could he not order it so but that there entreed cows and buffles for six weeks together.

I think the thing that made the *marquis* proceed with so much leisure and moderation was that he waited for my death and that of Monsieur de Strozzy; making account that we being once dead, and Monsieurs de Lansac and de Fourquevreux taken prisoners, our people, wanting a Frenchman to head them, would deliberate to retire: Monsieur de Strozzy nevertheless recovered, and being told that I was dead (for by reason I had for three dayes been looked upon as a dead man, no one entering into my chamber but the priests to take care of my soul, for my body was given over by the physicians, they had sent him such word), Monsieur de Strozzy, I say, seeing Monsieur de Lansac taken, and me dead, would venture to come from Montalsin, and to put himself into Sienna.

According to this resolution then he departed in the beginning of the night from Montalsin, and six companies of foot and two troops of horse, one of which was commanded by my nephew Serillac, who before he set out bethought himself to borrow three or four trumpets of his companions, fearing that would fall out which did; for Monsieur de Strozzy could not so secretly depart but that the *marquis* had intelligence of his design, and with all his camp lay in wait for him about Fontebrando and all along the River Tresse.

Monsieur de Strozzy had placed all his foot before and his cavalry behind, being himself mounted upon a very little horse, and having his leg sustained in a scarfe fastned to the pummel of his saddle, and with him was the bishop of Sienna.

So soon as our Italian foot came into the enemies *ambuscado*, they fell upon them with so great a fury and so sudden a terror that without much resistance they betook themselves to flight, and bore Monsieur de Strozzy over and over, who with the bishop got amongst the ruins of some old houses, where he staid holding his horse in his hand. The noise was so great that it was heard to Sienna, it being not above a mile off at the furthest. The enemy followed their victory with great execution, when Serillac with his trumpets charged through the middest of them; who hearing so many trumpets, and seeing the horse fain in amongst them, faced about in rout and confusion, and ran full drive upon the *marquis*, who seeing the disorder, was constrained to retire to Arberiotte.

Now those who had given the charge, and who also had received it, were Spaniards and Italians mixt together, insomuch that our people fled on the one side, and the enemy on the other. Two or three hundred Italians of ours recovered the walls of Sienna, others fled away twelve miles from thence, and old captains too, whom the *mareschal* very much esteemed: but the bravest men in the world having once lost their judgment, and giving all for lost, know not where they are. By this you may see how great the dangers of war are, and how infamous a thing it is to run away without first seeing an apparent danger. During this bustle the day began to appear, when Serillac remaining upon the place found he had lost no more than three or four of his troop only, who were also run away with the foot: but I believe there were not many left of the other troop, they having only a lieutenant to command them.

Monsieur de Strozzy hearing now no more noise, with much ado again mounted on horseback, beginning to discover our cavalry, and was looking if he could find Serillac amongst the dead bodies: when seeing him come to him, I leave you to judge what joy there was both on the one side and on the other, and so they marcht together straight towards the city. Now I must needs say that Monsieur de Strozzy herein committed one of the greatest follies that any man in his command ever did, as I have told him an hundred times since; for he knew very well that had he been taken all the world could not have saved him from being put to an ignominious death by the Duke of Florence, so profest and inveterate a hatred he had conceived against him. And although Serillac be my nephew, I may with truth give him this honour and commendation that he was the only cause of Monsieur de Strozzy's safety; which I may the better be bold to write because Monsieur de Strozzy himself told me so.

His troop indeed was a very good one, being for the greatest part Gascons and French; for it was the old company of Monsieur de Cypierre. Of captains there came to the town only Caraffa, who was since cardinal, and another as I was told, whose name I have forgot, and two or three hundred souldiers whom Monsieur de Strozzy would not suffer to come into the town but that night sent them away with the aforesaid captain and kept Caraffa with him.

So soon as Monsieur de Strozzy came into the city he presently enquired how I did, and was answered that for three or four dayes they had begun to conceive some hopes of my life, whereupon he came and alighted at my lodging, the bishop and the said gentleman being with him, where he found me so miserably worn away that my bones had pierced through my skin in several parts of my body.

He comforted me after the best manner he could, and there staid twelve dayes expecting how God would dispose of me; when seeing me from day to day recover strength and grow into a better posture of health, he resolved the thirteenth day in the beginning of the night to depart, without acquainting any one with his intention but myself only. A little before he took horse he and the bishop came to take their leaves of me, knowing very well that his being there would cause the *marquis* to proceed with greater vigour against the town, and also that being abroad he might find some way or other to relieve me; where at parting I promised and assured him to hold out to the last gasp.

The *mareschal* had set guards upon all the roads to catch him, but he chose to retire by a way by which of all other the *mareschal* never suspected he would attempt to pass: for he went out at the Port Camoglia, from whence he descended on the right hand down into the valley, leaving the fort of Camoglia above, and going all along by the river towards the palace of Dian. During his stay in Sienna he presently recovered of his wounds, so that he armed and mounted himself upon a good horse. He met by the way fourty or fifty of the enemies' foot, which gave him some alarm, but he still held on his way without losing any but some few servants only belonging to some gentlemen who went out of the city to attend him.

It was not however without peril. In a few dayes he escaped three great dangers. A little after his departure I recovered my health, and caused myself to be carried in a chair about the town. The *marquis* losing no time shut us up on every side, and every day we had very handsome skirmishes: but I knew very well that the *marquis* would have me for want of bread; which was the reason that I made this harangue to the captains, whom I had assembled together to that effect.

Gentlemen, I believe there is none of us who does not desire to come off from this siege with honour and repute; the thirst of honour has brought us hither. You see we are here shut up for a long time, for we are not to imagine that the enemy will ever rise from before us till he have us by one way or another, seeing upon the reducing of this place depends his victory.

You see also that the king is at a great distance from us, and that therefore of a long time it will not be possible for him to relieve us, forasmuch as he must of necessity draw our succours from Germany, and out of his own kingdom of France, the Italians themselves without the help of others not being sufficient to raise the enemies' siege, who have not only the forces of Italy but moreover of almost all other nations. Now in expectation of this relief we are to have a long patience in husbanding as much as is possible our provisions; in order whereunto I am to tell you that I have deliberated to lessen the size of bread from four and twenty to twenty ounces.

I know very well the souldiers would murmur at this if you did not remonstrate to them how far we are distant from the king;

that His Majesty cannot suddenly relieve us, and that you will rather die of famine than that it shall be laid in your dish that had you had the patience to lessen your diet the town had not been lost. It would be an infamous reproach to have it said that you filled your bellies to starve your honour; you have not shut yourselves up within these walls to occasion the loss and ruine of the city, but to defend and to save it. Represent to them that they are here amongst strange nations, where they may set a mark of honour upon their own. What glory do men acquire when they not only obtain honour and esteem for their own particular persons, but moreover for the nation from whence they come?

'Tis what a generous heart should principally propose to himself for the reward of his doing and suffering. You Germans shall return home proud of the hardships you have susteined and the dangers you have undergone, and we Frenchmen also: and as for you who are Italians, you shall acquire this renown, with invincible courages to have fought for the liberty of your country, a reputation we can none of us obtein but by a long patience in giving the king my master time to relieve us; and believe, I beseech you, that his most Christian Majesty will in nothing fail of the friendship he has promised and sworn to you. If you remonstrate all this to your souldiers, and that they see and know that you yourselves are thus resolved I am assured they will follow the same wayes you take.

Therefore, gentlemen, never think to excuse yourselves upon them; I have never known a mutiny happen (and yet I have seen many) thorough souldiers alone, if they were not by their officers set on and encouraged to it. If you lead them the way, there is nothing they will not do, no incommodity they will not suffer. Do it then I beseech you, or resolve betimes to discover the bottom of your hearts, and plainly tell us you have no mind to undergo the length and inconveniences of a siege, that such as had rather dishonourably spend their time in eating and drinking than stake their persons upon an account of honour, may depart and not divert others from nobler resolutions.

Now because the Germans did not understand my gibberish, I had the *rheincroc's* interpreter tell his master what I said, which he did, and the *rheincroc* made answer that both he and his souldiers would put on the same patience that we ourselves did: and that although it was said of the Germans that they could not endure without eating and drinking their fill, both he and his upon this occasion would manifest the contrary. I was in plain truth the most afraid of these people, because they love to make good chear more than we. As for the Italian, he is more enured to hardship and suffering than we are.

Thus then everyone retired to his own quarters to call their companies together, to whom they accordingly remonstrated the same things that I had represented to them before. Which having heard, the souldiers all held up their hands, and swore they would suffer to the last gasp of their lives before they would yield or do anything unbecoming men of honour. I then sent to the Senate, entreating them the next morning to assemble all the chief men of the city to the palace, to hear a remonstrance I had to make to them that concerned them and their affairs, which they did, and there in Italian I made them the following oration.

Gentlemen, had Almighty God been pleased sooner to restore to me my health and memory, I had sooner thought of what we are to do for the conservation of your liberty and the defence of this city. You have all seen how I have by sickness been reduced to the very door of death, and how God at last has rather by miracle than any operation of nature raised me up again to do yet more service for this republick in such and so great a necessity. Now, gentlemen, I very well see that the conservation of your city and liberty consists in nothing but the making your provisions hold out; for should the *marquis* attempt to have us by force, we shall I hope give him such an entertainment as shall make him curse the hour that ever he came to besiege Sienna: but I perceive he has no mind to go that way to work. On the contrary, he intends to reduce us by famine; against which we must if possible provide, and defeat him of that expectation. I yesterday called together the colonel of the Germans and his captains, Signior Cornelio here present with his, and Combas also with his French officers, to whom I remonstrated that to prolong time and to give the most Christian king leisure to relieve us, it would be necessary to lessen the souldiers' bread from four and twenty to twenty ounces. Telling them that so soon as all the world should know, and particularly the king, that we are resolved to hold out to the last morsel, it will incite

His Majesty to fall speedily in hand with levying of succours, that so many brave men may not be lost, and that he may not seem to abandon those he has taken into his protection in a time of the greatest necessity and danger.

Now, by what I have been told you have, during the time of my extremity, taken account of your provisions, and have only found so much as to last to the fifteenth of November. Of which you have also sent word to His Majesty, a thing that may very well give him occasion to grow cold in sending us relief, considering the great distance betwixt him and us, and that also winter is drawing on. Armies do not fly nor ride post. His succours will be worthy a great prince, suitable to the friendship he bears to you, and sufficient to force the enemy from your walls, and therefore cannot so suddenly be set on foot. Now (gentlemen) after I had remonstrated thus much to the captains, I found them all ready to suffer to the last gasp of their lives, and nation for nation went to make the same remonstrance to their souldiers, whom they found all willing to have patience, and so have both promised and sworn.

See then what you Siennois ought to do, seeing it concerns the loss of your liberties and *seigneuries*, and peradventure of your lives; for you are to expect no good usage, having put yourselves under the king's protection. I beseech you therefore, that since we who have nothing here to lose, neither wives nor fires, have shewed you the way, you will consider of it, to regulate the expence, and appoint commissaries to take an account of all the corn you have in the city, and also of the mouths; and this being done, begin to reduce your bread to fifteen ounces, for it is not possible but you must have some little conveniency in your houses, that the souldiers cannot have.

And of all this good order I shall advertise the king's ministers at Rome, and from thence shall cause a gentleman to go on forwards to the king himself, to the end that His Majesty may judge what time he may have wherein to relieve us, and for the rest rely upon me, who will have no more priviledge than the meanest citizen. The fast that we shall keep shall not only be for our sins, but also for the saving of your lives; for the conservation of which I will willingly lay down my own. *Credete Signiori, che fin a la morte, io vi gardaro quello che vi o promisso, riposate vi sopra di me.*'

They then returned me very many thanks for the good advice I had given them, which only tended to their own preservation, entreating me to retire to my lodging forasmuch as they would go into the great hall, where all the most eminent persons of the city were assembled, to whom they would give an account of what I had said to them, and that within two hours by two of their senators they would return me an answer, and so I departed from them. They were as good as their words, and my proposition being represented in this assembly, they at last all with one voice resolved to eat to their very wives and children rather not to wait the king's pleasure, upon the confidence they reposed in him of a certain relief, and immediately went about taking of order for the contracting the allowance of bread, and for the taking an inventory of both corn and other provision, which in five or six days was dispatched.

I then sent away Monsieur de L'Escussan, but with very great difficulty, for the *marquis* caused strict guard to be kept to hinder any from bringing us in any provisions, and as many countrymen as were taken attempting so to do were immediately hanged without mercy. L'Escussan went first to Montalsin, there to give Monsieur de Strozzy an account of all proceedings, that he might give notice thereof to the king's ministers at Rome, and from thence went to His Majesty to represent unto him the miserable condition of the Siennois, and I had given him in charge to do, and this might be about the middle of October.

From this time forward I could do nothing worth speaking of until Christmas Eve, saving that a little after the departure of the said L'Escussan, we again abated the souldiers' bread to eighteen ounces, and that of the city to fourteen, though all the while there were frequent skirmishes, and very handsomely fought on both sides.

Upon Christmas Eve, about four of the clock in the afternoon, the Marquis de Marignano by one of his trumpets, sent me half a stag, six capons, six partridges, six *borachio's* of excellent wine, and six loaves of white bread, wherewith the next day to keep the feast. I did not wonder at this courtesie, because in the extremity of my sickness he had permitted my physicians to send men through his camp to fetch certain drugs from Florence, and had himself three or four times sent me a very excellent sort of birds, a little bigger than the *beccasicco's* that are taken in Provence. He had also suffered a mule to enter the town laden with Greek wine, which was sent me by the cardinal of Armagnac, my people having sent the cardinal word that in the height of my sickness I talkt of nothing but drinking a little Greek wine. Whereupon he so ordered the business, that the cardinal de Medici writ to the *marquis* his brother to suffer it to come in to me, it being sent under pretence of making me a bath.

The wine came at a time when I was at the last gasp, and so was not delivered to me; but the half of it divided amongst the big-bellied women of the town. Whilst Monsieur de Strozzy was there I gave him three or four bottles of it, the rest I drank as they do Hippocras in the mornings. All these civilities I had received from the *marquis* before, which made me nothing wonder at the present he sent me now: Part of which I sent to the *seigneury*, part to the *rheincroc*, and the rest I reserved for Signior Cornelio, the Count de Gayas, and myself, because we commonly ate together. Such little civilities as these are very gentile and commendable, even betwixt the greatest enemies; if there be no thing particular betwixt them, as there was not betwixt us two. He served his master, and I served mine:

He attaqued me for his honour, and I defended myself for mine. He had a mind to acquire reputation, and so had I. 'Tis for Turks and Sarazens to deny an indifferent courtesie even to an enemy: but then it must not be such a one, or of such importance as to break or endammage your design.

But whilst the *marquis* caressed me with his presents, which I only payd back in thanks, he was preparing for me another kind of feast; for the same night about an hour after midnight he with all his army gave a *scalado* to the cittadel, and to the Fort Camoglia. 'Tis a strange thing that above a month before my mind gave me, and seemed to presage that the *marquis* would give me a *scalado* and that Captain St Auban would be cause of the loss of the fort. This was evermore running in my head, and that the Germans also would occasion the loss of the cittadel, into which an ensign of that nation every night entred, to keep guard there; and that was the reason why I placed an ensign of Siennois in guard overagainst the gate of the cittadel. Signor Cornelio prevailed so far with the *rheincroc*, that he promised him that in case of an alarm, and that the enemy should offer an assault to the cittadel, the German captain that he placed there every night upon the guard should from him have command to let in the Siennois to help to defend it, though I think he that night forgot so to do.

Every night I went to see a company of French foot mount the guard in the Fort Camoglia, and another of Siennois betwixt the fort and the gate of the city, under a great market-house, which on the two sides was enclosed with a little trench; but in the front of it, which went directly to the fort, it was all plain with the pavement, and it might be from this court of guard to the foot threescore or fourscore paces, and as much to the gate of the city. I placed this guard there for two reasons, whereof one was to relieve the fort if occasion should be, as the other company of Siennois was to do the cittadel, and the other to watch that the enemy did not storm the wall of the city; forasmuch as on the left hand, at the going out of the town, the wall was very low, and moreover a part thereof fallen down.

I had several times before said to Signior Cornelio, and to the Count de Gayas, seeing Captain St Auban's company enter into the fort, these words. Would you believe that it eternally runs in my mind that we shall lose this fort thorough the default of Captain St Auban and his company? I never saw him enter into it, that it did not put me into a fit of an ague, out of the ill conceit I had of him. I could never fancy him in my heart, because he never had twenty men of appearance in his company, for he valued a Teston more than the bravest man under the sun, and as to himself he would never stir from his lodging, for anything either I or any of his companions could say to him. I could have wisht him far enough off, I had so strange an aversion to him. And these were the reasons why I ever fancied that this man would bring upon me some mischief or other.

Our fort of Camoglia was environed with a ditch of a pike's length in wideness, and as much in depth, and not much more on three sides; and in the front of it which butted directly upon the Siennois court of guard, nothing but a little rampire of six or seven foot high, and no more; and about the middle of the rampire there was a little lench or half pace, where the souldiers had so much room only as to sustein themselves upon their knees. The enemy had another fort three times as big as ours, and just opposite to it, within an hundred and fifty paces the one of the other.

So that neither they nor we durst pop up a head without being hurt from that quarter; and in ours there was a little tower exactly overagainst theirs, where for greater security we had evermore three or four souldiers which served us for centinels, and who got up into it by a little hand ladder, as they do into a pidgeon-house. The said tower had been broke through on that side towards the enemies' fort, and we had there placed barrels filled with earth, for the hole had been made by the artillery from their fort. Which fort of theirs Monsieur de Termes had caused to be made; but when he went away it was not wholly finished: nevertheless when the Duke of Florence broke with the king, the *marquis* in one night made a very long march, carrying a great number of pioneers along with him, and possessing himself of it, (for there was no guard kept there) immediately put it into defence.

Now, as I have said before, at one of the clock in the night the *marquis* at once gave me a *scalado* both to the cittadel and the Fort Camoglia, where by ill luck the company of St Auban was this night upon duty. The *marquis* with the Spanish and German foot assaulted the cittadel, where by good fortune they had but three ladders long enough, and at the very first so overcharged those three with men, that one of them broke. Our Germans defended, and the Siennois presented themselves at the gate, as they were appointed to do. But the captain of the Germans who had the command of the gate would by no means let them in.

This dispute lasted for about half an hour, during which five or six of the enemy entred, and forct the Germans, who began to turn their backs and fly. They then opened the gate to the Siennois, who ran to the head of the cittadel, where the enemy began to enter, and met these five or six who were already entered, whom they cut in pieces, two of them being the *marquis's* kinsmen, one whereof did not immediately die; and this cooled the courage of the rest who were upon the point to enter. At the same time they gave a *scalado* to the Fort Camoglia. St Auban was in the city, in bed at his ease, and his lieutenant, called Comborcy, was at the fort, a young man of no experience; but that I think had he had good men in his company would have done his duty. They are both of them turned Hugonots since. So soon as the enemy presented their ladders by the three courtins, all his company betook them to their heels, and the enemy consequently entred in; and of the four that were in the tower, three threw themselves headlong down, and the fourth beat down the barrels from the hole, and drew the enemy in.

This rogue had been taken a few dayes before, and had remained above ten dayes prisoner, and I do believe it was upon his account that the *marquis* resolved upon this *scalado*; for he went away with them, and we never saw him after. Now Signior Cornelio and the Count de Gayas were lodged near unto the Fort Camoglia, who immediately upon the alarm ran to the gate, where they found the greatest part of the company of the Siennois before it, and the rest were firing at the enemy who sallyed out of the fort to fall upon them. Signior Cornelio then left the Count de Gayas at the gate, and came running to give me the alarm, where he met me coming out of my lodging with two pages, each of them carrying two torches, and whom I immediately sent back, bidding him both he and the Count de Gayas to go out, and of all things to take care that the Siennois did not forsake their Court of Guard, and to encourage them the best he could, for I would presently come out after him.

He did as I bid him, and came in so opportune a season that he found all abandoned, and gave the enemy a charge with the Siennois, and beat them back into the fort they had taken. The alarm was already throughout the whole city, and some ran to the cittadel, and others to the fort of Camoglia. As I arrived at the gate there came to me la Moliere and l'Espine, both on horseback, the one being mustermaster and the other treasurer, whom I commanded the one to the Port St Mark and the other to Porto Nuovo, and that by the way as they went they should cry out *victory, the enemy is repulst*. Which I did, fearing lest some in the town might have intelligence with the enemy, who hearing this cry would not dare to discover themselves. In the meantime I was at the gate of the city, sending out the captains and French souldiers to succour Signior Cornelio, and when I saw that there were enow gone out, I commanded the lieutenant of Captain Lussan to stay at the gate, and to shut the wicket so soon as ever I was out, and that in case I should be beaten back, he should by no means open it, but rather suffer us all to be killed without, and me in the first place.

I then went out with my four torches, and found Signior Cornelio, the Count de Gayas, and the other captains I had sent out, who had recovered the rampire and had placed the souldiers upon the little half pace upon their knees, who shot at the enemy into the fort, and they again at ours, who could not put up their heads without being discovered, and on the other two sides the enemy assaulted, and ours defended.

Now whilst I was putting the men out at the wicket, St Auban slipt by without my seeing him. The gate into the fort which we had lost was contrived after the manner of a hole, having one step forwards, and another on one side, waving and winding to and fro, and so straight that one man only could enter a breast. In this entry I found Captain Bourg, who was ensign to Captain Charry, Signior Cornelio, and the Count de Gayas close by him. Monsieur de Bassompierre master of the ordnance was always with me, and one of his canoneers. I saw very well that the fight was like to continue, and fearing lest our powder should fail us, bad Monsieur de Bassompierre dispatch away two of his canoneers to fetch more, which he did, and I dare boldly say he was as much the cause of our safety as all our fighting, as you shall hear.

Those that we fought withal were Italians, for the Spaniards and Germans stormed the cittadel. I continually ran first to one and then to another, crying out to them, '*Courage friends, courage comrades,*' and presently on that side on the right hand of the gate where the three forenamed stood, I spyed St Auban, to whom (running to him, and setting the point of my sword to his throat), I said 'Rogue! Son of a whore! thou art the cause that we shall lose the city, which notwithstanding thou shalt never live to see, for I will at this instant kill thee if thou dost not immediately leap into the fort': to which (sufficiently terrified) he made answer, 'Yes Sir, I will leap in,' and then called to him Lussan, Blaçon, and Combas, who were his companions, saying to them, 'Come on comrades, second me, I pray leap in after me'; to which they made answer, 'Do thou leap, and we will follow.'

Whereupon I said to him, 'Take thou no care, I will follow thee myself,' and we all set foot upon the hair pace with him, and immediately after this first step, without any more delaying (for if he had he had died for't) he threw himself desperately in, having a target upon his arm, and his companions also, for he was no sooner in the air, but the rest were also with him, and so all four leapt in together, and it was within two steps of the entry, that le Bourg, Signior Cornelio, and the Count de Gayas disputed. I then immediately made fifteen or twenty souldiers leap in after the four captains, and as all these were within, le Bourg, Signior Cornelio, and the Count de Gayas passed and entred into the fort. I caused the torches to be set upon the rampire, that we might see, and not kill one another, and myself entred by the same way Signior Cornelio had gone before me.

Now neither pikes, halberts, nor harquebuzes could serve us for any use here, for we were at it with swords and steeletto's, with which we made them leap over the curtains by the same way they had entred, excepting those who were killed within. There were yet however some remaining in the tower, when Captain Charry came up to us, though but eight days before he had received an harquebuz shot in his head, and such a one as that thereupon we had given him for dead, notwithstanding there he was with his sword and target, and a morrion upon his head over the cap that covered his wound: a good heart will ever manifest itself; for though he was desperately hurt, yet would he have his share of the fight. I was at the foot of the ladder, and had sent Signior Cornelio and the Count de Gayas out of the fort to encourage those who defended the flanks, bidding them take the one the one side, and the other the other, as they did, and found work enough to do.

I then took Captain Charry by the hand, and said, 'Captain Charry, I have bred you up to die in some brave service for the king, you must mount the first'; which said, he (who was certainly a man of as much courage as ever any man had) without any more dispute began to climb the ladder, which could not be above ten or twelve staves, and he was to enter by a trap-door above, as I have said before. I had very good harquebuzeers, whom I made continually to shot at the hole of this trapdoor, and put two of the said harquebuzeers upon the ladder to follow after him: I had two torches with me (for the other two Signior Cornelio and the count had taken along with them) by the light whereof we saw so clearly that the harquebuzeers did no hurt to Captain Charry, who mounted step by step, still giving our harquebuzeers time to fire, and so soon as he came to thrust up his head into the trapdoor, they fired two harquebuzes, which pierced through his target and morrion without touching his head. The harquebuzeer who followed next after him discharged his harquebuz under his target, by which means Captain Charry advanced the last step, and so they all three leapt in the one after the other, where they killed three of the enemy, and the rest leapt out at the hole. Those in the flancks were also beaten off, and so our fort was regained on every side.

Now the *marquis* had given order to him that commanded at the *scalado* of the fort, which was the governor of their fort of Camoglia, that in case he, the *marquis*, should first enter by the cittadel, that then he should come away to him with all his Italians, and if also he should first gain the fort, that then he would come with his Spaniards and Germans to relieve him. According to this agreement, so soon as the governor of the fort had gained ours, he presently sent to acquaint the *marquis* with it; but there being several little valleys betwixt the cittadel and the Fort Camoglia, the said *marquis* could not come so soon as he would, though he had made so good haste that when we had thought all had been at an end, we saw their whole camp coming upon us, having above an hundred and fifty torches with them; at which time by good fortune Bassompierre's two canoneers returned with the powder, which in great haste we divided amongst the harquebuzeers, for they had none left, and turning about, I bad him send

125

them again for more.

At the same instant la Moliere and L'Espine returned to me, when I immediately sent back la Moliere to the standard-bearer of St Martin to send me two hundred of the best harquebuzeers he had, and send them by the son of Misser Bernardin, a young man that carried the colours in his regiment, full of courage, and of whom I had taken particular notice in several skirmishes, who accordingly came in all haste and found us at it with the whole camp. I then left Signior Cornelio and the Count de Gayas with the other captains to defend the fort, and myself, Bassompierre, and the muster-master went along the flancks, doing nothing but run up and down from place to place to encourage our people. It might be about three hours after midnight when we rebegan the fight, and it lasted till the day took them off.

They there committed one of the greatest pieces of folly that ever men did; for by the light of so many torches we saw them more plainly than if it had been broad day, whereas had they taken the advantage of the night, and advanced with few lights, they had put us a great deal more hardly to't than they did. The two hundred Siennois harquebuzeers that the son of Misser Bernardin brought did us notable service, as also did the powder that Bassompierre sent for, for we had use for it all before we parted, by reason of the long continuance of the fight, where it was well assaulted and better defended.

This was the issue of the fight, the greatest and of the greatest duration without a battail wherein I have ever been, and where I believe God Almighty did as much assist me, if not more, preserving my judgment all the while entire, as at any time in my whole life; for had I failed in the least particle of command we had all been lost, and the city to boot; for on that side we had not fortified at all, and all our confidence was in this fort: I protest to God, that for at least three months after my hair stood on end, so oft as I called to mind the danger we had been in. The enemy there lost six hundred men killed and wounded, as we were enformed by prisoners we took, and we lost but an hundred and fifty in all, both hurt and slain.

That which made them lose so many was the light of the torches, which gave our men such aim that they could not miss, especially being within a pike's distance or two at the most of one another, which was a great incongruity in the *marquis*, as I said before: for we having but little light, and they so much, we discovered them so plain as gave us a mighty advantage. So soon as it was fair light day we went to take a view of what dead we had in the fort amongst theirs, where I found my *valet de chambre* and my groom, who both leapt in after the captains; in my life I never had two better servants.

Signior Cornelio and the Count de Gayas went likewise to visit the cittadel, for I was no longer able to stand, being yet so weak with my great sickness, that with a puff one might have blown me down; so that I wonder how I was ever able to take such pains: but God redoubled my forces in time of need; for in truth during all this great and tedious fight I never ceased running and skipping, now here, now there, without ever feeling myself weary, till there appeared no more an enemy to molest us. They came and gave me an account of all that had past, and there found a kinsman of the *marquis*, who was not yet dead, whom they caused to be carried to their lodging and his wounds dressed.

I will not forget to insert here for an exemple to others that if ever man was well seconded in a time of so great danger, I was, and would for no consideration deprive the chiefs who were there of their due honour, nor the common souldiers, for from the time that Signior Cornelio and the count went out before me and charged the enemy, neither after I was gone out to them, did so much as any one man ever offer to come in again (as Lussan's lieutenant, whom I had left at the gate, swore to me) excepting Bassompierre's two canoneers, who were sent for powder. All the whole city remained in arms during the whole time of the fight, and I will give the Siennois this commendation, with truth (as God is true) that there was no so much as any one man, who staid in the houses, and who did not take arms, both young and old, nor a man that discovered the least affection to the emperor; which gave me a great assurance of two things, one of their loyalty, and the other of their courage.

Three dayes after the *marquis* sent me a trumpet (the same who had brought me the present before) to see if any one of those was living who had entred the cittadel, and that he would not deny to me but that there were two of his kinsmen; Signior Cornelio then carried him to look upon that who was yet alive, and he proved to be one; whereupon the trumpet immediately returned to the *marquis* to acquaint him with it, who at the same instant sent him back again, entreating me to restore him back to him, and that he would be responsible to me for his ransome, which I did in a litter he had sent to that purpose: but he died three dayes after he came into their camp.

Methinks you governors of places ought here to take a fair exemple to present yourselves to the fight: For there are some who say, that a governor or a lieutenant of a province never ought to hazard his own person, arguing that if he chance to miscarry all is lost. I grant them that he ought not to expose himself at all times, and upon every light occasion, like an ordinary captain; but when all lies at stake, what is it that you are made governors and lieutenants for? what question will be made of your courage? and how will your honour and reputation be brought into dispute? Will it, think you, acquit you to say, I would not hazard myself in the fight lest my losing self I should lose all; especially in the night to relieve a fort or a cittadel, considering I was however able to defend the town?

This excuse will not serve your turn; and believe the loss of a fort is of so great importance that your enemy has by that means one foot upon your throat already, you are therefore to die or to recover what you lost, as I did, having at my going out caused the wicket to be shut, to take from us all hopes of retreat, being resolved to die or to expel the enemy, and also letting them alone with their conquest I had been infallibly lost.

And you captains my *camrades*, take notice and exemple by St Auban, that you may value valiant men above money, for the love of money will lead you to the loss of your lives and reputations, and valiant men about you will defend both one and the other, and preserve you from danger and dishonour. Admire, and follow as near as you can the great heart of Charry, who although half-dead, would yet come to the fight, and presented himself to enter the first, and pass by a ladder through a hole, then which a more dangerous passage could not possibly be; for in such a place an enemy has a mighty advantage. No danger nevertheless could deterre this brave souldier from running the hazard.

To conclude, I shall tell you governors of places, that whenever you entertain an ill opinion of an officer, you provide against his remissness, cowardise, or infidelity, as I did, by placing the companies near to the forts. But I had done better, St Auban being suspect to me, since I could not totally rid my hands of him, to have employed him in some other place. It has since taught me to be wiser, and I have found advantages by it, having never since that time entrusted any man of whom I had a mislike. There are wayes enow to shake them off, without either offending any other or disincouraging the party himself.

A little after, as we understood, there came a gentleman of the emperor's bedchamber, who brought letters to the Duke of Florence, and to the said *marquis*, wherein he writ them word that he thought it very strange this war should continue so long, and that he very well knew Sienna was not a place to resist canon, but that it was the *marquis* his custom evermore to spin out a war in length. In answer whereunto the *marquis* remonstrated that he had done all that in him possibly lay, and knew very well that artillery could not take the town, for I had valiant men within, and the whole city was resolute to stand to me to the last, speaking more honourably of me than I deserved, commending my vigilancy, and the provision I had made for my defence, so that he very well knew by the good order I had taken in the city he should but lose so much time by attempting to batter.

Notwithstanding the gentleman being come from the emperor to this effect, and having already spoke with the Duke of Florence, they together ordered it so that they made the *marquis* at last resolve upon a battery. He had before omitted nothing that a good souldier ought to do, having coopt us close in, without any hopes of relief, and yet he was accused of a design to protract the war: But it is the ordinary reward of a man's endeavour when things do not succeed according to the appetite of such as talk of things at their ease. The desires of those we serve and fight for run a great deal faster than we are able to follow.

About the twentieth of January we had notice that the artillery set out of Florence, to the number of six or eight and twenty canon or double culverine to come to the camp. The Siennois hearing this news were so curious as to send out a spy that they might be certain of the truth of this report, who at his return bringing them word back that the artillery was already come as far as Lusignano, it put the whole city into some apprehension, and made them resolve the next day to assemble all the gentry and the chief of the city to the palace, there to determine amongst themselves whether they should abide the assault or surrender upon composition.

Now I was not to huffe and vapour with these people, for they were stronger than I: I was therefore necessitated to win them by gentle remonstrances, and civil perswasions, without the least heat or shew of anger, and you may believe it was not without great violence to my own nature that I proceeded after this manner, contrary to my disposition and the image the constable had represented of me to the king, as he had seen me in my younger and more precipitous age. A prudent and staid governor when he is amongst strange nations must try as much as in him lies to conform himself to the humour of the people with whom he has to do.

With the Germans and Swiss you must be cholerick and rough:

with the Spaniards you must observe their starcht face and formality, and pretend to be a little more religious and devout than you perhaps really are: with the Italians you must be discreet and circumspect, neither to offend them in themselves, nor to court their wives: as for the Frenchman he is for anything: but so it was that God gave me the grace, who am a Gascon, sudden, cholerick, willful, and froward, so to deport myself with this jealous and mistrustful nation that not so much as one citizen could ever complain of me.

Now as all the gentry and the heads of the corporation were going to the palace, Misser Hieronimo Hispano, a gentleman of Sienna, a principal man in the city, and one of the eight of the Council of War, before he went to the palace came in all hast to speak with Signior Cornelio, where he told him that all the chief of the city were summoned to repair to the palace, and that it was to determine whether they ought to stand out a battery or to enter into capitulation with the Duke of Florence and the Marquis of Marignano, and that he had already heard that the major part of them had voted that they ought to condition, and not to endure a battery and an assault, for fear they should come by the worse; that he was now going thither to them, wherefore he entreated him to give me notice of it.

Hereupon Signior Cornelio came to me, and found me ready to take horse to go view the Guards: but so soon as he had told me the news we both went up into my chamber, where we long debated by what means we might divert this blow; and whilst we were in this deliberation came Signior Bartolomeo Cavalcano, who told me as much as I had heard before, and moreover that he thought the resolution was already taken throughout the whole city, and that he only went to the palace to cast in his lot, and that after the lots should once be cast it would be too late to speak.

We were all three in a very great straight, they which way to advise me, and I was as much to seek what advice to take. In the end I resolved to go to the palace, and to take with me the *rhinecroc* and his captains, Signior Cornelio with his Italians, and Captain Combas with the French officers. Our Germans began to suffer much for want of wine, and their bread was very small, for as for flesh there was no more talk of any, unless of some horse or some ass that was exposed to sell in the butchery, and as for money there was no such thing in nature; for Monsieur de Strozzy had no possible means to send any in to us: all which considered, it put us into some fear lest the Germans should joyn with the city to enter into composition, which was the reason I desired Signior Cornelio to go to the *rhinecroc* and entreat him from me to bear me company to the palace, and to bring his captains along with him, and that he would in the meantime leave his lieutenants and ensigns everyone in his own quarters, to the end there might be no surprise about the walls whilst we should be at the palace.

I wisht him also himself to do the same, and ordered Captain Combas to come likewise, which being done, I sent Bartolomeo in all haste to the palace, to try if he could secretly gain any one to his party that might help to break this design: for I had an opinion that if I could but divert this one blow I would deal with so many people afterwards that the blancks should be the greater number in the lottery, and so they all went out of my chamber without being further acquainted by me what I intended to do.

I was yet so extreamly lean and worn with my late sickness, and the cold was at this time of the year so very great and sharp, that I was constrained to go continually with both my body and my head so wrapt and muffled up in furrs, that as they saw me go up and down the streets of the city, no one had any hopes of my recovery, believing that my inwards were decayed and perished, and that I would fall down and die on a sudden. 'What shall we do,' said the ladies and the citizens' wives, 'what will become of us if our governor should die? we shall all be lost; for next after God all our hope is in him: it is not possible he should escape.'

I do verily believe that the prayers of those good women redeemed me out of the extremity and languishing weakness I was in, I mean that of my body; for as to the vigour of my mind, and the quickness of my understanding, I never perceived any decay there. Having then before been accustomed to go so wrapt and muffled, and observing what moan the people made for me, to see me in so lamentable a plight, I called for a pair of breeches of crimson velvet, which I had brought from Alba, laid over with gold lace, finely cut and very neat, for I had made them at a time when I was forsooth in love. We had there leisure enough for those follies whilst we lay in garrison, and having little else to do, it was fit to give the ladies some part of our time.

I put on a doublet of the same, under which I had a shirt finely wrought with crimson silk and gold twist very rich: (for in those dayes they wore the neck-bands of their shirts a good way falling over the collar) I then took a buffe collar, over which I put on the gorget of my arms, which was very finely gilt. I at that time wore gray and white, in honour of a fair lady to whom I was a servant when I had leisure; I therefore put on a hat of gray silk of the German fashion, with a great silver hatband, and a plume of heron's feathers, thick set with silver spangles; the hats they wore in those dayes were not so broad as they wear them now: I then put on a short cassock of gray velvet garnisht with little plaits of silver at two fingers distance from one another, and lined with cloth of silver all open betwixt the plaits, which I wore in Piedmont over my arms.

Now I had yet two little bottles of Greek wine left of those had been sent me by the cardinal of Armagnac, with which I wet my hands, and with them rubbed my face till I had brought a little colour into my cheeks, and then drank a small draught with a little bit of bread, after which I lookt myself in the glass. I swear to you I did not know myself, and methought I was yet in Piedmont, and in love as heretofore. At which I could not forbear laughing, for methought I had got on a sudden quite another face.

The first that came to me with his captains was Signior Cornelio and the Count de Gayas, Monsieur de Bassompierre and the Count de Bisque, whom I had also sent for; who finding me dressed after this manner, all fell a laughing. I strutted up and down the room before them like fifteen Spaniards, and yet had not strength enough to kill a chicken, for I was so weak as nothing more. Combas and the French captains came also, and the whole farce tended to nothing but laughter for all the company: the last that came was the *rhinecroc* and his captains, who seeing me in this posture, laught to that excess that he sobbed again, when pulling him by the arm, I said to him, 'What colonel, do you think me to be that Montluc that goes every day dying through the streets? No, no, you are mistaken, that fellow's dead, and I am another Montluc sprung up in his room.'

His interpreter told him what I said, which made him laugh still more, and Signior Cornelio had already acquainted him with the reason why I had sent for him, and that it was necessary by one means or another to dispossess the Siennois of their fear. Thus then we went all on horseback to the palace, where so soon as we were got up to the top of the stairs, we found the great hall full of gentlemen, and such other *burgers* of the city as were of the council.

Within the great hall on the left hand there is a lesser room, into which none were to enter but the captains of the people, the twelve counsellors, and the eight of the Council of War, all which are called the magistracy. Thus then I entred into the great hall, where I put off my hat to them, but was known by nobody at first; they all believing me to be some gentleman sent by Monsieur de Strozzy into the city to command at the assault, by reason of my great weakness.

I then entred into the little hall, with all the colonels and captains after me, who kept at distance by the door whilst I went and sat down by the captain of the people, in the place where those who represented the person of the king were used to sit, as I myself upon that account had often done. In going up with my hat in my hand, I smiled first upon one and then upon another, they all wondering to see me, and two had already delivered their opinions when I began to speak to them in Italian to this effect.

Gentlemen, I have been told that since the time you have been certain of the truth of the enemies bringing up artillery to your walls, you have entred into some debates which have rather begot amongst you fear and astonishment than any noble resolution to defend your city and liberty by arms. Which I have thought very strange, and greatly wondred at, not being able to perswade myself to believe any such thing. However in the end I resolved with the colonels and captains of all the three nations the king my master has in this city, to come to you in this place, and to understand from your own mouths the truth of all that has passed.

Now I besiech you gentlemen, weigh and consider well what you shall determine in this council to which you are called; for upon this council, and the resolution that shall be the issue of it, depends all your honour, greatness, authority, and the security of your State, your lives and honours, and the conservation of your ancient liberty; and on the contrary, all the shame, dishonour, and reproach, with a perpetual infamy to your posterity, and dishonour to your famous ancestors, who have left you for inheritance the *grandeur* you now possess and uphold, having themselves ever defended and maintained it by battels, with their weapons in their hands, against all those who have attempted to take it from them.

And now when you ought to have purchast the occasion that presents itself at the price of half your wealth, that therein you might to all Christendom manifest and approve yourselves the true legitimate sons of those ancient warlike Romans, and of those noble ancestors who have so often and so bravely fought to assert and maintain your liberty, is it possible that so great and so generous hearts as those of the Siennois should enter into astonishment for hearing talk of canon? will you be afraid for this? I cannot think that this proceeds from you, who have given so many, and so ample testimonies of your valour; neither is it out of any want of friendship to the most Christian king, nor out of any distrust you have in him, that he will not certainly relieve you, neither can it be out of any diffidence you have in one another, by reason of any factions in your city, for I have never observed the least division among you: But on the contrary, the greatest unanimity for the conservation of your liberty and republick. I have ever seen you resolute to dye with your swords in your hands, rather than suffer it to be ravished from you.

I have ever seen all men of all conditions move with the same motion and inspired with the same resolution. Neither can it be for want of courage, for I never saw you sally out to skirmish that some of your young men did not evermore signalize themselves above our people, though much older souldiers than they, who in a longer practice of arms have performed acts worthy to be praised and esteemed of all. I cannot then believe that men who do so well, should for the noise of canon, which brings more terror than harm, enter into astonishment and resolve to surrender themselves slaves to that insolent and insupportable Nation of the Spaniards; or your neighbours, your ancient and professed enemies. Since then this apprehension cannot proceed from any defect in yourselves, it must of necessity proceed from me, who have the honour to be lieutenant for the King of France, your good friend and protector.

If as to what concerns me, you apprehend that I shall want health and vigour to undergo that toil and labour that will be necessary and required at the time when the enemy shall assault us, by reason of the weakness wherein I now am through my great sickness; that consideration ought not to beget in you the least distrust; arms and legs do not do all: The great Captain Antonio de Leva, gouty and impotent as he was, has won more victories in his chair than any other of our age has done on horseback.

God has ever been pleased to preserve my judgement to preserve you. Have you ever known me fail? Was I then stretched at ease in bed when the enemy gave you the great *camisado*, and *scalado?* Do but mark I beseech you, gentlemen, the great grace God was pleased to shew me on a sudden, supplying me with as much strength as I had never been sick; by which you may perceive that Almighty God loves us, and that he will not that either you or we perish. I feel myself strong enough to wear my arms, you shall no more see me swathed and furred up as before.

If perhaps you do it out of my incapacity, or little experience, you do therein a great wrong to the king, that being as much as to give all the world to understand that His Majesty has hither sent you a man void of all ability and poorly experimented to know how to order what should be done for the defence of your city? What? do you believe the king has so little kindness for you, as to send me hither, had he not had a great confidence in my capacity, and beforehand made sufficient tryal elsewhere both what I am and what I can do? I shall tell you nothing of myself, it would not become me to be my own trumpet, something you have seen yourselves, and the rest you may have heard from others.

You may then well judge that the king has not singled out me amongst so many gentlemen of his kingdom, and has not sent me to you, without having well weighed what I am able to do by the long experience he has had, not only of my politicks in point of government, of which you may hitherto have taken some notice: But moreover, of my conduct in matter of arms, when an enemy would carry a place by fine force. Do you fear, gentlemen, my courage will fail me in time of need? what then do all those testimonies I have given you since my coming hither being sick avail? You have seen me sally out from the time I have been able to mount to horse, to go to see the skirmishes so near that my self-commanded them.

And have you altogether forgot the day, that I entred into this city, and the great skirmish I then made? Your people saw it and had a share in the fight; and upon Christmas Eve yet a greater, where the fight lasted for six long hours together? Did I not then fight in my own person? Did you not then see that I neither wanted judgment to command nor valour to fight? I am ashamed to say so much of my self; but seeing you all know it to be true I need not blush to speak it. I will tell you nothing but what yourselves have seen. I am no bragging Spaniard, I am a Frenchman, and moreover a Gascon, the most frank and plain dealing of all that nation.

Now, methinks, gentlemen, you have so much experience of yourselves as will render you worthy of a perpetual reproach, should you go less in your resolution, besides the ruine it would infallibly bring upon you. Methinks you ought to know me sufficiently, having been so long amongst you, and that I have omitted nothing of what the king proposed to himself I should perform for his service and yours in the greatest necessity and danger. All this that I have remonstrated to you, as well for what concerns your own particular, as what relates to myself, ought to make you lay aside all apprehension, and to assume the courage and magnanimity that your predecessors and selves who are now living have ever had.

Wherefore, I beseech you that you will unanimously take up such a resolution as valiant men such as you are ought to take, that is to dye with your weapons in your hands rather than to loose your sovereignty and the liberty you have so long exercised and enjoyed. And for what concerns me and these colonels and captains whom you see present here, we swear in the presence of God that we will dye with you, as at this instant we will give assurance. It is not for our benefit, nor to acquire riches, neither is it for our ease, for you see we suffer both thirst and hunger: it is only in pursuance of our duty, and to acquit ourselves of our oath, to the end that it may one day be said, and by you, that it was we who defended the liberty of this city, and that we may be called conservators of the liberty of Sienna.'

I then rose up, bidding the German interpreter to remember well all I had said, to repeat it to the *rhinecroc* and his captains, and then directed my speech to the colonels, and said to them '*Signori mi e fratelli juriamo tutti e promettiamo inanzi Iddio, che noi moriremo tutti l'arme in mano conessi loro, per adjutar li a deffendere lor sicuressa e liberta: e ogni uno di noi s'obligi per lei soi soldati, e alsate tutt le vostre mani.*'

Which being said, everyone held up his hand, and the interpreter told it to the *rhinecroc*, who also held up his hand, and all the captains crying '*Io, io huerlie,*' and the other '*Ouy, ouy,*' we promise to do it, everyone in his own language. Whereupon the captain of the people arose, and all the council, returning me infinite thanks; and then turned towards the captains, whom he also very much thanked, and with great chearfulness. They then entreated me that I would retire to my lodgings till such time as they had spoken with all the council who were in the great hall without, and given them an account of what I had remonstrated to them; which I accordingly did, and at my going out of the little room, I there met with Misser Bartolomeo Cavalcano, who knew nothing of the proposition I had made (for he entred not into the council chamber) who told me in my ear that he thought they had all taken a resolution not to endure a battery.

I then carried him back with me to my lodgings, and three hours after, came four of the magistracy, of which Misser Hieronimo Espano was one, having in charge from all the *signeury* in general to return me infinite thanks; and he told me that Misser Ambrosia Mitti had made a speech in the accustomed chair, which is in the middle of the great hall, against the wall, giving them to understand what a remonstrance I had made to them, wherein he forgot nothing (for he was a man of great eloquence and wisdom) and the oath that all the colonels and captains had taken, finally exhorting them to resolve all to fight. I do not remember whether they put it to the balotte, or if they held up their hands as we had done.

But they all four assured us that they had never seen a greater joy then what generally appeared amongst them, after the proposition of the said Ambrosia Mitti. Telling me, moreover, that after I had been in the said hall and made an end of the forementioned harangue, the two gentlemen who had delivered their opinions before, that they ought to capitulate and come to a composition with the enemy, had requested the Senate to do them that favour as to conceal what they had said and take no notice of it, but give them leave to vote anew; which being accordingly done, they again delivered their opinions that they ought to fight, and enter into no kind of composition, but rather dye with their arms in their hands. I then told Misser Hieronimo Espano, that I would retire myself for all that day and for all that night to write down the order of the fight; which having done, I would immediately send it to the Germans in their language, and to the French in theirs.

Governors and captains, you ought to take some example here, forasmuch as there are some who say they have surrendered a place that the souldiers would not defend, and moreover, that the inhabitants of the town went about to betray them, and by that means compelled them to capitulate. These are mere excuses, believe me they are mere excuses. The thing that compels you is your own want of experience. Gentlemen and *camrades*, whenever you shall happen to be at such a wedding, put on your best clothes, make yourselves as fine as you can, wash your faces with Greek wine, and rub a good colour into your cheeks, and so march bravely thorough the streets and amongst the souldiers with your faces erect, having nothing in your mouths, but that very soon, by God's help and the strength of your own arms, you will in despite of them have the lives of your enemies, and not they yours; that it is not for them to come to attaque you in your own fort; that it is the only thing you desire, forasmuch as upon that depends their ruine, and your deliverance.

And by carrying yourselves after that manner, the very women will take courage, and much more the souldiers: But if you sneak up and down with a pale face, speaking to nobody, sad, mellanchollick and pensive, though all the city and all the souldiers had the hearts of lyons, you will make them as timerous as sheep. Speak often to those of the city in four or five words, and likewise to the souldiers saying to them:

> Well friends, are you not in heart? I look upon the victory as
> our own, and hold the death of our enemies already for certain:
> For I have I know not what prophetick spirit, which whenever
> it comes upon me, I am always certain to overcome, which I
> have from God and not from men. Wherefore rely upon me,
> and resolve all of you to fight, and to go out of this place with
> honour and reputation. You can dye but once, and 'tis a thing
> that is predestined, if God has appointed it so, it is in vain for
> you to fly. Let us then dye honourably; but there is no appear-
> ance of danger for us, but rather for our enemies, over whom
> we have the greatest advantage imaginable.

And who governors and captains, would you have dare to say he is afraid, seeing you so bravely resolved? Let me tell you that though they trembled before, they will lay aside their fear, and the most cow-ardly will become as bold as the most couragious of the company. The souldier is never astonished so long as he sees the confidence of his chief continue firm and unshaken. As the chief therefore carries away all the honour, and the rest have nothing but what he shall give them in his report of their valour to the prince; so ought he to resolve never to discover the least shadow of fear: For behaving himself after that fearless manner, the souldiers themselves will be sufficient testimonie for him, so that the reputation he shall have acquired shall remain in-disputably his own, without anyone being able to contradict it.

I do not then advise you anything I have not first tryed myself, not only here but in many other places also; as you will find in this book if you have the patience to read it. Now this is the order I set down for the fight, and for all the whole city, all which particularities I represent to you, without contenting myself to say that Sienna was besieged, where I nine or ten months sustained the seige, and was at last constrained to capitulate by famine; for of such a general account as that, a king's lieutenant, a captain, or a souldier, can make no benefit. This is the historians way, and of these kind of writers there are but too many: I write of myself, and will instruct others that come after me; for to be born for a man's self only is in plain English to be born a beast.

I then ordered in the first place that the city should be divided into eight parts, of which the eight of the Council of War should have everyone a part; that every one of the Council of Eight should appoint a person for whom he should himself be responsible to take a list of the quarter should be assigned him, how many men, women and children there were in that division, from twelve the males to sixty, and the females to fifty years of age, which were to carry baskets, barrels, shovels, picks, and mattocks, and that each one of his own quarter should make captains of every trade, without mixing them together: that everyone should be commanded upon pain of death so soon as ever their captain should send for them to come to the place appointed, immediately to haste away, as also the women and children; that everyone should forthwith make provision of such things as were proper for his or her employment, and that the masters of men-servants and maids, or their mistresses, should be obliged speedily to take order that their men and maids be furnisht with tools and utensils wherewith to labour at the work for which they shall be appointed, upon pain of two hundred crowns.

And the city to furnish the poor who have not wherewith to buy them, at the expense of the publick treasure: that the said deputies shall make their catalogues, and shall go from house to house to register their people; and that so soon as the captains, everyone in his own quarter, should cry out 'Force, Force,' everyone both men and women should run to their tools, and present themselves at the place to which the captain should lead or appoint them to come; and that the deputies should deliver in the lists of all, both men and women, they shall have found in their respective precincts to each of the eight of the Council of War, quarter for quarter; that the old men and women above the forementioned ages shall remain in their masters' houses, to get meat and to look to the house. That the said deputies should take a list of all the masons and carpenters who should be found in their quarter, which list they should also deliver to him of the eight of the Council of War by whom they shall be deputed. And this was the order for the laborers and pioneers.

The order for those who bore arms was that the three standard bearers, namely of St Martin, of Ciotat, and of Camoglia, should forthwith take a view of all the companies, which were four and twenty, and examine every man's arms if they were in good order for fight, and if not to make them presently to be repaired: that they should refine all the powder, and cause great store of bullet and match to be made: that the three standard-bearers should each keep in his own quarter without stirring thence till one of the Eight of War should come to give them order what to do; that the antient gentlemen who were not able to bear arms nor to work should present themselves to sollicit the pioneers of that quarter where their houses stood, and to assist the captains of the said pioneers.

Now I had ever determined that if ever the enemy should come to assault us with artillery, to entrench myself at a good distance from the wall, where the battery should be made, to let them enter at pleasure, and made account to shut up the two ends of the trench, and at either end to plant four or five pieces of great canon, loaden with great chains, nails, and pieces of iron. Behind the retirade I intended to place the muskets, together with the harquebuzeers, and so soon as they should be entred in, to cause the artillery and small shot to fire all at once, and we at the two ends then to run in upon them with pikes and halberts, two handed swords, short swords, and targets.

This I resolved upon, as seeing it altogether impossible for the king to send us relief, by reason that he was engaged in so many places that it would not be possible for him to set on foot forces sufficient to raise the siege, neither by sea nor by land; and Monsieur de Strozzy had no means to relieve us, wherefore I would permit them to enter, and make little defence at the breach, to the end that I might give them battail in the town, after they had past the fury of our canon and smaller shot: For to have defended the breach had in my opinion been a very easie matter; but then we could not have done the enemy so much mischief as by letting them enter the breach, which we would have pretended to quit, onely to draw them on to the fight.

For five or six dayes before the artillery came I every night sent out two peasants and a captain or a sergeant, as centinels *perdues*, which is a very good thing and of great safety; but take heed whom you send, for he may do you a very ill turn. So soon as the night came the captain set a peasant centinel at some fifty or sixty paces distant from the wall, and either in a ditch or behind a hedge, with instructions that so soon as he should hear anything he should come back to the captain at the foot of the wall, which captain had in charge from me that immediately upon the peasant's speaking to him they should clap down upon all four, and so creep the one after the other to the place where the peasant had heard the noise, or rather fall down upon their bellies close to the earth, to discover if there were not three or four who came to view that place, and to observe if they did not lay their heads together to confer; for this is a certain sign that they came to view that place in order to the bringing up of artillery.

To do which as it ought to be done, they ought to be no other than the master of the ordnance, the colonel or the camp-master of the infantry, or the engineer, the master carter, and a captain of pioneers, to the end that according to what shall be resolved upon by the master of the ordnance, the colonel, and canoneer, the master carter may also take notice which way he may bring up artillery to the place; and the canoneer ought to shew the captain of the pioneers what is to be done for the esplanade, or plaining of the way, according to the determination of the rest. And this is the discovery that is to be made by night after you have discovered a little at distance by day; for if those within be an enemy of any spirit, they ought either by skirmishes or by their canon to keep you from coming to discover at hand.

The captain had orders to come and give me a present account of what he and the peasants had heard or seen, and to leave the peasants still upon their *perdue*, and a souldier in his own place till his return. Three times the enemy was discovered after this manner, and immediately upon the notice, having also the list of the eight quarters, and of the Eight of War who commanded those quarters, I suddenly acquainted Signior Cornelio, who could presently tell me both the quarter against which it was, and the gentlemen of the Eight of War that commanded it. I had never discovered my intention to anyone, but to Signior Cornelio onely, who was a man of great wisdom and valour, and in whom I reposed a very great confidence; who, so soon as he knew that I meant to give them battail in the city, we did nothing of one whole day but walk the round both within and without, taking very good observation of all the places where the enemy could make a battery, and consequently by that knew where to make our retirade.

And so soon as ever notice was given me by the captain who stood centinel without the city, I presently advertised the commander of that quarter, and he his deputy, and his deputy the captain of the pioneers, so that in an hours' time you might have seen at least a thousand, or twelve hundred persons beginning the retirade. Now I had ordered the city to make great provision of torches, so that those who had discovered were hardly returned to the *marquis*, but that they saw all that part within the town covered with torches and people, insomuch that by break of day we had very much advanct our trench, and in the morning sent back those to rest, calling in another quarter to the work till noon, and another from noon till night, and consequently others till midnight, and so till break of day, by which means in a little time we performed so great a work, that we could by no means be surprised.

After this manner I still turned the defences of the town towards the *marquis's* attempts, who lodged at the house of Guillet the Dreamer, (phrase signifying that a man is nonplust, and knows not what to do, which is properly to lie at the house of Guillet the Dreamer), and Signior Fernando de Sylva, brother to Signior Rigomez (who commanded on that side towards the observance, with whom I had some discourse upon the publick faith, the Friday before we departed out of the city, betwixt their quarters and the Fort Camoglia) told me that the *marquis* had some jealousie that someone of their council betrayed to me all their deliberations, seeing he had no sooner designed to batter any part, but that we alwayes fortified against that place; for by night the least noise is easily heard, and so great a bustle cannot be concealed; and because he told me that he had compiled a book of the particularities of the Siege of Sienna, he entreated me to tell him by what means I so continually discovered their intentions, whereupon I told him the truth.

But to return to our subject, the *marquis* in the end came and planted his artillery upon a little hill betwixt Port Oville and the great observance. The choice of this place put me, who thought my self so cunning, almost to a nonplus, forasmuch as at Port Oville there is a very spatious antiport, where the houses of the city almost touch, having nothing but the street between, time to make the necessary retirade, to do which I must be constrained to beat down above an hundred houses, which extremely troubled me; for it is to create so many enemies in our entrals, the poor citizen losing all patience to see his house pulled down before his eyes. I gave to the Count de Bisque the charge of terrassing up this gate, for which use we took the earth out of the gardens, and vacant places that lie a little on the left hand. Oh the rare exemple that is here, which I will commit to writing that it may serve for a mirror to all those who would conserve their liberty.

All these poor inhabitants, without discovering the least distaste or sorrow for the ruine of their houses, put themselves their own hands first to the work, everyone contending who should be most ready to pull down his own. There was never less than four thousand souls at labour, and I was shewed by the gentleman of Sienna a great number of gentlewomen carrying of baskets of earth upon their heads. It shall never be (you ladies of Sienna) that I will not immortalize your names so long as the book of Montluc shall live; for in truth you are worthy of immortal praise if ever women were.

At the beginning of the noble resolution these people took to defend their liberty, all the ladies of Sienna divided themselves into three squadrons; the first led by Signiora Fortaguerra, who was herself clad in violet, as also all those of her train, her attire being cut in the fashion of a nymph, short, and discovering her buskins; the second was la Signiora Picolhuomini attired in carnatian sattin, and her troop in the same livery; the third was la Signiora Livia Fausta, apparelled all in white, as also her train, with her white ensign, In their ensigns they had very fine devices, which I would give a good deal I could remember. These three squadrons consisted of three thousand ladies, gentlewomen, and citizens, their arms were picks, shovels, baskets, and bavins, and in this equipage they made their muster, and went to begin the fortifications. Monsieur de Termes, who has often told me this story (for I was not then arrived at Sienna) has assured me that in his life he never saw so fine a sight. I have since seen their ensigns, and they had composed a song to the honour of France, for which I wish I had given the best horse I have that I might insert it here.

And since I am upon the honour of these women, I will that those who shall come after us admire the courage and virtue of a young virgin of Sienna, who, though she was a poor man's daughter, deserves notwithstanding to be rankt with those of the noblest families. I had made a decree at the time when I was dictator that no one upon pain of severe punishment should fail to go to the guard in his turn. This young maid seeing a brother of hers who was concerned to be upon duty not able to go, she took his morrion and put it upon her head, his breeches, and a collar of buff, and put them on, and with his halbert upon her neck, in this equipage mounted the guard; passing when the list was read by her brother's name, and stood centinel in turn, without being discovered till the morning that it was fair light day, when she was conducted home with great honour. In the afternoon Signior Cornelio shewed her to me.

But to return to our subject, it was not possible of all that day nor the night following for the count to perfect his terrass, nor we our retirade, at which we wrought exceeding hard, leaving about fourscore paces to the *marquis*, if he had a mind to enter there. We had made a traverse by the Port Oville, where we had placet three great culverins, laden as I have said before, at which place were Signior Cornelio, the Count de Gayas, and three canoneers, who were there left by Monsieur Bassompierre. On the right hand upon an eminence was the great observance, betwixt which and the walls we had planted five pieces of canon ramed with the same, which the said Bassompierre commanded in his own person; yet both the one and the other were so well concealed that the enemy could discover nothing from the little hills about us.

Well did they perceive, that above at the observance there were people; for they had evermore a clap at that: but we were all behind a trench we had cast up betwixt the observance and the wall of the city, tapist and squat, so that we could not be seen. The souldiers were all before the houses, through which they had pierct several holes to come and go under cover. Behind the retirade, which was not much above the height of a man, they were also sheltred from being seen. Signior Cornelio was also under cover, by reason that he lay in a low place and under the shelter of a very thick wall which joined to Port Oville. The order of the fight was thus.

Signior Cornelio had with him one ensign of Germans, two of French, four of Italians, and four of Siennois, having also the Count de Gayas to assist him; and with me at the observance was the *rhinecroc*, with three companies of Germans, two of French, two of Italians, and four ensigns of Siennois. In all the two troops both of Signior Cornelio's and mine there was not so much as one harquebus, but pikes, halberts, and two hand-swords, (and of those but few) swords, and targets, all arms proper for close fight, and the most furious and killing weapons of all other; for to stand popping and pelting with those small shot is but so much time lost; a man must close and grapple collar to collar if he mean to rid any work, which the souldier will never do so long as he has his fire-arms in his hands, but will be alwaies fighting at distance.

All the night the enemy were placing gabions for six and twenty or seven and twenty pieces of ordnance, and by break of day they had planted twelve, as they would in that time have done all the rest had it not been that they had been necessitated to draw their canon up to this mountain by strength of hand. The wall is good enough, which not long since by one of the two Popes Pius's, who were of the house of Picolhuomini, and of the order of the people, had caused to be made. At break of day they began their battery within a foot or two of the bottom of the walls, at the distance of about an hundred paces; which they did to cut the wall by the bottom, making account the next day with the rest of the artillery in a short time to beat down the whole wall: but for all that the Count de Bisque ceased not continually to fill the antiport, leaving us flanckers, so that we could see all along the breach.

About noon they gave over their battery below, and began to batter the middle of the wall, when so soon as I saw them begin to let in light, I left Signior Cornelio, who continually went up and down from place to place, and took Monsieur de Bassompierre, with whom I went to the Fort Camoglia, from whence we could plainly see into the recoyle of their canon, but I shall leave this discourse to finish the order.

I left a French company at the Fort Camoglia, another at the citadel, there being already two companies of Siennois at each, more than two companies of Germans at the place, each a part by themselves; one of Italians at the Port St Mark, and all along the wall towards Fontebrando, Siennois, and towards Porto Novo the same, having given the word to the two French companies that in case I should stand in need I would send for them, leaving the Siennois still in the citadel, and in the fort.

The same instructions I left with the Germans, and had taken order that from six hours to six hours we would change the word, as well by day as by night, to the end that whilst everyone lay close at his post, if there should be any traytor amongst us, he might go to no place where he might have any intelligence with the enemy to draw men from that part to weaken that post, to carry them to another: but that no one should be believed if he did not bring the word, in changing of which it should be carried to the Siennois by two of the Council of Eight, by the one to the one half, and by the other to the other; so that unless those themselves brought the word they were not to stir from their post. I was ever afraid that the *marquis* had some intelligence in the city, which made me take this course to prevent him.

The Germans who were at the great place had the same command, and moreover that an officer or a sergeant of the others should come to fetch them: to which end there were six sergeants chosen out of our Italian and French companies, who had in charge that during the time of the battery or of an assault they should continually be moving along the curtain of the wall to the quarters I had appointed, and never to abandon their quarter. It was also ordained that no one upon pain of death, of what nation soever, not so much as the Siennois themselves should dare to abandon the retirade, being of the number of those who were there appointed for the fight, and the same was carried quite round the walls of the city.

It was also ordered that of eight of the Council of War four were continually to remain with me and Signior Cornelio, to the end that the two who remained with him might go continually on horseback with the word to fetch such succours as Signior Cornelio should send for, to relieve him if occasion should be, and my two the like; that is to say of the captains of the city, and the other four should go to the places where the six sergeants were appointed to be, to the end that they might joyntly encourage the souldiers to fight if necessity should require. And there, where there was no business to be done and that any came to them with the word for succours, they should deliver him the one half and keep the rest to defend that post.

That the officers of the king, as controulers, commissaries of victual, treasurers, or their deputies, should ordinarily be, part by day and part by night, still on horseback, riding up and down the streets of the city, and that from hour to hour one of them should bring me news how all things stood in the body of the city and about the walls, bringing us still some token or another that they had spoke with the four of the council and the sergeants who were deputed with them. This was the order I gave, at least as much as I remember, never failing myself every day to visit the companies and to encourage the inhabitants to do well.

I now return to what we did at the Fort Camoglia: Monsieur de Bassompierre ran to fetch a canon we had in the citadel, but as he went about to remove it the carriage broke, so that instead of it he brought a demy-canon, which a Siennois the said Bassompierre had enterteined in the quality of a canoneer evermore shot in, and so well that he could hit with it as small a mark as if it had been a harquebuz. He was assisted by some Italian and French souldiers of the citadel to bring it, whilst I was making ready a platform with the souldiers of the fort, till my company of pioneers came which I had sent for in all haste, and in less than an hour and a half we dispatcht it where I mounted my demy-canon. I gave ten crowns to our Siennois, that he might make some good shots with that piece here as he had done several at the citadel before. The enemy had placed gabions on the flanck of their battery towards us.

Bassompierre and I went a little on the right hand, and observed the bullet in the air like a hat on fire, flying very wide on the right hand, and the second as much on the left, which made me ready to eat my own flesh for rage: Monsieur de Bassompierre always assured me that he would presently take his level right, and still went and came to and fro betwixt him and me. The third shot light upon the bottom of the gabions, and the fourth playd directly into their artillery and there killed a great many of their men, whereupon all those that assisted fled behind a little house which was in the rear of their canon. At which I ran and took him in my arms, and seeing him with his linstock ready to fire again, said to him, '*Fradel mio da li da seno, per dio facio, ti presente dalteri dieci scoudi, e d'une biechier de vino Graeco.*'

I then left him the French captain, who had the guard of the fort, to furnish him continually with such things as he stood in need of, and Monsieur Bassompierre and I returned to our post. There then advanct a German ensign to the enemies' battery, who came along by the other gabionade with his colours flying, and this might be about four of the clock in the afternoon, we could see him march from behind the observance, and was no sooner come to the artillery but our piece fired and killed the ensign, upon which the Germans immediately fled away, retiring to the place from whence they came. And this Siennois made so many brave shots that he dismounted them six pieces of canon, and their artillery remained totally abandoned till the beginning of the night, without playing any worse than two pieces of canon that were covered with gabions and flanckt towards the Fort Camoglia, which our artillery could not touch, because they shot over by reason of the height of the gabions, and in the twilight they made seven or eight shots at the observance where we were, and the houses adjoyning, and of all night after shot no more.

We worked exceeding hard all night to finish our retirade, and the Count de Bisque was no less diligent at the antiport, so that two hours before day all was perfected and everyone settled in his post where he was to fight. That which made us make so much haste was that we heard a great noise at their artillery and thought they were bringing up the rest, which made me put out a man to discover their battery, who brought us word that they had cut above fourscore paces of the wall, within a spar or two of the bottom, and that he believed in a few hours they would have beaten it totally down, which we did not much care for though they did, for we hoped to sell them their entry very dear; and about an hour before day they ceased their noise, which made us think that they only expected the break of day to give fire.

I then mounted upon the wall, having Captain Charry always with me, who by main force would needs have me down when the day began to break, and soon after I perceived that at the windows of the gabions there was no artillery, and that instead of planting more they had drawn off those that were. I then called out to Signior Cornelio that we were out of danger of an assault, and that the enemy had drawn off their canon; at which news everyone began to come upon the wall, where the Siennois sufficiently rated the enemy in their language, saying 'Coioni marrani, venete qua vi metteremo per terra vinii brassi di muri.' They were constrained to stay three days at the foot of the mountain to repair their carriages, which the demy-canon we had brought to Fort Camoglia had broken and spoild them.

Now (as I have already said) the gentleman of the emperor's bedchamber had all the while kept a great deal of clutter what canon would do to the winning of the town: but after he had been an eye witness of all that has been related, and that the *marquis* had remonstrated to him that the retirade and those other fortifications I made within was to let him enter, and to give him battail in the city (for if I knew what he did, he was no less enformed of my proceeding, there being evermore one traytor or another amongst all people) he then was of the same opinion with the *marquis* and the other captains that the town was never to be taken by force; but that it was to be reduced to famine, and therefore thought it convenient that the artillery should be sent back to Florence.

He then returned back to his master to give him an account of what he had seen, and that the *marquis* could do no more than what he had already done. I do not know whether or no he acquainted the emperor with the fright he had been in, which the *marquis* himself gave me a relation of at my going out of Sienna, as he went along with me above two miles of my way, where he told me that at the time when their artillery was forsaken by reason of the havock our demy-canon made amongst them, he was close by the side of the little house in his litter, being then very lame of the gout, where his litter being set down upon the ground, this gentleman of the emperor's was talking to him, having his hands upon the cover of the litter, and his head within it, whispering with the said *marquis*; when our governor seeing the artillery abandoned, and everyone retyred under the shelter of the little house, made a shot at it, with which a part of the wall which was of brick fell upon the litter, so that the said gentleman was by it beaten down upon the *marquis's* legs, so astonisht as nothing more, and the *marquis* swore to me that in his life he was himself never in so much fear of being killed as at that time: that they drew the gentleman out from off his legs, and himself after with much ado, all the litter being full of the ruine and covering of the said house.

And the said *marquis* moreover told me that at the great fright he was in his gout left him, for the whole ruine fell at once upon him and upon the gentleman, who verily thought himself to be killed. I have often heard that the apprehension of death has cured many diseases; I know not if the *marquis's* gout be returned since, but he assured me he had never had it after from that fright till the time I saw him. If it be returned or no I leave others to enquire.

This might be about the middle of January, and not above eight dayes after we began to perceive that the Germans grew very impatient at the little bread they had, having no wine, which was the most insupportable of all. The *rhinecroc* himself, who was sickly, could no longer endure, there being nothing to be had unless it were a little horse flesh or a piece of an ass. Signior Cornelio and I then began to contrive which way we might get these Germans out of the city, and conceited that if they were gone we could yet keep the town above two months longer, whereas if they staid we should be necessitated to surrender: we therefore concluded to send a man privately to Monsieur de Strozzy to remonstrate all this to him, and to entreat him to send for them after the most plausible manner he could (which I also directed him how to do), and sent to him Captain Cossel, who is now my ensign, very well instructed.

It was with exceeding great difficulty that he was to pass, which that he might do we were to fight two courts of guard, by reason that the *marquis* had already cast up a great number of trenches which came up close to the walls of the city on every side. Of these Captain Charry fought the one, and the Count de Gayas with a company of Italians the other: so that whilst they were fighting he got over the trench and recovered the rear of the camp with his guides, and two dayes after returned in company with an Italian gentleman called Captain Flaminio, who brought letters to the *rhinecroc* and to me also, wherein Monsieur de Strozzy writ to me to send the *rhinecroc* with his companies out to him, for that he intended to set on foot a flying army, having with him great store of Italian horse and foot, and that without some of those tramontane sinews he should never be able to relieve me, and that he would protest against me if the city was lost.

To the *rhinecroc* likewise he sent very obliging letters, having beforehand made Captain Flamino very perfect in his lesson. The *rhinecroc* upon the receiving these orders broke out into very great complaints, saying that Monsieur de Strozzy reduced him to the greatest extremities, and that it was impossible for him to get away without being defeated: but that he would however speak to his officers, which he did, and which begot a very great dispute amongst them.

At length one of them in whom he reposed the greatest confidence, and who served him in the quality of camp-master, remonstrated to him that he had much better hazard with his sword in his hand to make his way through the *marquis's* camp, than stay to die of famine, or by a capitulation to surrender himself to the enemies' discretion, which however in a few days he must of necessity do; for there was nothing left to eat, and their souldiers began to murmur insomuch that they evermore expected when a great part of them should go give themselves up to the enemy, which made them resolve to depart.

The *rhinecroc* was not much to be blamed for his unwillingness, it being a very perilous journey, for at the very sallying out of the gate, he was of necessity to fight several Spanish guards, and half a mile from thence another at a trench the enemy had cast up near unto a certain mill which was in his way. Upon their determination to depart, I gave express charge that no one living should speak of this sally, causing the gates of the city to be close shut, and at the beginning of the night they all came with their baggage to the great place before Porto Novo.

The Siennois, who understood nothing of all this, at the seeing the Germans in this marching posture, began in all haste to repair to the pallace in very great despair. I then caused three companies to sally out, two of French and one of Italian; the first whereof was led by Captain Charry, the second by Captain Blacon (who since dyed a Hugonot at Xaintonge), and the third by the Count de Gayas. Captain Charry had orders to fight the first Court of Guard, which was in a great street of the suburbs, the second was at the Augustins in the same street, and the third at S. Lazaro. They had a command from me, never to give over till they had fought all the three courts of guards, and the Count de Gayas took the way on the outside of the suburbs on the right hand all along by the houses, still marching softly on to rally our men together, as they should be separated and scattered by the fight.

The *Tertia* of Sicily lay at the charter-house, consisting of very good souldiers, and the *rhinecroc* at the going out of the gate took on the right hand, entring into a valley, and the Count de Gayas remained upon the eminence moving still softly on, which produced two effects for the relief of our people, the one as has been said by gathering our squandred men together, and the other to succour the *rhinecroc* also if he should stand in need; and so we began to open the gate, it being about one of the clock in the night. Captain Charry marched out first (for it was he who alwayes led the dance), Blacon after him, the Count de Gayas next, and then the Germans, who in a trice put themselves into the valley. We immediately heard the fight betwixt our French and the Spaniards: Captain Charry routed the two courts of guards, the one after the other, and beat them up as far as that of St Lazaro: whereupon those of the charter-house came out to relieve their people, and came to the Augustins (where Blacon had made a halt expecting Captain Charry) and there clapt in betwixt them. Captain Charry having done his business, thought to return (hearing very well that they were fighting with Blacon) and met the enemy, which redoubled the fight.

The Count de Gayas could not come to assist him by reason that I had expressly forbid him to engage in the fight till he should first be sure that the Germans were out of danger: but in the end he was constrained to do as the rest did, our two French companies being driven upon him. The fight continued above a long hour, Signior Cornelio and I were without the gate by the portcullis, and nothing was open but the wicket, and there as the souldiers came one after another we put them in, when on a sudden we heard the fight coming towards us, some crying '*France*,' and others '*Spain*,' when at last they all came up pel mel together to the portcullis. We had torches within the gates, and through the wicket saw a little light, by which we drew the souldiers in.

I must needs say there were very valiant men both on the one side and the other; for not so much as either French or Italian ever once ran furiously upon us, but still faced about at the portcullis, and never retired, but step by step, till we pulled them in. All the three captains were wounded, and we there lost, what slain and wounded, above forty of the best souldiers we had, both French and Italians, and in the end we got in all the rest of our people. And because before the sally, the Siennois were astonished at the departure of the Germans, I made Signior Cornelio to go about the several guards and to the forts to reassure our men, for no one knew that the Germans were to go away, and I myself went to the palace where I found all the Senate in a very great distraction, to whom spoke as followeth:

I see well (gentlemen) that you have here assembled yourselves upon the occasion of the Germans departure, and that you are entered into some apprehension and jealousie that by that means your city will be lost: But I must tell you it is the conservation and not the loss of your city; for those six ensigns devoured more than the twelve of the Italians and French. On the other side, I know you must have heard that the said Germans already began to mutiny, being no longer able to endure. I also discovered well enough that even their captains were not like to govern them, themselves apprehending that they would go over to the enemy, and you yourselves have for five or six days last past heard the enemy call out to us at the very foot of our walls that we were lost and that our Germans would soon be with them.

Yet did not this proceed from any default in their officers, but from the impatience of the common souldiers who were no longer able to suffer. Now (gentlemen) should you appear dejected upon their departure; the world would say that both your courage and ours depended only upon theirs, and so we should dishonour ourselves to honour them; to which I shall never give my consent: for you knew all the great fights that have hapned in this siege have been performed by you and us only, and they have never so much as sallied out of the town, save once only, that in spite of me the *rhinecroc* would send out his people under the conduct of his nephew and his camp-master, and would accept of no one of any other nation than his own, at which time you saw how soon and how easily they were beaten back even into the ditch of the ravelin of Porto Novo; so that if, by good fortune, I had not been there and had not made the Italian guard sally out to their rescue, not a man of them had come off alive.

I will not disparage them, but they are much more proper for a battel than a siege. Why then (*signiors*) should you be concerned at their departure? I will say one thing more to you, that although I had also sent away the twelve companies that remain with me in this town, I would yet undertake to defend your city, provided the captains stayed behind to relieve me. You must make your ensigns captains of the watch by turns, who shall have two nights of intermission, and ours shall have but one, and we must begin to contract our allowance of bread to fourteen ounces, and you of the city to ten.

You must also put the useless mouths out of town, and appoint six persons to take a list of their names tomorrow, without further delay, and that without regard of persons, and speedily thrust them out of your city, by which expedient we shall make our bread last three months longer, which will be a sufficient time for the king wherein to relieve us, especially now that the spring is drawing on. Cease therefore your apprehensions, and on the contrary approve what I have done in order to your service. If have done it without pre-acquainting the Senate with my design, it was not out of disrespect to them but to keep this departure secret, which was of very great consequence, as you yourselves may have observed; I having been constrained to put Monsieur de Strozzy upon the business to deliver myself from a people so entirely devoted to their bellies.

The Senate having heard my remonstrance desired me to go to my repose and that they would consider of what I had said, rendring me very many thanks for the comfort and good counsel I had given them. In the morning my whole speech was divulged all over the city, and there was no more thought of fear amongst them: But they could not well agree amongst themselves about the unprofitable mouths, forasmuch as everyone was willing to favour his own relations and friends; wherefore by ballotte they created me their dictator general for the space of a month, during which time neither the captain of the people nor the magistracy had any command at all, but I had the absolute authority and dignity anciently belonging to the old dictators of Rome. I thereupon created six commissaries, to take a list of all the useless people, and afterwards delivered the roll to a Knight of Malta, accompanied with five and twenty or thirty souldiers, to put them out of the town, which in three days after I had delivered in the list, was performed.

A thing that I had not very good witness of, both of the Siennois, the king's officers, and the captains who were then present in Sienna, I should not however have mentioned in this place, lest the world should take me for a lyar: but it is most perfectly true. The list of these useless mouths I do assure you amounted to four thousand and four hundred people, or more, which of all the miseries and desolations that I have ever seen was the greatest my eyes ever yet beheld, or that I believe I shall ever see again; for the master was hereby necessitated to part with his servant who had served him long, the mistress with her maid, besides an infinite number of poor people, who only lived by the sweat of their brows; which weeping and desolation continued for three days together: and these poor wretches were to go thorow the enemy, who still beat them back again towards the city, the whole camp continuing night and day in arms to that only end: for that they drove them up to the very foot of the walls that they might the sooner consume the little bread we had left, and to see if the city out of compassion to those miserable creatures would revolt; but that prevailed nothing, though they lay eight days in this condition, when they had nothing to eat but herbs and grass, and above the one half of them perished, for the enemy killed them, and very few escaped away.

There were a great many maids and handsome women indeed, who found means to escape, the Spaniards by night stealing them into their quarters, for their own provision, but it was unknown to the *marquis*, for it had otherwise been death: and some strong and vigorous men also forced their way, and escaped by night. But all those did not amount to the fourth part, and all the rest miserably perished. These are the effects of war. We must of necessity sometimes be cruel to frustrate the designs of an enemy. God had need to be merciful to men of our trade, who commit so many sins, and are the causers of many miseries and mischiefs.

You captains and governors of places, if you be not perfect already, lessen these arts and stratagems: It is not all to be valiant and wise, you must also be circumspect and cunning. Had I entreated the *rhinecroc* to depart the city, he would have been displeased and have reproached me that I sent him to the slaughter, but I proceeded more discreetly, serving myself with the authority of Monsieur de Strozzy, wherein I had no other end but to gain time to tire out my enemy, and to give the king leisure to relieve us: But as I have said before, he employed his forces there where he had the most concern. *Nearer is the skin than the skirt.* Never fear to discharge yourselves of useless mouths, and bar your ears from all crys of the afflicted: Had I obeyed my own disposition, I had done it three months' sooner, which if I had, I might peradventure have saved the town, or at least I had longer held my enemy in play; and I have a hundred times since repented me that I did not.

The *marquis* seeing that I had put the Germans out of the town (who were the greatest part of them defeated by the way, and thorough their own great fault, which I shall not however give any further account of, for they were not defeated about Sienna, but elsewhere upon their march, where their own fear surprized them, without any great reason) and seeing also that I had driven out the useless people, both which would help to prolong the siege, with the contracting our allowance of bread (which he had also learned from those that went out) these things made him to think of some other way to bring us to his bow, fearing lest some snow should fall in the spring (as it often falls out in those parts at that time of the year) which should it so happen, he should then be constraind to raise the siege and repair to the cities to eat, for he was almost in as great necessity as we, and the souldiers of his camp were fain to eat mallows and other herbs, as well as ours, by reason that oftentimes their provisions could not be brought in due time; for it all came from about Florence, which was thirty miles off, and upon little asses, excepting 100 mules, and those were to bring sufficient to serve whilst they could go and come, which was five or six days, and every return some of their beasts of burthen dyed.

For about the camp there was no more so much as one herb, neither hay, straw, nor grain to be found, and much less any one Inhabitant within ten miles of the road. And all his cavalry lay yet ten miles beyond Florence, excepting the company of Signior Cabri the *marquis* his nephew, which consisted of no more than fifty horse, and was also every fifteen days to be relieved by fifty others that were quartered at Banconvent. So that had God been pleased to send us a little snow, though but for eight days only, his camp would have been necessitated to rise and to shift for themselves in the most commodious quarters abroad in the country.

All these things together put the *marquis* upon an attempt to shorten the war, wherein his design was one way or another to sow division amongst the quarters of the city, seeing us weak, and knowing very well that although we had yet twelve companies, there was nevertheless not eighteen hundred men: To which effect by those of the Siennois who were banished from the city, and were with the *marquis*, an invention was found out to gain a citizen of the town called Messer Pedro, a man with one eye, and of the order of the people (which was that wherein we most confided, together with the order of the reformators) and that by the means of certain little boys who went with little sacks to gather herbs in the meadows upon the River Tresse. By whom the *marquis* so ordered the business that he corrupted this man, and made him a traytor to his people and countrey; and the form of this practice was that Messer Pedro should receive several blancks, signed by the Siennois, who were in the *marquis's* camp, which he himself should write over at his own discretion.

The plot of this design was thus, that Messer Pedro should in his letters write these words:

That they wondered they should thus suffer themselves to be so manifestly abused by the Signeur de Montluc; and that a child might discern all the assurances he gave them of relief from the King of France to be no more than gulleries and deceits: That although they had unworthily been thrust out of the city yet did they nevertheless, with tears in their eyes, infinitely lament to see them so miserably lose themselves, and that if they would send out a man to go so far as Rome, to enquire if the king was raising an army for their succour, they would then infallibly discover the cheat: That they begged of them not to suffer themselves to be reduced to the last morsel, which if they should do, they would not then come off cheaper than at the price of their heads, the ruine of their estates, their wives and children: That they had yet means to make their peace with the emperor by the mediation of the *marquis* if they would let him into the town, which was a thing easie enough to do, if they would consult and joyn with some of the city, who had already engaged themselves to them; and that they might know who were of the intelligence, they were to go into such a street and where they should see a little white cross under the door the master of that house was one.

This one eyed dog performed his office exactly well, and directed his letters to one of those in whom we reposed an absolute trust, being very certain that he would forthwith carry it to the magistrate, and that the magistrate would also in the morning send into the street mentioned in the letter and would seize upon the gentleman of the house at whose door the cross should be found. However he resolved ever to make his cross at some house of the Orders of the Novi and the gentlemen, forasmuch as the other two orders had them in suspicion, and the *marquis* thought (knowing the humour of the Siennois, and the hatred they bore one to another) that immediately so soon as that person should be taken, they would hurry him without any other form of justice to the scaffold, by which means those two Orders of the Novi and of the gentlemen would enter into so great an animosity and despair that to save their lives they would be constrained to betake themselves to arms to possess themselves of a canton of the city near into the walls, to favour the enemy, and to help them into the city.

This cursed rogue then began to forge his first letter, and by night went and thrust it under the door of the house of one of the gentlemen, who was unsuspected, and made his little cross in another street at the house of one of the richest gentlemen of the Order of the Novi; so that in the morning the gentleman to whom the letter was directed found it in the entry of his house, presently read it, and carreid it to the magistrates, who so soon as they had looked upon it immediately sent it to me by Misser Hieronimo Hispano, sending me word withal that they had determined to go apprehend the said gentleman, and forthwith to carry him directly to the scaffold. Whereupon I sent the Signiors Cornelio and Bartolomeo Cavalcano back to them to entreat them not so precipitously to proceed to blood, for that it might be an invention of the *marquis* to set division amongst us: but that they might do well to commit him to prison, which they accordingly did.

Two days after there was another letter found in the same manner in the house of a gentleman of the Order of the Novi, a man no more suspected than the other, and the little cross under the door of one of the gentlemen: At which the Senate was so incensed that I was fain myself to go to the pallace, where I had much ado to obtain the favour that they would defer execution for five days only to see if in that time God would please to give us further light into this fact. All the whole city was enraged and talked of nothing but cutting off heads. As God help me it could never sink into my head that it was any other than a device of the *marquis*, for I knew very well with whom I had to do. I then entreated Messer Bartolomeo Cavalcano that he would never cease day or night, to go visit the said gentlemen, and the citizens of the Order of the Gentlemen, and the Novi, whom the misfortune concerned, to entreat them not to despair, and to tell them that I would take order no blood should be shed and that I gave no credit to those letters and crosses. Signior Cornelio also assisted me very much

157

in this affair, who had a very great interest in the city, by reason of the cardinal of Ferrara with whom he had always lived during his abode in this city.

Now three or four days after this, thinking the fury to be over, behold another letter and another cross found in the same manner as before: At which everybody lost all patience, and would immediately drag all three to execution. I then ran to the pallace, taking Signior Cornelio and Signior Bartolomeo along with me. As I was going, it came into my head that I had no way to divert this blow, but by a colour of devotion, and so soon as I came there, I found the great hall already almost full of men of the reformators, and of the order of the people: when so soon as I entered into the hall of the magistracy, they all began to cry out that it was now no longer time to forbear, but that they were to proceed to a speedy execution of justice; whereupon having taken my place, I spoke to them in Italian, as at other times, after this manner.

> Gentlemen, since the time that I have had the honour to command in your city, by the appointment of the king my master, you have never undertaken anything whether as to matters of war or as to the government of your corporation, without first communicating to me your intention, and asking my opinion and advice. Wherein, by God's good pleasure, I have been so happy that I have hitherto never advised you to anything which has not succeeded to your advantage and honour; neither would I do it for the world, my own life and safety not being dearer to me than your preservation. Seeing then (gentlemen) I have been so fortunate as ever to have given you sound and useful counsels; let me beseech you to retain the same opinion of me now, and to give credit to me in an affair of so great importance as this that presents itself before you, with which your judgements seem to be very much perplexed.
>
> I beg of you with joyned hands, and in the name of God, that of all things you take heed of embruing your hands in the blood of your citizens till the truth shall be fully known; neither can it possibly be long concealed: 'tis to much purpose to cover the fire, the smoak will however issue out; in like manner they may endeavour to mask and disguise this practice, but the truth will infallibly appear. All the world (and I beseech you be of my opinion) cannot make me believe, that this is any other than an

artifice and a trick of the *marquis*, who having found that the lyon's skin will do him no good, has therefore put on that of the fox the better to bring about his design. Which to do, he had no better nor more subtile way than by sowing division in the heart of your city. And which way could he better do it than by making you believe there are traytors among you and within your own walls?

Knowing very well that that would make you not only to imprison such suspected persons, but also to put them to death, and by that execution to set discord in your city, for true blood cannot lye. The parents and friends of the sufferers will bear the death of their kindred, though it should be just, with great sorrow and discontent, and will endeavour to revenge them; by which means behold you have created so many domestick enemies, much more dangerous than those without, and you will be perplexed about the death of your own people at the time when you meditate that of your open and declared foes. See then (gentlemen) what joy, what satisfaction and delight, you will administer to your enemies when they shall know that you busie yourselves about cutting off the heads of your own citizens, and of those who I dare say and swear are innocent.

However it may prove to be, the expectation of the truth can no ways be prejudicial to you, for you have them in sure hold: you are secure of your prisoners, you have them under safe custody. I will also be vigilant on my part, why then should you make such haste to put them to death? For the honour of God believe me you will not repent your patience. I have no interest but yours, let us have recourse to God in so great a necessity. Command that all your clergy tomorrow ordein a general procession throughout the whole city, and let everyone be enjoyned to be assisting at it, and let them joyn in prayer that it may please God to do us that grace as to discover to us the truth of this affair, the treason, if treason there be, and the innocency of the prisoners, if there be none, I assure myself that God will hear us and you will soon be satisfied of the truth, after which you may proceed to justice against the guilty if cause require: but to do it before, and in heat to embrew your hands in the blood of your citizens, without having maturely weighed every circumstance, you would in my opinion do very ill, and bring a great mischief upon your city.

159

Gentlemen, the sole affection I have to your service, your safety, and conservation, has made me speak thus freely to you without any other consideration, and I once more most earnestly beseech you to grant me this favour, as for a few dayes to supersede your sentence, which in the meantime we will employ in prayers and supplications, that God will please, by manifesting to us the truth, to direct our justice.

I had no sooner ended my speech, but that a confused murmur arose throughout the whole hall, some saying I, and others no, for there will be evermore some opposers; but in the end my advice was followed, and presently intimation given to the churches and to all the people to prepare themselves against the next day for a general procession, to pray unto Almighty God; for as for fasting we had enough of that already. I was my self-assisting at the procession, and all the captains together with all the gentlemen and ladies of the city, the kindred of the prisoners followed weeping: and to be short, all the whole body of the city this day and the day following were in humiliation and prayer, everyone beseeching of God that he would please to afford us that grace, as to discover the truth of this treason.

In the meantime I slept not, for all the night Signior Cornelio and I were in consultation which way this practice of the *marquis* could be set on foot. I considered with myself, that the business being gone thus far, he who carried on the designe would not rest there, and that the council of the city would not be kept so secret that the *marquis* would not infallibly have intelligence of what had been concluded, there being evermore some tell-tales in these great assemblies; and then very well knew that I had committed an error in so openly declaring that I was assured it was a trick of the *marquis*, it being to be feared that it would make him enter into some jealousie of his agent. Now because it was likely he would by his letters and tickets give us some new alarm, I thought fit to cause certain men to walk up and down the streets of the city by night, after the most private manner they could, to try if by that means something might not be brought to light, and after this manner caused centinel to be made two nights together.

By day I caused the people to be taken up with processions in their respective parishes, and when any of the *signiory* came to tell me that it was so much time lost, and that they must proceed to justice, I entreated them to have patience, assuring them that I began to discover some light into the business; for it was necessary to proceed after this manner to restrain the fury of the people.

Now it hapned that the third night about midnight this Messer Pedro was seen to pass by, and stopping at a house, put his hand to a casement, which was low and hapned to be shut, and one of the three letters had been found to have been put into a low window as that was. He then kneeled down, and under the door put in the letter as far as he could thrust his arm, which having done he went his way along the street. A gentleman who lay at watch went presently after him, and taking him by the arm said, '*che fiete voi?*' to whom the other replyed, '*Io sono Messer Piedro*' (I cannot remember the sir-name of this rascal) the gentleman then knew him, and said to him '*dove andate?*' who made answer '*me ne vo à la guardia,*' to which the gentleman returned, '*adio adio*'; which having done he knockt, and made them open the door, where he found the letter of the same contents with the former.

He then immediately went and carried it to the magistracy, who sent me two of their council, to give me an account of the whole business, and those two went and called up Signior Cornelio, who came along with them; where amongst us it was concluded that the gates should not be opened in the morning, nor the guards and centinels relieved, till he was first taken; and in the morning Signior Cornelio went with a hundred men to beset the house both before and behind. Signior Cornelio knew the man, and so soon as he had placed his souldiers, knockt at the door, where he found him yet in bed, and presently sent me word of his being taken.

Whereupon, the time of my dictatorship being expired, I made use of entreaties, as before, requesting the Senate that he might be forthwith put upon the rack, for he both denied the letter and also that he had seen the gentleman of all that night. As he was upon the rack he begged that they would torment him no more, for he would confess the truth, which he did from point to point, together with the *marquis* his practices to set division in the city. Upon which confession they would in the heat have presently hanged him at the windows of the palace: but I entreated them not to do it yet, and so he was clapt up in a dungeon. I then entreated the captain of the people to deliver to me the three gentlemen who were prisoners, for that I had a desire to talk with them at my lodging; which he accordingly did.

They were brought by Signior Cornelio and Bartolomeo Cavelcano, and so soon as they were come to my lodging I remonstrated to them, 'that they ought by no means to stomach their imprisonments, nor to bear the Senate any ill will for seising of their persons, affairs being reduced to such terms that the father ought not to trust his son, nor the son his father, since it concerned no less than their lives and fortunes, and that therefore I desired they would go to the magistracy to give them hearty thanks that they had not proceeded to speedy execution, but had had patience till such time as God had discovered the truth.'

They returned me answer that I should pardon them, that being a thing they would never do; neither was it they that had saved their lives, but that it was I, and that they would give God thanks and me; but that they had no obligation to them at all. We were all there above a long hour labouring to perswade them, where I remonstrated to them that not to do the thing I requested of them, was to accomplish the *marquis* his designe, and to give him his heart's desire, which was that they should remain in division and mortal hatred; and whatever else I could contrive to say that might any way serve to perswade them to go, I represented to their consideration to pacific and appease them. In the end remembring how highly they stood obliged to me for the saving their lives, they promised me that they would do it, and Signior Cornelio and Messer Bartolomeo at my request went along with them, for I was afraid they might repent by the way.

Where so soon as they came before the magistracy, one of them spake for the rest, remonstrating their innocency and the wrong that had been done them; which nevertheless they would no more remember, considering the necessity of the time and the estate of the city, affectionately beseeching them to esteem them for their good citizens and friends, and loyal to the commonwealth; and that for the time to come neither they nor their posterity might have any blemish upon their names upon this occasion, they desired they would please to grant them patents sealed with the broad seal for their satisfaction. The captain of the people then made them a very ample remonstrance, wherein he entreated they would excuse them, if the publick safety being in question they had been constrained to shut their eyes to particular interests, and by the importance of the affair had been constrained to be so severe in their inquisition: but that they did acknowledge and esteem them to be good and loyal citizens. Whereupon they all descended from their seats and embraced them, and as Messer Bartolomeo told me, the most of them with tears in their eyes; and so everyone retired to his own house.

Now because this one-eyed villain was of the Order of the People, which was the greatest party in the town, and wherein was most souldiers, I was afraid that should they put him to death those of his order might make some stir in the town saying that now it was well enough known of what order the traitors were, which might occasion some mutiny or sedition, and make them in the end betake themselves to arms, which was the reason that I made a request to the Senate to give me his life, and to banish him for ever, that all things might be husht up, and that the *marquis* might not say that any of his policies had succeeded any more than his attempts by arms. And thus were all things discovered and hudled up, for the Senate granted my request.

I have often since wondered how I came to be so discreet and so moderate in an affair of this importance, considering how reasonable it was that an exemple should be made; but it would peradventure have done more hurt than good. We must not alwayes be so severe, and the seeing of others so hot upon blood I do believe made me a little more temperate. And you (gentlemen) who have the charge of places, do not suffer yourselves to be transported at the first appearance of things, nor upon too light information; consider and weigh the circumstances, and hinder the violence of the people over whom you command by one pretence or another, as I did, amusing them with processions; not that that was not nevertheless well done, but I would see if time would make any discovery; and had I suffered these men to have been put to death, their kindred might perhaps have been prompted with some spirit of revenge.

Above all things endeavour to preserve union amongst those over whom you shall happen to command, as I did in this city, where all was accommodated and appeased. Consider also with what enemy you have to do; for you may well imagine that he will leave no stone unremoved nor no artifice untried to set division in your city; as I have formerly read in Livie, the great Captain Hannibal did to sow dissension amongst the Romans. Your wisdom and prudence (governors of places) must discern if there be appearance in the thing; whether or no the party accused be a man capable of practice, or have any means whereby to bring his purpose about, and whether or no he have done anything any wayes tending to such a design. If in apprehending him you discover any confusion in his countenance or variation in his answers. You ought in this to be very circumspect and discreet, and to consider that there is nothing more easie than to calumniate a man. God be praised, all here passed with moderation, and the prisoners with their friends came to give me thanks.

Now after the *marquis* saw himself disappointed of his expectation, and that all his plots and stratagems came to nothing, he suffered us to rest in peace, not expecting to have us till we should be reduced to the last morsel of bread; and we began to enter into the month of March, when we were in the greatest recessity of all things; for of wine there had not been one drop in the whole city from the middle of February: We had eaten all the horses, asses, mules, cats, and rats that were in the town. Cats sold for three and four crowns a piece, and a rat for a crown. And in all the whole city there was onely remaining four old mares, so lean as nothing more, which turned the mills, two that I had, the Controller la Moliere his, the Treasurer L'Espine another, Signior Cornelio a little bay pad-nag that was blind with age, and Misser Hieronimo Hispano a Turk of above twenty years old.

These were all the horses and mares that were left in the city in this extremity, which was greater than I can represent it, and I do believe there is not in nature so dreadful a thing as famine. We had from Rome some hopes sent us of succours, and that the king was sending away the Mareschal de Brissac to relieve us, which was the reason that we again lessened our bread to twelve ounces, and the souldiers and citizens of the town to nine: whilst in the meantime by little and little we lost several inhabitants and souldiers, who fell down dead as they walked the streets, so that they died without sickness. At last the physicians found it out that it was the mallows they fed upon, that being an herb that does relax the stomach and obstructs digestion.

Now we had no other herbs all along the walls of the city, they having been all eaten before; neither could we come by these without sallying out to skirmish, and then all the women and children of the town went out to gather them. But I saw I lost so many men in these skirmishes that I would no more permit any one to sally out. Now to hear any more news of the Mareschal de Brissac was henceforward impossible, for the trenches were brought up to the very gates of the city, which trenches the *marquis* had also redoubled for fear we should sally out upon him in despair and give him battail, as the Siennois in their antient wars had formerly done, as themselves report.

In this condition we languished on till the 8th of April, that we had lost all manner of hopes of relief, and then it was that the *siegneury* entreated me not to take it ill if they began to think of their preservation. When seeing there was no other remedy, unless to eat one another? I could not deny them, cursing to the pit of hell all those who engage men of honour in places, and then leave them in the lurch. Yet did I not herein intend to speak of the king, my good master, he loved me too well for that; but those who gave him ill counsels to the prejudice of his affairs, and I have ever observed more evil than good counsellors about princes. They then sent out one of their people to the *marquis* to entreat of him a safe conduct for two of their Senate, whom they would send to him, which he granted, and they began to capitulate.

The *marquis* himself did very much facilitate the treaty, and they began to enter into great confidence of him, for he very well saw that to cause the city to be sacked and ruined would be no profit, neither to the emperor, nor the Duke of Florence, and would only benefit the souldier, and on the other side he feared lest if the Siennois could obtain no good conditions, we should sally out upon him, *a la desesperade*, having already lost above the third part of his men, who were either dead through the length of the siege, or run away, so that he had almost no Italians, who were quartered at the Fort St Mark; and the *marquis* had remained for above a moneth with no more than six ensigns for the guard of his own person, all the rest being in the trenches; neither could he ever relieve them with more than ten ensigns, and those had only one night of intermission, and some such guards there were that were not relieved in six days.

To this condition was he reduced without, as well as we within; neither could he make any use of his horse, no more than Monsieur de Strozzy could of the cavalry he had, by reason that there was no manner of thing upon the ground to give the horses to eat from Montalsin to Sienna and from Sienna to Florence.

I will now give an account of myself after what manner I lived. I had no manner of advantage, no more than the meanest souldier, and my bread weighed no more than twelve ounces, and of white bread there was never above seven or eight made, whereof three were brought to my quarters, and the rest were saved for some captain that was sick. Neither those of the city nor we from the end of February to the 22th of April ever eat above once a day; neither did I ever hear so much as any one souldier complain, and I can assure you the remonstrances I often made to them served to very good purpose; for if they would have gone over to the enemies' camp the *marquis* would have treated them very well; for the enemy very much esteemed our Italian and French souldiers, and in the skirmishes that had happened betwixt us had had very sufficient tyral of their valour. I had bought thirty hens and a cock to get me eggs, which Signior Cornelio, the Count de Gayas, and I eat, for we all three constantly eat together, at noon in one place and in the evening at another; but towards the end of March all these were eaten, the cock and all.

'Twas pitty we had no more: and so I remained without flesh and without eggs and had nothing to eat but my little loaf with a few pease boyled with a little bacon and mallows, and that but once a day only. The desire I had to acquire honour, and to put this bafflle upon the emperor, so long to have held his army in play, made me find this so sweet that it was no trouble to me to fast: and this pittiful supper with a bit of bread was a feast to me, when returning from some skirmish I knew the enemy to be well drubed, or that I knew them to suffer under the same necessities we did.

But to return to the capitulation; the *marquis* sent to the Duke of Florence, and Don Juan Manricou, who was embassador from the emperor to the Pope, and resided at Florence by reason of the siege; whereupon the said duke sending a safe conduct, the Siennois also sent to the Pope (which was Pope Julio, who died two or three days after) from whom they received a very scurvy answer, he reproaching them with their obstinacy, and commanding them to submit to the Duke of Florence his mercy without any condition. He was a terrible Pope: but the duke proceeded after a more modest and courteous manner, as a prince ought to do, who would gain the hearts of a people, and indeed he was one of the greatest politicians of our times. It behooved him so to be to establish his principality, in the time of two of the greatest and most ambitious princes that ever were, who had both of them a great mind to get footing in Italy.

But the Spaniard was more subtle than we, and this duke managed his business very well; his name was Cosmo, and I believe he is yet living. In the meantime commissioners for eight dayes together went and came betwixt Florence and the camp, and upon Monday night the capitulation was brought to Sienna, and the morning before the *marquis* had sent a trumpet to me, entreating I would send two gentlemen out to him in whom I might confide, he having something to say to them that he desired I should know, and that he was come to St Lazare to that effect.

I thereupon sent out to him Signior Cornelio and Captain Charry, who being come to him, he there acquainted them with the terms of the capitulation which would that night be brought to the city, and that amongst other things there was one article which exprest that the Sieur de Montluc with his Italian and French companies, and all the officers of the king, should march out with bag and baggage, colours flying, drums beating, with match lighted, and bullet in mouth: but

that this article would do me no good, forasmuch as we did not belong to the Siennois, but to the King of France; and being we did not
belong to them, they consequently had no power to capitulate for us;
that therefore I was myself to capitulate in the name of the king my
master, which if I thought fit to do, he assured me I should have what
conditions soever I would demand, and that his service to the emperor
excepted, he would do as much for me as for the cardinal his brother:
that he and I were two poor gentlemen, who by our arms were arrived to such degrees of honour that the greatest both of France and
Italy would be glad to have our places, telling them withal he would
there stay to expect my answer.

They found me at Porto Novo walking with Messer Hieronimo
Espanos, where, after I had received his message, I bad them go back
and tell him that I very well knew he had read the Roman history
wherein he might have taken notice that in the times of the antient warlike Romans they had sent one of their colonies to inhabit
Gascony, near to the Pyrhenean Mountains, of which province I was
a native, and that if he would not content himself that the Siennois
had comprised me in their capitulation I would at my coming out let
him see that I was descended from those warlike Romans who would
rather have lost a thousand lives, could they have had so many to lose,
than an inch of their honour: that I had rather the Siennois should
capitulate for me, than I for them, and that for my part the name of
Montluc should never be found subscribed to a Capitulation. They
then returned to him, to whom having repeated my answer, he said
to them in Italian. '*Che vol dir questo? mi pare che vol jocar a la desperata.
Altre volte io rose due forteresse con ragone, ne per questo ne sui maj represso
de l'Imperatore, e no resta su Majesty a servir si di me.*'

Signior Cornelio then told him that I was positive in this determination and would rather put all to the hazard of the sword than to the
hazard of a capitulation.

'Well then,' said he, 'recommend me to him, and tell him I will let
him see that I am his friend, and that he may march out in all assurance upon the capitulation of the Sennois, or after what manner he
pleases himself'; and so they returned.

Oh *camrades*, you have here a fair exemple before you, when you
shall find yourselves in such an affair, never to discover any fear, for
nothing in the world so much startles an enemy as to see the chief
with whom he has to do to be undaunted in all extremities, and that
he gives him to understand he will rather run the hazard of a fight

than a capitulation; nothing so much puzzels him as that, besides the encouragement it gives to your own people. I was as much afraid as another, seeing myself so desperately engaged, and no news of any relief, neither of victuals nor men: but ask anyone who is yet living whether they ever saw me any more dejected than the first day I came into the city. And at the last of all, when we were reduced to the extremest necessity of all things, I was more resolute to fight than before, which I believe conduced much to the obtaining of so good conditions both for the Sennois and for us, as we could have had, had we capitulated the first day the enemy sat down before us.

Late at night came the capitulation, and upon Tuesday morning four of the Senate brought it to me, wherein I found an article that everyone of what mean condition soever should go out with bag and baggage, their wives and children, who had a mind to depart the city, except the exiles and rebels to the State of the Emperor, the King of England (which was King Philip), and the Duke of Florence.

I then very well understood that this article would fall heavy upon the poor Florentines who were with us in the city, and who had been banisht upon Monsieur de Strozzy's account. There were also Neapolitans, and Millanois; so that I there clearly saw above a hundred men thrown away, and their heads surrendered to the scaffold, which made me desire the senators to return, and that in an hour I would come to them to the palace, and shew them the deceit that was couched in their capitulation, entreating them in the meantime speedily there to assemble all the principal members of the city, which they did, and I took along with me Signior Cornelio and Bartolomeo Cavalcano who was ready to die for fear when he understood my proposition, for he was a Florentine; where being come I made to them this remonstrance.

Gentlemen, I have seen your capitulation, which tends rather to the cutting off of your heads than to any indemnity for your lives and estates. You have there one article that everyone generally shall enjoy the benefit of the capitulation, their lives and estates saved, excepting such as are rebels to the Emperor, the King of England, and the Duke of Florence. Now you know very well that the emperor has caused you all to be declared rebels in his Imperial Chamber, as Subjects of the Empire, for having rebelled against him. By which you see you are declared subjects, and you say you are not subjects, but only stand in recommendation to the Empire.

The dispute is not yet determined, whether you are subjects or recommended, and when the enemy shall once be got within your walls, and that you are in their power, what judges will you have to determine of the question, except the hangman and with your heads, for it will certainly be by that way that they will go about to assert their title. Behold then you will all be put to death, your estates confiscated, and your wives and children a prey to the conqueror.

As for me and the souldiers, they will permit us safely to depart, for souldiers pass in all places, and even better cheaper than other sorts of men. They know we have nothing to lose but our arms, and that we are bound to obey our prince; should they offer any outrage to us we shall have our revenge in turn at one time or another, for men do sooner meet than mountains: But all the mischief will fall upon you, considering the hatred the emperor and the duke have conceived against you.

A prince rarely pardons subjects who have once rebelled against him; but if ever he can pick a hole in their coats he will be sure to take hold of the occasion. Since then we have so long lived together, without ever having so much as one unkind word pass betwixt us, and that I have received so many honours at your hands, if you will take my advice we will make the *marquis* think of something he never thought of yet, that is we will sally out with our weapons in our hands to the fight and give him battail, and we ought to believe that God will be on our side and assist us, considering the cruelty they would exercise upon you.

For my own part, I freely offer you my life and those of all my captains and souldiers to die with you, that as we have lived, so we may die together, rather than to see you so basely betrayed and sold to slaughter.

Credete à me, à me dico che son vechio, e à cui sono pessate molte cose inanti li occhi.'

Now I knew very well that this exception did not point at the Siennois, but only at those I named before, so that this was only a device of mine to make the Siennois engage with us in the fight, for I had rather have put all to the hazard of the sword then that any one of those who were within with us and who upon my account had been obstinate in the defence of the city should be lost.

They took it however for current pay, and after I was departed from them, all of them resolved to fight it out to the last man. I then presently sent them word what they were to do, which was that the standard-bearer should command all their powder to be refined, their swords, halberts, and pike-heads to be scowred and ground: that upon pain of death everyone who was able to bear arms should be ready in two days, and that the priests and *religieux*, who had taken arms for the defence of the town at the battery, should now take them again under the same captains they did before; insomuch that I do believe that for two or three days so great a bustle in the city had never been seen.

The two deputies hereupon of the Duke of Florence and the *marquis*, who had safe conduct into the city, returned about three of the clock in the afternoon back to the *marquis*, where they shewed him this article, which had put not only the whole city but also the souldiers into despair of fair quarter, telling him how we were all resolved and by what means they came to understand the hubub and preparation that was making in the city to give him battel, which was the reason that he sent all night to the Duke of Florence and Don Juan Manricou, whom I since saw with the Queen of Spain at Bayonne, giving them an account how all things stood, and entreating them withal that since he was now upon the point to have the town surrendered to him they would not for this one article put him in danger of losing all; but consider that he had to do with a great captain and an old souldier, commending me more than I deserved: that as themselves very well knew he had lost near upon the one half of his army, and had a great many sick of those he had left, and that he had not twenty horse, there being nothing upon the place to support them, nor any means by which to bring them away from other places; and that they would do well to weigh and consider of this affair, for as for his part, he must discharge himself upon them, if anything fell out amiss.

So soon then as the Duke of Florence and Don Juan saw the Siennois resolution, they dispatched to him le Cousignou, the duke's chief secretary, with a blank to put in whatever we would demand, for he stood upon thorns till he was master of the city. It was upon Wednesday morning that the Cousignou came to the camp, when the said *marquis* sent for the two deputies, who had been on Tuesday night returned into the city, where they inserted in the articles that all those who had been banished, and rebels of the State of the Emperor, Empire, and Duke of Florence, should go out in all security, as well as the rest, and in this posture we remained till Sunday morning the 22 of April, that we went out in the order following:

Before anyone of us stirred out of the town, I restored the citadel and the Fort Camoglia into the hands of the Siennois, where they put an ensign of the city into each, as I also made them to place an ensign at every gate of the city that stood open, which being done, I returned to Porto Novo. The *marquis* had planted all his Spanish foot all along the street that leads to S. Lazaro, on both sides the street, his Germans were drawn up in battalia a little on the right hand in a camp, and at S. Lazaro was Signior Cabry his nephew with fifty or threescore horse, which was all they could make (as I have said before), and three hundred Italian harquebuzeers, which they had drawn out of the forts of Camolia and S. Mark and was the convoy the *marquis* had appointed to conduct us.

Signior Cornelio then, and the Count de Gayas, armed at all points, with their pikes shouldred went out side by side, with a company of harquebuzeers at their heels, after them went out two captains at the head of the pikes, amongst whom were a great company of corslets, and in the middle of the pikes, the ensigns displayed and advanced, and in the reer of them the rest of the harquebuzeers, with two captains in their reer.

I had overnight sent to the *marquis* that he would be so civil to the ancient women and children who were to go out with us as to lend them forty or fifty of his carriage mules; which he did, and which before I went out I distributed amongst the Siennois, who put upon them the ancient women and some children in their laps.

All the rest were on foot, where there were above an hundred virgins following their fathers and mothers, and women who carried cradles with infants in them upon their heads, and you might have seen several men leading their daughter in one hand and their wife in the other, and they were numbered to above eight hundred men, women, and children. I had seen a sad parting at the turning out the useless mouths; but I saw as sad a one at the separation of those who went out with us and who remained behind.

In my life I never saw so sad a farwel; so that although our souldiers had in their own persons suffered to the last extremes, yet did they infinitely regret this woful parting, and that they had not the power to defend the liberty of these people, and I more than all the rest, who could not without tears behold this misery and desolation of a people who had manifested themselves so devout for the conservation of their liberty and honour.

So soon as Signior Cornelio was gone out, all the Italians followed, and the citizens in the rear of the Italians. Then at the head of our French went out S. Auban and Lussan armed, with pikes upon their shoulders, and a company of harquebuzeers after them, two captains at the head of the pikes, with another company of harquebuzeers led by Charry and Blacon, having each of them a halbert in his hand, and the ensigns in the middle of the pikes, after the same manner the Italians had past before.

After these I went out armed, and Messer Hieronimo Espanos side by side with me, for I was afraid they would have seized upon him, he having been a principal actor in the revolt of the city. He was mounted upon an old Turk, and I upon another, miserably lean and haggled out, notwithstanding which I set a good face on the matter and made the best meen I could, I left two Siennois ensigns at the gate, entreating them to clap to the gate immediately after me, and not to open it till the *marquis* himself came.

The said *marquis* rid up and down, and Signior Chiapino Vitelli with him through all the files, to take care that no one meddled with the Siennois, for as to our baggage, it was so little as it made no number. The Spanish camp-masters then came to salute me, and all their captains. The camp-masters alighted not, but all the captains did, and came to embrace my knee, after which they again mounted on horseback and accompanied me till we came to the *marquis* and Signior Chiapino, which might be about 300 paces from the gate, where we embraced, and they placed me betwixt them.

After this manner we passed on discoursing all the way of the siege, and the particularities had hapned upon it, attributing much honour to us, the *marquis* particularly saying that he had great obligation to me, for that besides he had learned several stratagems of war, I was the cause he had been cured of his gout; telling me the fear that both he and the emperor's gentleman had been in, which did not pass without much laughter: Whereupon I told him that he had put me into a much greater fright the night of the *scalado*, and yet that I was not for all that cured of my feaver; adding moreover, that he had done very ill to come upon me, as the Jews did to take our Lord, for he brought along with him lanthorns and torches, which gave me a great advantage: to which he replyed bowing his head (for he was a very courteous gentleman) '*Signior, un attre volte fero piu savio.*' I then told him that had he continued his battery, he would have had no very good bargain of us; for the Gascons were an obstinate people, but that they were flesh and bone as other men were, and must eat.

With this and other discourse of the same nature we entertained ourselves till we were got a mile beyond S. Lazaro, and there the *marquis* bad Signior Chiapino Vitelli go to the head of our people and speak to Signior Cabry, to take care there should be no disorder, and that if any one offered to take anything from us he should kill all such as should attempt it, and that he should give the same command to the captain of the three hundred harquebuzeers.

So soon as Signior Chiapino was gone from us, the *marquis* embracing me in his arms said these words in as good French as I could have spoke myself. '*Adieu* Monsieur de Montluc, I pray present my most humble service to the king and assure him that I am his most humble and affectionate servant, as much (my honour safe) as any gentleman in Italy.'

I then returned him thanks for the good inclination he had towards the king, and the courtesies I had received at his hands, which I would proclaim in all places wherever I should come, and when it should ever lie in my power to do him service would requite. He offered me the same, and so we fell to embrace again. He had then no more than four or five horse with him, they being all behind in the same order he had left them, and so he returned back towards the city, and soon after Signior Chiapino Vitelli returned, where we also embraced and parted.

We then went to Arbierroute, a little village upon the tresse, or else the river itself is called Arbie, and there we found eighteen asses loaden with bread, which the *marquis* had sent thither to distribute amongst us upon the way; of which one part I gave to the Siennois, another to the Italians, and the third to the French. To do which, as I passed through the Spaniards, I saw that the souldiers had also purposely brought bread along with them to give to our people. I dare boldly say, and that by the testimony of those who were then with me, that this bread saved the lives of two hundred persons, and there are many who will affirm that it saved the lives of four hundred, and yet could it not go so far that there was not above fifty who dyed that very day; for we had been from Wednesday till Sunday without eating any more than six ounces of biscuit a day a man, and upon the Thursday, of two horses I had, I killed one that would now be worth 900 crowns, he was then indeed very lean, which I divided amongst the Italian and French companies, causing all the oyl to be taken out of the lamps in the churches, which I likewise divided amongst the souldiers, who with mallows and nettles boiled this flesh and oyl and so susteined themselves till Sunday morning when not a man amongst us at our going out, had eaten one bit of anything in the world?

The *marquis* also caused four *borachio's* of wine to be brought for me, together with five or six loaves of white bread, and so soon as we came to Arbierroute we halted and under some sallows that were by the riverside, eat our bread. I gave two of my bottles of wine to the Siennois, the other two we drank ourselves, each one a little, and afterwards went on our way directly towards Montalsin, when so soon as we came to Bonconvent, Signior Cabry made the foot convoy to return: but till he saw Monsieur de Strozzy, who came out with a party of horse to meet us, would himself never leave us; and then he bade me farwel, taking me in his arms, as he did Signior Cornelio, the Count de Gayas, and all our captains, for he was a very worthy gentleman and a brave souldier as any they had in their camp.

So soon as we came up to Monsieur de Strozzy, we embraced without being able either of us to utter one word; neither am I able to say which of us had his heart the most full of the remembrance of our fortunes. In this manner then, nothing but skin and bone, and more like ghosts than men, we arrived at Montalsin, which was upon Sunday, and all Monday and Tuesday we were shut up with the treasurers and comptrollers, to examine and state our accompts, and to see what I had borrowed to lend the souldiers, where we found that the king was four months to us in arrear, and Monsieur de Strozzy gave me 500 crowns of his own money to carry me into France. I dare sware he had not half so much more left; for Signior Cornelio and I had been constrained to borrow 400 crowns to disengage his great Order, which he had pawned to a Jew at the beginning when he came to Sienna. I would afterwards have restored it to him, and namely at Thionville, though he would never receive it, but laughed at me; and this was the end of the siege.

★★★★★★

I know very well (gentlemen) that many of you will take delight in what I have to say to you concerning the government and conservation of places, and that others will make little account of it, forasmuch as there are a sort of people so good natured as to think they know all things of themselves, and nothing value the knowledge and experience of other men, as if God had sent them into the world like St. John Baptist, inspired from their mothers' wombs. Which is the reason

174

we are not to wonder, that so many fall into mishaps; for their own arrogancy and self-conceit leads them by the hand till they come to a precipice, from whence they tumble headlong from the top to the bottom with so great a fall that they are never able to rise again. Yet was this nothing, if the fall hurt nobody but themselves; but the king and his people suffer also by it.

Do not then disdain to learn, and although you may have great experience of your own, yet can it do you no great harm to hear and read the discourses of old captains. When I was but five and twenty years old I took more pleasure in hearing an old souldier talk than ever I did to sit and chat with the finest woman that ever I was in love with in my life; therefore I beseech you take a little notice of what I am going to say.

When your prince shall give you a place to keep, you are to consider three things; first the honour he does you in reposing so much confidence in your valour and wisdom, as amongst others to make choice of you to entrust with a command of that importance. Wherein the honour he does you is no little one, forasmuch as he does not only honour you in your own person, but moreover sets a mark of reputation upon your whole race, by entrusting in your hands a key of his kingdom or some city of very great importance to him as this was, the siege whereof I have related to you.

This honour, I say, that he does you draws so long a train after it that your renown does not only spread itself through the whole kingdom from whence you come, and the countreys adjoyning to the place you defend, but moreover throughout the whole world.

Everybody is curious to enquire who does well or ill, and who is a good or bad commander; nay, although we have no concern in the affair, yet are we evermore inquisitive after news, for such is the nature of man: by which means thorow all foreign nations your name will be for ever known, either to honour or infamy. For whatever is done, is committed to History, without which the greatest part of men or honour would not care for acquiring renown, it costs so very dear. Never did any man ever purchase it upon harder terms than I; but the laudable desire we have to perpetuate our names, makes the pain seem easie to him who has a generous heart.

Methought all the time when I read Titus Livie that I saw all the brave Scipio's, Cato's, and Caesar's alive, and when I was at Rome, and saw the Capitol, calling to mind the things I had heard (for I for my own part was ever a bad reader), methought I ought to find those ancient Romans there. The historians then who omit nothing of any kind in their writings will mark your name in white or black, with glory or with shame, according to your desert, as you see they have done by so many captains who have gone before us.

The second thing that you ought to set before your eyes is to consider if you lose the place committed to you, first what a loss it will be to the king, it being part of his estate and his house, there being no garrison that is not properly the king's own house, besides that the revenue is his, of which you deprive him in losing the place, enrich his enemy and augment his reputation, whilst you dishonour your own master, who shall read in the histories dedicated to eternity that in his reign such a town, such a castle, such a fortress was lost.

You ought then to reflect upon the miseries you bring upon his poor subjects, how many curses will they load you with, who shall be neighbours to the place you have lost: for they will certainly be destroyed, and by your carelessness or cowardize ruined and undone. They will curse the hour that ever you was born, and especially the poor inhabitants who through your fault must either change their king and master, or taking their children upon their backs be constrained to seek another habitation.

O that the poor English who had above three hundred years been settled in the town of Calice, have reason to curse the cowardize and treachery of him who so infamously lost so strong a place! How can you ever have the confidence to look up should you once fall into such a misfortune as this?

Before you were honoured and esteemed, and every one rejoyced at your coming, praying to God to preserve and bless you; but should you once fall into a misfortune like this, instead of prayers and acclamations you shall meet with affronts and injuries, for prayers maledictions, and they will curse you to all the devils in Hell. Instead of caressing, they will turn their backs upon you, everyone will point at you, so that a hundred times a day you will curse the hour that you were not killed upon a platform or in a breach in the defence of your garrison rather than so shamefully to have given it up to your enemy.

And not only your master, the princes and lords, will look upon you with an eye of contempt, but the very women and children; nay, I will say more, your own wife, though she make a shew of love, will hate and despise you in her heart; for the nature of all women is such that they hate all poltrons let them be never so proper men, or never so handsomely dressed, and love the bold and couragious let them be never so slovenly or deformed.

They participate of your shame, and although being in your arms in bed, they may pretend to be glad of your return, they wish in their hearts you had been smothered or carried away by a canon shot: for as we conceive it to be the greatest disgrace to a man to have a whore to his wife, the women also think that the greatest shame can befal them is to have a coward to their husband: and thus *Monsieur le Gouvernor,* you who have lost your place, you will be in a marvellous happy condition when you shall be cursed in your own bed.

But what shall we say of your children? People will not only reproach them that they are the sons of a cowardly father; but they will moreover themselves see his name in print and the mischiefs of which his cowardize has been the cause. For a town is never lost, let it be never so inconsiderable, that it does not draw a great deal of inconvenience along with it. It brings so mighty an inconvenience upon your children that to extinguish your ill repute and to raise their own to some tollerable degree of esteem, they must hazard their lives upon all occasions, without either fear or wit, and few escape being killed, who by this means to wipe of the stain from their family would signalize themselves.

How many have I seen in my time who by endeavouring to repair some notorious fault have lost themselves and exposed themselves to death upon the first occasion has presented itself, being ashamed to live. And though your children should escape these dangers, yet will the king be afraid (what great reputation soever they may have acquired) to trust a town to their custody, lest the son should take after the father, as it ordinarily comes to pass. Thus shall you not only ruine yourselves, but your whole family.

To avoid and to break the neck of your ill fortune, and of all these mishaps, there is a good remedy, which I have learned myself, and am willing to teach it you, if you know it not already. First you ought to consider all this that I have told you, and set on the one side the shame and on the other the honour you will obtain if you bravely defend your place, remaining victorious; or at the least having done all that a man of honour could do to come of triumphant, and like a conqueror, though you be overcome, as you see I did in this siege. Imagine still that you see your prince and master before you, and what countenance you ought to hope for if by your cowardize you lose his place.

And seeing nothing ever had a beginning but that it had likewise an end, consider from the beginning what the end is like to be, and remember that your master has not entrusted this place in your hands to deliver it up but to defend it; that he has put you into it not to live there only, but to dye there also bravely fighting, if occasion be. If you ask him at your going away to your command, 'Sir, must I dye before I surrender the place you have given me in trust?' he will tell you, that you are to fight to the last moment of your life; for being you are his subjects, your life is his.

The Seigneur de Jarnac one day told the king that it was the greatest craft and policy that even kings found out to make their subjects believe, that their lives were theirs, and that it was the greatest honour they could have to dye for their service: but that it was a great simplicity in us to believe it, and to keep such a clutter with this fine bed of honour. It is nevertheless true that our lives and estates are the kings, our souls belong to God, and our honour is our own, for over my honour the king has no power at all.

To return to what I was saying before, if in accepting the charge committed to you, you have not this resolution within yourselves, you would do a great deal better to make an excuse. There are ways enow to put it off, and there will be enow who will be glad to accept of what you refuse. If you accept it with a resolution to bring it to a handsome issue, do one thing, never think of dying.

'Tis for a coxcomb to fear death, till he see it within three inches of him, and yet cannot he forbear representing it to his imagination, though it be a hundred leagues off. On the contrary, meditate how to kill your enemy; for if you once enter into an apprehension and fear of death, you may assuredly give your place for lost; for that is to take away your understanding and your judgement, which is the best piece in your harness.

'Tis to much purpose to be valiant, if this fail you at need; which if you intend to preserve, you must by no means enter into this fear of dying; for fear is of itself and by the frailty of your own nature too apt to intrude upon us, without our needing to assist it with our own imagination. If then it present itself before you, you must reject it, and have sudden recourse to the intention of the king, and to what end he placed you there. Think of the shame and dishonour you are running into. Read often, or cause to be read to you, books that speak of the honour of great captains, principally those of our own times; as for example, Langey and another, who has writ in Italian (I cannot think of his name) who has writ so well since King Charles the Eight. I have often read him, and he is a very good author. Would to God that all of us who bear arms would take up a custom to write the things we see and do; for I am of opinion it would be better done by our hands (I mean as to feats of war) than by these lettered men, for they too much disguise the truth, and this relishes of the clerk.

Read then these books, and meditate with yourselves, if I do like Antonio de Leva at Pavie, the Sieur de Lude at Fontarabie, the Siegneur de Bouillon at Peronne, the Signior de Sansac at Miranda, and Montluc at Sienna, what will they say of me? what honour shall I carry back to my own house? and on the contrary, if I surrender, what shame and infamy for me and mine? Then apply yourselves to Almighty God, and beg of him that he will defend you from falling into these misfortunes, resigning up all things into his hands.

After this assist yourselves with all that he has put into the power of men, as you see I did in this siege, and above all things be always diligent and vigilant, evermore mindful of your charge, if you do this (forgetting withal death and danger) you will find means to defend your place, though it were but a dove-coat; and though it should be lost, you having performed your duty, you must conclude it to be by the hand of God.

We must however always trie; for I have seen a place lost that was never suspected to be in danger, and such a one saved as has been given over for gone. If you there die in your defence, you will neither dishonour yourselves nor your posterity, but shall be laid in your grave with an immortal renown, which is all that a man of arms ought to desire. For a man that fears to die ought never to go to the wars, there being in the world so many other employments to which he may apply himself, especially in the kingdom of France, where there are so many orders, that of justice, and that of the finances; too many indeed for the good of the king and of his kingdom, such a brave and numerous youth living idle, who would be fit to bear arms.

As I have entred sometimes into the Parliament of Tholouze and Bordeaux, since my being the king's lieutenant in Guienne, I have a hundred times wondred how it was possible so many young men should eternally amuse themselves in a palace, considering that the blood ordinarily boyls in young men; I believe it is nothing but custome, and the king could not do better than to drive away these people, and to enure them to arms. But to return to you who have the government of places, and you who have a mind to put yourselves into a town to defend it, if you so much fear death, never go, though it be but a folly to fear it, for those that blow the fire at home in their own houses are no more exempt than the others, and I do not know what choice there is betwixt dying of a stone in the kidneys, and being knocked o' th' head with a musket bullet, though if God would give me choice, I should not be long in choosing.

MONLUC HAS HONOURS THRUST UPON HIM

About this time the Duke of Florence procured the Duke of Ferrara's peace with the King of Spain, but it was with the knowledge and content of the king, otherwise the said duke would not have done to have saved his dukedom, he was so good a Frenchman; and when the peace came, which was five and twenty dayes after I entered into Versle, I took my leave of the prince, and returned to Ferrara, where it is not to be asked if I was welcome to the duke, the dutchess, and the cardinal; for I do not think they ever caressed any man of what condition soever he was, or could be, more than they did me; and when he died I might well say, as I now do, I lost one of the best friends I had in the world: and when I departed from Ferrara to go to Versel, the duke examined a secretary of mine what store of money I had, and he telling him I had not above two hundred crowns, he sent five hundred crowns to my said secretary, who had the ordering of my expence; and when three dayes after my return I took my leave of him, the dutchess, and the cardinal, the said duke seeing me have a great many gentlemen of quality in my train, and knowing I could not have money enough to defray my journey, he sent me five hundred more.

And thus I returned rich from my command in Tuscany. This money carried me to Lyons, where I found two thousand and four hundred *francs*, which the king had caused to be paid for two years' salary of my place of gentleman of the chamber, and that Martineau had then deposited for me in the hands of Cathelin Jean the post-master, which brought me to Paris.

Immediately upon my coming to Paris I went to kiss His Majesties hand, he being then at Cressy, where I was as well received by His Majesty as at my return from Sienna, and he was very well satisfied with what I had done for the Duke of Ferrara. Monsieur de Guise, who had not seen me before, embraced me three or four times in the presence of the king himself, and His Majesty commanded the said Monsieur de Guise to cause a thousand crowns to be given me, wherewith to return and to sojourn some time at Paris, which he presently did. And thus was my return out of Italy into France; the last time that I was in those parts, and the services I did there, wherein I cannot lie; there being so many yet living who can bear testimony of what I have delivered.

By this (captains) you may see, and take notice what a thing reputation is, which also having once acquired, you ought rather to die than to lose; neither must you do like men of the world, who so soon as they have got a little repute are content with it, and think that whatever they shall do afterwards the world will still repute them valiant.

Do not fancy any such thing; for by performing from time to time still more and braver things, young men rise to greatness, have fire in their pates, and fight like devils; who when they shall see you do nothing worth taking notice of, will be apt to say that the world has bestowed the title of valiant upon you without desert, will set less value upon you, use you with less respect, and behind your back talk of you at their pleasure, and with good reason; for if you will not still continue to do well, and still attempt new and greater things, it were much safer for your honour to retire home to your own house, with the reputation you have already got, than by still following arms to lose it again, and to be scouting at distance when others are laying about them.

If you desire to mount to the highest step of the stairs of honour, do not stop in the mid-way, but step by step strive to get up to the top without imagining that your renown will continue the same as when it was obtained at first. You deceive yourselves, some newcommer will carry the prize, if you do not look well about you, and strive to do still better and better.

The same day that I went from Cressy back to Paris, Monsieur de Guise departed also to go to Metz to execute the enterprise of Thionville. The king from the time of his return out of Italy had made choice of him for his lieutenant general throughout his whole kingdom, so that before my coming I found that he had taken the town of Calice, and sent back the English to the other side of the sea, together with Guines, and that he was now upon the Siege of Thionville. Two dayes had not past before the king sent for me to come to him to Cressy, without giving me notice what it was about, and I heard that the next morning after I departed from thence the king had caused Monsieur d'Andelot to be arrested about some answer he had made him concerning religion.

So soon as I was come, the king sent for me into his chamber, where he had with him the Cardinal of Lorrain, and two or three others (whom I have forgot, but I think the King of Navarre and

181

Monsieur de Montpensir were there) and there the king told me that I must go to Metz to the Duke of Guise, there to command the foot, of which Monsieur d'Andelot was colonel.

I most humbly besought His Majesty not to make me to intermeddle with another man's command, which rather than I would do, I would go serve His Majesty under the Duke of Guise in the quality of private souldier, or else would command his pioneers, rather than take upon me this employment. The king then told me that Monsieur de Guise, so soon as he had heard of Andelot's imprisonment, had himself sent to demand me to exercise the said command.

Seeing then I could get nothing by excuses, I told His Majesty that I was not yet cured of a dyssentery my disease had left me, and that this was a command which required health and disposition of body to perform it; which were neither of them in me; whereupon His Majesty told me that he should think this command better discharged by me in a litter, than by another in perfect health, and that he did not give it me to exercise for another, but that he intended I should have it for ever; to which I made answer that I gave His Majesty most humble thanks for the honour he deigned me herein, and made it my most humble request that he would not be displeased if I could not accept it.

Whereupon His Majesty said to me these words, 'Let me entreat you to accept it for my sake,' and with that the cardinal reproved me, saying, 'You dispute it too long with His Majesty, 'tis too much contested with your master,' to which I replyed, that I did not dispute it out of any disaffection to His Majestie's service, nor that I was unwilling to serve under the Duke of Guise, I having upon my first coming to Paris laid out money to buy me some tents and other equipage in order to my attendance upon him, having engaged myself before at Rome so to do; but only upon the account of my incapacity in that posture of health wherein I then was.

His Majesty then told me that there was no more to be said, and that I must go; after which I had no more to say. And I fancy the King of Navarre, and Monsieur de Montpensier both fell upon me to persuade me to accept of this command, forasmuch as I remember the king said to me, 'there is no more excuse, for you see all the world is against you,' and thereupon commanded the cardinal to order me another thousand crowns towards my equipage, which he presently did. I then returned to Paris, where I stayd but two dayes to provide myself of such things as I wanted, and so went away to the Duke of Guise to

Metz. I found him just mounting to horse to go to discover Thionville, but he would not suffer me to go along with him, by reason of my long journey, and to speak the truth I was not very well; and the same night he returned and told me that if God would permit us to take that place, there was honour to be got.

He was alwaies wont when disposed to be merry to call me his heart, and smiling, then said to me, 'Courage my heart, I hope we shall carry it.' And in the morning we departed, for he had all his tackle ready. I must needs say one thing with truth, and without flattery, that he was one of the most diligent generals that I had served, of eighteen under whom I had the honour to bear arms for His Majestie's service; and yet he had one fault, which was that he would write almost everything with his own hand, and would not trust to any secretary he had.

I will not say this was ill done, but it rendred him a little slow, and affairs of war require so prompt a diligence that a quarter of an hour's delay sometimes endangers the success of the greatest enterprise.

One day I came from the trenches to demand of him four German ensigns to reinforce our guards, for we began to approach very near to the town; and because the artillery from the walls had forced him from his first quarter, he was lodged in a little low house, which had one little chamber only, the window whereof was just over the door: I there met with Monsieur de Bourdillon, who was since Mareschal of France, whom I asked where the duke was; he told me he was writing;' the Devil,' said I, 'take all these writings for me, it seems he has a mind to save his secretaries a labour, 'tis pitty he was not a clerk of the Parliament of Paris, for he would have got more money than du Tillet and all the rest of them put together.'

Monsieur Bourdillon was ready to die with laughing, because he knew (which I dreamt not on) that the duke heard every word I said, and therefore egged me on still to descant more upon this clerk: when presently Monsieur de Guise came out laughing, and said, 'How now my heart, what do you think I should have made a good clerk?' but in my life I was never so out of countenance, and was furiously angry with Monsieur de Bourdillon, for having made me talk at that rate, though the duke laught at it only, and gave me Count Rocquendolf with four ensigns.

But to return to what I was saying of his diligence, there was not anyone who did not acknowledge him for one of the most vigilant and diligent generals of our times, and withal a man of so great judgment in deliberation, that he having delivered his opinion and advice, a better was not to be expected.

And to the rest, a prince so discreet, affable, and familiar, that there was not a man in his army who would not cheerfully run all hazards for the least word of his mouth; so great a dexterity he had in gaining hearts.

THE TAKING OF ARLON AND THE DINNER THAT SUCCEEDED IT

Three days after the taking of Thionville, the army marched directly to Arlon, a little town, but a very neat one for its circuit. 'Tis a great fault in a general to lie still after the taking of a place, as I have known them often do. This both encourages your enemy, and gives your own men opportunity to steal away; whereas their honour will oblige them to stay, when they see themselves employed: I mean, if the army be not totally broken or ruined, for then necessity compels you so to do: but otherwise to repose after a conquest, and to lose never so little time, is very prejudicial to His Majestie's service.

I with our foot quartered round about the town, Monsieur de Guise lay a quarter of a league behind, and told me he was almost moaped for want of sleep; for that since the beginning of the siege of Thionville till now he had not had so much sleep in all as he was wont to have in one night at other times (and I had had less than he) entreating me to make the approaches that night, that he would send me the commissaries of the artillery with four pieces of canon, to consult where they should be planted, and that he would give the sack of this town to the souldiers, in recompense of that of Thionville: Which having said, he retired himself into a little thatched house, where he was to lie.

There was in the town a hundred and fifty Germans, and four hundred Walloons, the Germans kept one gate, and the Walloons another; when, so soon as I had placed the centinels, and the courts of guards very near to one another (because it was said that some succours would enter in that night) they within set a very good face on the matter, which made us think that they lookt for some relief, I began to make the esplanade by the gardens of the town, to bring up the artillery, resolving to make my battery a little on the left hand the gate, to assist myself at the assault with the ladders of a little breach they had made themselves, through which to carry up earth to the terras they were making in that place; which to do they had made steps in the very earth itself, both at the descent into the grasse, and likewise in the ascent on the other side up to the terras.

I came up close to the ditch of the town, and to another little ditch there was near unto the way, which I caused to be discovered by a souldier; and I had three or four captains with me in this little ditch. The souldier found the steps, by which he went down, and afterwards mounted three or four of those that went up to the terrass, and there stayed without being perceived.

When having stayed a while he returned to me, and told me that there was no centinel upon the terrass; so that he thought if we should throw ourselves desperately upon the terrass we should carry the town. Hearing this, I caused a court of guard (that was much stronger than the rest, it being designed to guard the artillery) to come up to me, making the souldiers to creep on their hands and knees, and to put themselves into the ditch.

I then made the souldier return to the ditch, with three or four harquebuzeers, and two captains with targets, of which Monsieur de Goas was one. The night was so very dark that a man could not see a step from him, and this souldier was a Fleming. He goes down into the ditch, the captains after him, and the three or four harquebuzeers after them; and so soon as they were in the ditch they planted themselves on that side of it towards the town, and as near as they could to the steps.

The enemy hearing the noise began to cry '*who goes there?*' and the souldier answered them in their own language, '*a friend, a friend*'; they then demanded of him what he was, to which he made answer that he was a Fleming, and that being their countryman, he very much lamented their ruine, for that all the artillery Monsieur de Guise had would be planted in battery by morning, and that they were not to trust to the Germans who were with them in the town, for they were assured to have no harm, nor the least offence from our people, they having already made them that promise by a German souldier who stole out in the close of the evening to speak with us; so that all the slaughter would fall upon them if they did not surrender, which also would be too late after the canon had once playd.

Upon this they sent immediately to the Germans' quarters, and found that a souldier of ours who spoke Dutch was talking to them; so that so soon as their messenger returned, this souldier heard them all in a hurly-burly within, and began to ask them if they would make him drink, to which they answered they would, and bad him come up boldly upon their word and faith.

I heard every word, for I was not above six paces from the brink of the grasse, and made the other two captains go one after another into it, and three or four sergeants with halberts after them. The souldier then mounted the steps till he came to the edge of the terrass, where he again spoke to them, saying that Monsieur de Guise had made fair war with those of Thionville, and would do the same by them, still amusing them with fair speeches, and they fetcht him some drink. Monsieur de Goas was just behind the souldier, and three harquebuzeers one after another (for they could mount but one by one) in heels of him whom this first souldier so shaded with his body, that they could not see down the steps.

The other captain followed in the rear of the three harquebuzeers, and the sergeants after him, insomuch that all the steps were full from the top to the bottom; which when Monsieur de Goas saw, he pusht the souldier that was before him upon the terrass and the other captain the other three harquebuzeers, and then the souldier began to cry 'goot krich,' which is to say, 'good quarter, good quarter,' the harquebuzeers gave fire, and the captains threw themselves upon the counterscarp, and everybody after them, and these poor people fled to their quarters, the souldiers chasing them through the streets. I then leapt into the ditch with the rest of my men, mounting the souldiers as fast as I could one after another.

The Germans who saw themselves surprised behind, at the request of the souldier that spoke Dutch very courteously opened a postern, and gave themselves up to the discretion of the souldiers, wherein our men did an act worthy the highest commendation, and by which they shewed themselves to be old souldiers, for there was not four men killed in the whole town, but on the contrary they themselves led our people to the houses where the best booty was to be had: and thus the town was taken.

Monsieur de Guise, who had given order that no one should disturb him, but let him that night sleep his fill, knew nothing of all this till break of day, that asking if the artillery had begun to play, they told him the town was already taken, from about midnight, and the artillery returned back to its place, which made him make the sign of the cross, saying 'this is quick work,' when presently making himself ready, and mounting to horse, he came up to us.

Now by misfortune the fire had taken in two or three houses by reason of some powder that was found in them, which in removing thence accidentally took fire and burnt four or five souldiers, so that the town being almost full of flax ready drest for spinning, and the wind being very high, so no good means could be used but that above half the town was reduced to ashes, by reason whereof the souldiers did not get so much as otherwise they had done.

The next day Monsieur de Guise marched away with his army, and never staid till he came to Pierre-point, where himself and all the gentlemen of his train lodged in the town, which was very large while we encampt without on both sides of the river; and there it was that the Swiss came to us, and John William Duke of Saxony, who broght a great and very brave troop of *Reiters* along with him, and, if I mistake not, a regiment of Germans also.

The king himself likewise came, and lay at Marches, a house be-longing to the Cardinal of Lorrain, which altogether made up the greatest and the bravest army that I think ever a King of France had; for when the king would see them all drawn into battalia, they took up above a league and a half in length, and when the van began to march, to go back to the rear and to return back to the front took up three hours' time.

Two hours before day Messieurs de Bourdillon and de Tavannes Mareschaux de Camp, came to the place assigned for the rendezvouz, where as we came they still drew us up, and before all the army was in battalia it was above eight hours, and was excessively hot; Monsieur de Guise came himself by break of day, and helped to put the army into battalia.

I with my French foot was placed betwixt the Swiss and a battalion of Germans, whereas Monsieur de Guise passt by the head of our bat-talion, he said, 'Would to God we had some good fellow here with a bottle of wine and a crust of bread, that I might drink a glass or two, for I shall not have time to go dine at Pierre-point, and be back again before the king comes.'

Whereupon I said to him, 'Sir will you please to dine with me at my tents? (which was not above a harquebuz shot off) I will give you very good French and Gascon wine, and a whole covy of partridges.'

'Yes my heart,' said he, 'but they will be garlick and onions': to which I made answer, that they should neither be the one nor the other, but that I would give him as good a dinner as if he was in his own quarters, and wine as cool as he could desire, and moreover Gas-con wine, and admirable good water.

'Are you in earnest my heart,' said he.

'Yes upon my faith am I,' said I.

'Why then,' said he, 'I would willingly come, but I cannot leave the

Duke of Saxony.'

'Why sir,' said I, 'in the name of God bring the Duke of Saxony and who you please.'

'But,' said he, 'the duke will not come without his captains.'

'Why,' said I, 'bring his captains too, I have belly timber for you all.'

Now I had overnight promised Messieurs de Bourdillon and de Tabannes to treat them at dinner, after they had drawn the army up in battalia; but they could not come, by reason that part of the cavalry, who were quartered a great way off, were not yet come up; and on the other side, I had one of the best *providores* in the army. Monsieur de Guise then went to find out the Duke of Saxony and his captains, and I sent in all haste to my steward to get all things ready. My people had made a cellar in the earth, where the wind and the water were as cool as ice; and by good fortune I had got a great many partridges, quails, turkies, leverets, and all that could be desired, wherewith to make a noble feast, with baked-meats and tarts: for I knew that Monsieur de Bourdillon and de Tavannes would not come alone, and I had a mind to entertain them very well, they being both of them very good friends of mine.

They were so well treated that Monsieur de Guise asking the Duke of Saxony by his interpreter what he thought of the French colonel, and whether or no he had not treated them well, and given them good wine? the duke made answer, that if the king himself had treated them, he could not have done it better, nor have given them better nor cooler wine.

The Duke of Saxony's captains spared it not but drank freely to our French captains that I had brought along with me, neither though Messieurs de Bourdillon and de Tavannes had also come had I been surprized for next to the Duke of Guise his own table there was not one in the whole army longer or better furnisht than mine.

A way that I have alwayes used in what command soever I had been, being willing thereby to honour the employments I have had from my masters, to encrease my expence; and have alwayes observed such as have lived after this manner to be in greater reputation, and better followed than others: for such a gentleman may be, and of a good family, that sometimes knows not where to dine, and knowing where a good table is kept, will be glad to be there, who if he follow you at your table, will follow you anywhere else if he have never so little good blood or breeding in him.

But to return to my guests, so soon as they rose from table Monsieur de Guise asked me what laundress I had that kept my table-linnen so white, to which I made answer that they were two men I had that did it; 'Believe me,' said he, 'you are served like a prince'; and thereupon entertained the Duke of Saxony upon that subject, speaking better things of me than I deserved; whereupon I took occasion to tell him, that he would do well to perswade the king to give me money to buy silver vessel, that another time, when he and the Duke of Saxony would do me the honour to come eat in my pavillions, I might serve them according to their quality.

Monsieur de Guise told the Duke of Saxony what I said, who made answer, that he would tell the king; when being about to mount to horse to return to the camp, word was brought that the king was upon his way from Marches, and coming to the camp; whereupon they two went out to meet him. and we returned everyone to his place, all of us I assure you very well drunk, and our pates full.

About a quarter of a league from the battalions they met the king, where His Majesty asked them if they had dined, to which Monsieur de Guise made answer, that they had, and as well as they had done of a year before: 'why,' said His Majesty (seeing them come fromwards the battalions) 'you did not dine at Pierre-point.'

'No Sir,' said Monsieur de Guise. 'Neither can your Majesty guess where we dined, nor by whom so well entertained.'

'I pray by whom,' said the king.

'Marry Sir,' replied Monsieur de Guise, 'by Montluc.'

'I believe then,' said the king, 'he feasted you with his own country diet, garlick and onions, and wine as warm as milk': whereupon Monsieur de Guise up and told him how I had entertained them, when the king asking the Duke of Saxony by his interpreter if it were true, the duke made answer, that if His Majesty himself had treated them, they could not have had better meat, nor cooler wine: and that since I was so good a fellow, His Majesty might do well to give me money to buy plate, nothing having been wanting but that, and that Monsieur de Guise and he had both promised me to make that request to His Majesty in my behalf; which the king promised them to do, and that since I was so honourable in my expense, he would give me means to do it, more than hitherto he had ever done.

Though this passage be not much to the purpose, yet I thought fit to insert it here, to the end everyone may know that avarice had never so great a dominion over me as to hinder me from honouring the employments I have had from my kings and masters; and I would advise you, fellow captains, who command over a great many men, to do the same, and never to suffer avarice to be predominant over you; the little you spend will procure you several and considerable advantages.

A captain's handsome table invites worthy men, especially that of a lieutenant of the king, to which the nobility and gentry repair, either for want of commodious quarter, or sometimes perhaps upon the account of other inconveniences, where if the said lieutenant be miserable and narrow souled, they will look upon him as a man unworthy to be followed.

I never did so, but on the contrary always spent more than I had, and have found that it has done me more good than harm; yet was not this my only way of spending, but I had a trick of giving horses and arms also, and oftentimes to men that were better able than myself. If the king or the prince you serve under know you to be of this humour, he ought also to be open-handed to you, knowing you to be of a liberal nature, and that you reserve nothing to yourself.

The Beginning of the Wars of Religion

King Francis being dead at Orleans, where I then was, I went to wait upon the queen mother, who although she was very ill nevertheless did me the honour to command, that they should permit me to enter into her chamber. I had taken notice of the practices were set on foot, which did by no means please me, and especially those of the estates then sitting, by which I saw we should not long continue in peace, and that was it which made me resolve to retire from court, that I might not be hooked in either by one faction or another; especially considering that I had been made guilty that way before (contrary to all truth, as God be my help) which was the reason, that taking leave of Her Majesty, and not thinking it fit to trouble her with much discourse in her indisposition, I said to her these words.

Madam, I am going into Gascony, with a determination to do you most humble and faithful service all the days of my life, which I most humbly beseech your Majesty to believe, and if anything fall out considerable enough to engage you to call your servants about you, I promise you, and give you my faith, I will never take other side than that of your Majesties, and my Lords your children; but for that will be on horseback so soon as ever your Majesty shall please to command me.

The very night of the same day on which King Francis dyed, I had given her the same assurance, for which she now did me the honour to return me thanks, when Madam de Cursol, who stood at her bed's head, said to her, 'Madam, you ought not to let him go, your Majesty having no servant more faithful than those of the family of Montluc.'

To which I made answer, 'Madam, you shall never be without Montluc's, for you have three yet remaining, which are my two brothers and my son, who with myself will dye at your feet, for your Majestie's service.'

For which Her Majesty returned me many thanks. She who had a great deal of understanding, and who has given very ample testimony of it to the world, saw very well, that having so many affairs upon her hands during the minority of her children, she should have use for all the servants she had, and may herself remember what she said to me, wherein if I have failed to execute her commands, it was because I did not understand them.

And so I took my leave of Her Majesty; Madam le Cursol followed me to the middle of the room, where she took her leave of me, and Madame le Curton did the same, and thus I returned to my own house. Some months after my return home, I had news brought me from all sides, of the strange language and most audacious speeches the ministers of the new faith impudently uttered, even against the royal authority.

I was moreover told that they imposed taxes upon the people, made captains, and listed souldiers, keeping their assemblies in the houses of several lords of the country, who were of this new religion; which was the first beginning and cause of all those mischiefs and massacres they have since exercised upon one another.

I saw the evil daily to increase, but saw no one who appeared on the king's behalf to oppose it. I heard also that the greatest part of the officers of the treasury were of this religion (the nature of man being greedy of novelty) and the worst of all, and from whence proceeded all the mischief, was, that those of the long robe, the man of justice in the Parliaments and Senachalseys, and other judges, abandoned the ancient religion, and that of the king, to embrace the new one. I met also with strange names of surveillans, deacons, consistories, sinods and colloquies, having never before breakfasted of such viands.

I heard that the surveillans had bulls pizzles by them called lohanots, with which they misused, and very cruelly beat the poor peasants if they went not to their conventicles; the people being so totally abandoned by justice, that if anyone went to complain, they received nothing but injury instead of redress, and not a sergeant that durst attempt to execute anything in the behalf of the Catholicks, but for the Hugonots only (for so they were called, though I know not why) the rest of the judges and officers who were Catholicks being so over-awed that they durst not have commanded so much as an information to be made for fear of their lives.

All these things together were presages to me of what I have since seen come to pass, and returning from another house of mine to that of Stillac, I found the town of La Plume besieged by three or four hundred men. I had my son Captain Montluc with me, whom I sent with all sorts of fair language (for I had no more than ten or twelve horse in my company) to try to perswade them to desist. Wherein he prevailed so far that he overcame the Brimonts, the principal heads of this enterprise (which was undertaken to rescue two prisoners of their religion, that the magistrates of La Plume had for some disorders committed.) My son having promised them that if they would retire I would cause them to be delivered; they took his word, and drew off from before the town. The next day accordingly I went to speak with the officers of the said city, to whom having remonstrated that for these two prisoners they ought not to suffer a sedition to be set on foot, they brought them out to me, and let them go.

★★★★★★

But to return to my first subject, having heard and seen all these affairs and novelties which still much more disclosed themselves after my return, and after the death of the king (for they now explained themselves in down-right terms) than before, I deliberated to return to court, no more to stir from the queen and her children, but to die at their feet in opposition to all such as should present themselves against them, according to the promise I had made to the queen, and put myself upon my way in order to this resolution. The court was then at St German en l'Aye. I staid but two dayes at Paris, and at my coming to St Germains found not one person of the house of Guise, nor any other but the Queen, the King of Navarre, the Prince of Condé, and the Cardinal of Ferrara, where I was very well received by Her Majesty, and by them all.

The Queen and the King of Navarre drawing me apart, enquired of me how affairs stood in Guienne; to which I made answer, that they were not yet very ill, but that I feared they would every day grow worse and worse, telling them withall the reasons why I conceived that it would not be long before they would break into open arms.

I staid there but five dayes in which time news came that the Hugonots were risen at Marmanda, and had killed all the religious of the Order of St Francis, and burnt their monastery: immediately came other news of the massacre the Catholics had made of the Hugonots at Cahors, with that of Grenade near unto Tholouze. After that came news of the death of Monsieur de Fumel, barbarously massacred by his own tenants who were Hugonots; which troubled the queen more than all the rest, and then it was that Her Majesty saw that what I had prophecied to her, that they would not long abstain from arms, was very true.

They were six dayes before they could resolve at which end to begin to extinguish this fire. The King of Navarre would that the queen should write to Monsieur de Burie to take order in those affairs; but the queen said that if none but he put their hands to the work, there would be no great matters done, by which she implied some jealousie of him; and I know what he said to me, 'A little thing will serve to render me suspected.'

I perceived also that the King of Navarre was not so kind to me as formerly: which I believe proceeded from my own behaviour, I being not so observant to him as at other times, and never stirring from the queen. In the end they resolved to send me into Guienne with a commission to raise horse and foot, and to fall upon all such as should appear in arms. I defended myself the best I could from this employment, knowing very well that it was not a work done, but a work that was only about to begin, and such as required a great master to execute it as it ought to be; and therefore remained at this bout constant not to take it upon me.

The next morning the Queen and the King of Navarre sent for me, and the queen had in the interval commanded Monsieur de Valence my brother to persuade me to accept of this commission; so that when I came before them, after several remonstrances they made me, I was constrained to accept of it, provided that Monsieur de Burie might be joyned in the commission, for I would have him have his part of the cake.

But the queen would by no means hear of it, alledging but too many reasons (princes may say what they please) till in the end I was forced to tell Her Majesty plainly, that in case he was not comprehended in the commission, he being the king's lieutenant as he was, would underhand strew so many traverses and difficulties in my way, that I should never effect anything to purpose; which at last they allowed to be a sufficient reason, and let it pass according to my own desire.

The same commission they gave me for Guienne, they also gave Monsieur de Cursol for the province of Languedcc, giving us both in charge, that which of us soever should first have dispatched our own business, should go help his fellow, if he should stand in need. Monsieur de Cursol was no more of this new religion than I, and without all doubt afterward turned to it more out of some discontent, than for any devotion, for he was no great divine, no more than I was; but I have known many turn to this religion out of pure spite, who have afterwards very much repented.

We both of us together took our leaves of the Queen and the King of Navarre, and went to Paris, and Monsieur de Valence with us. I demanded two counsellors of that part of France to sit upon life and death (fearing that those of the country would do no good, being that some of them would encline to the Catholicks, and others to the Hugonots) and had given me two of the damnedest rogues in the whole kingdom, one whereof was Compain a counsellor of the great council, and the other Gerard, lieutenant to the Prevost d'Hostel, who have since gained no better a reputation than they had before. I repented me I had demanded them; but I thought I did well in it, and so I came into Gascony in all diligence.

★★★★★★

I had scarce been four or five days in my house Estellac, when a minister called la Barrelle came to me on the behalf of their churches, telling me that the churches were exceeding glad of my coming, and the authority the queen had given me, being now assured to obtain justice against those that had massacred their brethren. To which I made answer, that he might be confident all such as should appear in fault, should be certainly punished.

He then told me that he had in commission from the churches to make me a handsome present, and such a one as therewith I should have reason to be well satisfied. I told him, that there was no need of any presents to me, forasmuch as my integrity would oblige me to do my duty, and that for all the presents in the world, I was never to be made to do anything contrary to it. He then told me, that the Catholicks had declared they would never endure to have justice executed upon them, and that therefore he had in commission from all the churches, to present me with four thousand foot in good equipage, and paid.

194

This word began to put me into fury, and made me angrily demand of him, what men, and of what nation must those four thousand foot be? to which he made answer, of this very country, and of the churches; whereupon I asked him, if he had power to present the king's subjects, and to put men into the field, without the command of the king, or the queen who was at this time regent of the kingdom, and so declared by the estates held at Orleans.

'O you confounded rogues,' said I, 'I see very well what you aim at, it is to set divisions in the kingdom, and 'tis you ministers that are the authors of this godly work, under colour of the Gospel'; and thereupon fell to swearing, and seizing him by the collar, said these words, 'I know not rascal, what should hinder me, that I do not myself hang thee at this window, for I have with my own hands strangled twenty honester men than thou.'

Who then trembling, said to me, 'Sir I beseech you let me go to Monsieur de Burie, for I have order from the churches to go speak with him, and be not offended with me, who only came to deliver a message, neither do or do it for any other end, but only to defend ourselves.' Whereupon I bade him go and be hanged to all the devils in Hell, both he, and all the rest of his fellow ministers, and so he departed from me, as sufficiently frighted as ever he was in his life. This action got me very ill repute amongst the ministers, for it was no less than high treason to touch one of them.

Nevertheless a few days after came another minister called Boenormant, *alias* la Piene, sent in the behalf their churches, (as he said) to entreat me to accept the present and offer that Barelle had made me, saying that it was not for the intention I imagined, and that without costing the king so much as a liard, I might render equal justice both to the one party and the other.

At this I was almost ready to lose all manner of patience, and with great vehemency reproached him with the levying of money and the listing of men, but he denied it all, whereupon I said to him, 'But what if I prove to you, that no longer since then yesterday, you listed men at la Plume, what will you say?'

To which he made answer, 'That if it was so, it was more than he knew.' Now he had a souldier with him, that had formerly been in my company in Piedmont, called Antragues, which made me turn to him, saying 'Will you Captain Antragues deny, that you yesterday listed men at la Plume?'

To which, seeing himself caught, he made answer, that indeed the

Church of Nerac had made him their captain. Whereupon I began to say, 'What the Devil Churches are those that make captains?' and fell to reproach him with the good usage and respect I had shewed him when he was in my company; forbidding them ever again to come to me with the like errand, which if they did, I should not have the patience to forbear laying hands upon them; and so they departed.

They afterwards began to rise at Agen, and to make themselves masters of the town, in which were the Seigneurs de Memi and Castet-Segrat, and the Seneschal of Agenois; Poton was also there, who did all that in him lay to pacific affairs, and came to me, entreating me to go to Agen, and that all obedience should be paid me there; there came a minister also along with him, who would engage his honour to me in the business, but I did not take that for good security.

The *seneschal* proceeded with integrity, and I believe it would have cost him his life as well as me mine, had I gone thither, for he would have defended me the best he could; and it came so near it, that at their importunity, I promised to be there the next morning. But the Sieurs de la Lande and de Nort in the meantime dispatched away a messenger in private to me, to give me warning not to come, if I had any care of my life, for if I did, I was a dead man; which made me send them word, that I would not pass over the river, but if they could come to a house at the ferry, I was content to give them the meeting there.

When they saw they could not inveigle me into their power, they consented to come to the place appointed, whither I accordingly went to meet them with five and twenty souldiers, whom I ordered not to stir from the water side, and there we dined together.

After dinner we fell to debate what was best to be done; where I told them, 'that in the first place, and before we proceeded to any further particulars, they were to content themselves with the church, that Monsieur de Burie had allowed them for their meetings, which was a Parish church, and that they must quit the Jacobins, and permit the religious to re-enter, to perform their offices there; that they must lay down their arms, and receive the one half of the King of Navarre's company into their city for a garrison, and the other half should remain at Condom.'

I could never perswade them to condesend to this; wherefore taking the Seneschal of Agen aside, I said to him, 'Do you not evidently see, that they aim at a subversion, and to make themselves masters of cities? I would not advise you to stay with these people; for you will be necessitated, either to let them do what they will, or resolve to have your throat cut, we have a fair example in Monsieur de Funill: consider with yourself what is best for you to do, and so farewel.'

And so without any more words, I abruptly left them, and returned to Stillac, where at my coming home I found a farmer of mine of Puch de Gontaut, called Labat, who came to tell me in behalf of their churches that I was too cholerick, and had not patience rightly to understand what the Ministers Barrelle and Boenormont had to say to me, and to present me withal, which was, that the churches made me a tender of thirty thousand crowns, provided I would not take arms against them, but let them alone, without desiring nevertheless that I should alter my religion, and that within fifteen days at the furthest, they would bring me the money to my own house.

In answer to which I told him, 'That were it not for the love I bore him, and also that he was my tenant, I would handle him after another manner than I had done Barrelle and Boenormont, and clap a dagger at his bosom, that he knew very well I had the knack on't, and therefore henceforward let neither he, nor any other be so impudent as to make any such proposals to me, for I would infallibly be the death of them if they did.' Whereupon, very sufficiently frighted, he immediately left me to return to Nerac, to carry back my answer to his church.

Eight days had not passed after this before Captain Sendat came again to tempt me with much greater offers then before; for he made me an offer of forty thousand crowns, he himself having made them a promise to be of their party, provided I did not take arms against them; for which they also gave him Two thousand crowns.

We talked a pretty while of the business, and when he saw he could no other way prevail with me to take their money, he prest and advised me to take it, and lend the money to the king, wherewith to make war against them. To which I made answer, that I very well perceived he did not understand what it was to bring the reputation of an honest man in dispute, said I:

> For in the first place they will not give me this money, without first making me take an oath not to bear arms against them, which engagement they will have in writing to shew to their churches, to make them part with their money; and besides, it is impossible but that this must come to light, for fire can never be so covered and concealed but that some smoak will issue out.

The queen will wonder that I sit still in my own house and do nothing, she will solicite me to take arms, which if I then refuse to do, will you not that both she and all the world believe I have taken this money, and am a bribed and corrupted fellow?

On the other side, should I give this money to the king, his council must needs take notice, that I have taken an oath not to bear arms, and yet they know, that upon my receiving the order, I have sworn to do it, and to defend his person and his crown against all the world. How then can you imagine, that either the queen now, or the king when he grows up, can look upon me as an honest man, when I have taken two oaths expressly contrary to one another? Some will say that I took the money at first upon the account of infidelity; but that afterwards repenting, I would palliate my knavery by giving it to the king. Others will say that the queen ought no more to repose any trust in me, having taken two oaths positively contrary to one another, and that since I made no conscience of cheating the Hugonots with an oath, I would make as little to deceive the king. Thus shall my honour be brought in question, and I with just reason sentenced for ever incapable of any place amongst honest men, and such as are good and loyal subjects to their prince. What will then become of me, and what a monster of men shall I be, when I have lost the honour I have fought for all my life, and parted with my blood to obtain? I will not only say, that the gentlemen of France will avoid my conversation, but even the basest of the people also will be ashamed of my company.

See then Captain Sendat what a fine condition I should be in, should I follow your advice: In return of which, I will give you better; I pray frequent these people no more, you have ever been brought up and born arms with the Montluc's, let me entreat you to take them up now for the service of the king, and do not go over to that ridiculous religion. Our forefathers were honester men than they, and I cannot believe that the Holy Ghost is amongst a people who rise in rebellion against their king; Here is a hopeful beginning.

He promised to follow my counsel, and so departed.

By my behaviour in this affair, I sufficiently manifested to all the world that avarice could never make me abandon my honour nor my conscience to falsifie the oath I have in the presence of God made to the king, loyally and faithfully to serve him, and to defend his person and his crown, and yet some have not been ashamed to accuse me of polling from the king's treasury, and of imposing taxes upon the country to enrich myself. God and the truth are on my side, and the testimony of the estates of Guienne, who will make it know to all those who have made all these false reports of me to their Majesties, that I have never done any such thing.

But letting this alone, I will return to the justice Monsieur de Burie and I did with our vertuous Commissioners Compain and Gerard, who remained a long time without appearing in any place, or it being so much as known where they were. Which made me solicite Monsieur de Burie to let us speedily fall to our business, and that since our commissioners did not come, we would make use of the counsellors of Agen.

Yet still we lingered away the time in delays, whilst I had intelligence daily brought me that the Hugonots continued their damnable conspiracies. There was at this time a lieutenant of the tribunal of Condom, called du Franc, a very honest man and a good servant of the king's, who was once half in mind to have gone over to this new religion (for he was not the son of a good mother, that was not one of them) this man was one day called to a council, in which there were some persons of a very great quality, and where he heard an accursed and execrable proposition, both being once proposed, he durst not when it came to his turn to deliver his opinion say otherwise than the rest had done, fearing should he contradict it they would put him to death, lest he should discover their council, and was therefore constrained to go through with it as the rest had done. I shall not say where this council was kept, much less name the persons who were present at it, for the council and the proposition signifie nothing now, and there were some in the company, who are since become very honest men.

He sent to me to entreat that he might have some private conference with me, betwixt Sampoy and Condom, and appointed an hour. I took no more company with me, but one footman only, and he another, for so we had agreed, and we met in a meadow that lay under the house of Monsieur de Sainctorens, where he told me all that had been said in the council, and what had there been concluded, which was such a conspiracy as (so God shall help me) made my hair stand on end to hear it.

After he had ended his story, he made me the remonstrance of an honest man, telling me that now an occasion presented itself wherein I might acquire honour to myself and those who should descend from me for ever, which was with a couragious and magnanimous heart to take arms, and to expose my life to all dangers for the safeguard of those poor children who were the sons of so good a king, and as yet in no better an age to defend themselves than if they were in their cradles, and that God would assist me, seeing me take arms to protect the innocent and those who were no way able to defend themselves.

To this, this good man added so many and so powerful remonstrances that (as I shall be saved) the tears came into my eyes, entreating me withal, not to discover him, for if I should, he was a dead man. He told me further, that as to what concerned myself, they had consulted about me, and determined to surprise me in one place or another, and that if they could get me into their hands, they would deal worse by me, than they had done by Monsieur de Fumel. Nothing of all their conspiracies was concealed from the said lieutenant, because they thought him sure of their side, so dexterously did he behave himself amongst them; but he afterwards shewed them the contrary, several times exposing his life in the city of Condom, with his sword in his hand, in defence of the king's authority.

But however it came to pass, he was afterwards either by poyson, or some other violent means, dispatched out of the world for this very business. I thought he had never discovered himself but to me only, but I found that he had told the same thing to Monsieur de Gondrin, who was a very intimate friend of his, and to Monsieur de Maillac, receiver of Guienne, for they were both as it were brothers. For my part, I never opened my lips concerning it to anyone living, but to the queen at Tholouze, by the chimney of her chamber, at which Her Majesty was very much astonished, as she had very good reason to be, for more horrid and diabolical designs were never heard of, and yet very great persons were of the conspiracy.

Having heard all these abominable designs, I retired to my own house at Sampoy; where I concluded with myself to lay aside all manner of fear, resolving to sell my skin as dear as I could, as knowing very well, that if I once fell into their hands, and was left to their mercy, the greatest piece of my body would be no bigger than my little finger. Moreover, determining to execute all the cruelty I could, and especially against those who spoke against the Royal Majesty; for I saw very well that gentle ways would never reclaim those cankered and inveterate rascals. Monsieur de Burie departed from Bourdeaux, sending me word of the day he intended to be at Clairac, that we might there together resolve where we ought to begin our circuit.

He sent me also letters the commissioners had writ to him, wherein they appointed us to come to Cahors, there to begin against the Catholicks; in answer to which I writ to him back again, that he should well consider the patent, and that there he would find the queen had commanded us to go and begin at Fumel. The letters of these two honourable gentlemen were of so audacious and impudent a stile as that by them they gave us to understand that they were the principal commissioners, and that we had no authority, saving to justifie their proceedings, and to be assisting in the execution of their decrees.

Now there was a village two leagues from Estillac, called S. Mezard, the greatest part whereof belonged to the Sieur de Rouillac a gentleman of eight or ten thousand *livers* a year. Four or five days before I came thither the Hugonots his tenants were risen up against him, because he offered to hinder them from breaking open the church, and taking away the chalices, and kept him four and twenty hours besieged in his own house; so that had it not been for a brother of his, called Monsieur de S. Aignan, and some other gentlemen his neighbours, who came to his relief, they had certainly cut his throat, as also those of Ostfort would have done to the Sieurs de Cuq, and de la Montjoye, so that already there began to be open war against the gentry.

I privately got two hangmen (which they have since called my lacquais, because they were very often at my heels) and sent to Monsieur de Fontenilles, my son in law (who carried my cornet, and was at Beaumont de Lomange, where he lay in garison), that he should come away upon Thursday in the beginning of the night, and by break of day be at the said S. Mezard, there to seize of those persons whose names I had sent him in writing, and whereof the principal was nephew to the advocate of the King and Queen of Navarre at Lectoure, called Verdery.

Now the said advocate was he that fomented all the sedition, and I had private word sent me that he would come that very Thursday to S. Mezard, for he had some estate there. I was resolved to begin with this fellow's head, forasmuch as having advertised the King of Navarre at court that the said Verdery and other of his officers at Lectoure were the principal incendiaries of rebellion, and having writ as much to the queen of the king's officers, she had writ back that I should begin with those people first, and the King of Navarre had writ in his letter that if I hanged the king's officers on the lower branches of a tree, I should hang his on the uppermost of all. But Verdery came not, which was well for him, for if he had I had branched him.

Monsieur de Fontenilles performed a very long march, and came by break of day to S. Mezard, where at his first coming he took the nephew of Verdery, and two others, and a deacon, the rest escaped away, there being not anyone who knew the houses, for there was not so much as any one man at arms or archer who had any knowledge of the place.

A gentleman, called Monsieur de Corde, who lived at the said place, had sent me word that when in the presence of the consuls he had remonstrated to them that they did ill, and that the king would be highly displeased with their doings, they made answer, 'What king? We are the kings, he that you speak of is a little turdy roylet, we'll whip his breech, and set him to a trade, to teach him to get his living as others do.'

Neither was it only there that they talked at this precious rate, but it was common discourse in every place. I was ready to burst with indignation at it, and saw very well that all this language tended to what had been told me by Lieutenant du Franc, which, in sum, was to make another king. I had agreed with Monsieur de Sainctorens that he should also take me five or six of Astefort, and especially one Captain Morallet, the chief ringleader of them all, and that if he could take him, and those I named to him, he should with good words bring them to me to S. Mazard, the same day that I performed the execution, which was upon a Friday, which nevertheless that day he could not do, but he snaped them the Sunday following, and brought them prisoners to Villeneufe.

So soon as I came to S. Mazard, Monsieur de Fonteneilles presented the three prisoners and the deacon, all bound, in the churchyard, in which there was yet remaining the foot of a cross of stone they had broken, that might be about some two foot high. I presently called Monsieur de Corde and the consuls, bidding them upon pain of death to deliver truly what words they heard these fellows speak against the king.

The consuls were afraid, and durst say nothing; whereupon I told the said Sieur de Corde that it belonged to him to speak first, and therefore bid him speak; upon which he maintained to their faces, that they had spoke the forementioned words, and then the consuls told the truth, and justified the same the Sieur de Corde had done. I had my two hangmen behind me very well equiped with their tackle, and especially with a sharp ax, when flying in great fury upon this Verdere, I took him by the collar, saying to him, 'O thou confounded rogue! durst thou defile thy wicked tongue against the Majesty of thy King and Sovereign'

To which he replyed 'Ah Sir, have mercy upon a poor sinner.'

At which more enraged than before I said to him, 'Thou ungracious rascal, would'st thou have me to have mercy upon thee who hadst no reverence nor respect for thy king,' and with that pushed him rudely to the ground, so that his neck fell exactly upon the piece of the cross, crying to the hangman, 'Strike villain,' which he did, and so nimbly, that my word and the blow were the one as soon as the other, which fetched off his head, and moreover above another half foot of the cross.

The other two I caused to be hanged upon an elm that was close by, and beeing the deacon was but eighteen years old, I would not put him to death, as also that he might carry the news to his brethren; but caused him nevertheless to be so well whiped by the hangman, that, as I was told, he dyed within ten or twelve days after.

This was the first execution I did at my coming from my own house without sentence or writing; for in such matters, I have heard, men must begin with execution, and if every one that had the charge of provinces had done the same, they had put out the fire that has since consumed all. However, this served to stop the mouths of several seditious persons, who durst no more speak of the king, but with respect, but in great privacy, and with greater circumspection carried on their practices and designs.

Two Commissioners Pass a Bad Quarter of an Hour at Monluc's hands

From thence we went to Cahors, where we found these venerable lords, who had begun and were already a good way advanced in their process against the Catholicks, and kept in prison Monsieur de Viole, Canon and Archdeacon of Cahors, and Chancellor of the University, a gentleman of a family of seven or eight thousand *livres* a year belonging to Monsieur de Terride, de Negrepelice, and other gentlemen of the country.

The Sieur de Caumont des Mirandes had married his sister into this family, and was there soliciting for the said de Viole, his brother in law with his children, and nephews of the said de Voile, and Madam de Bagua, sister to the said de Viole. Monsieur d'Aussan was come thither also, as being kinsman to his wife, and the whole city was full of gentry to solicit in the behalf of the said Sieur de Viole.

Our reverend commissioners had ordered their business so well that they had called in to their assistance nine judges, six whereof were Hugonots, and the other three they had so terrified with their power and authority that they pretended to have it in their commission, that none of them was to dare to contradict what the others said, and especially Judge Mage, being a timerous person, durst not pronounce a syllable but what the rest would have him say.

They there condemned fourteen or fifteen men, of which not above three had any hand in the massacre; but in revenge of the execution we had done at Fumel, they would put to death as many as they could, justly or unjustly, and caused them to be executed in the market-place of the city; at which both the magistrates and the clergy entred into so violent an apprehension that they gave themselves all for lost, seeing them to put Monsieur de Viole, and several others upon their tryal, who were none of them present at the massacre.

All the ladies were continually following after me, seeing they could obtain no satisfactory answer from Monsieur de Burie, and Monsieur de Caumont that now is come to speak to Monsieur de Burie, I think rather to take an occasion to quarrel me than for anything else, because I had said that he suffered a minister in the open pulpit to speak against the person of the king and his royal authority at Clairac, of which he was abbot, and he questioned me about it in the open hall before Monsieur de Burie; whereupon I told him, that I had said so, and that he stood so much obliged to the king for the benefits he had received, that he ought not to have endured it, to which he replied that the said minister had not preached before him, and that although he had, it was not to me to whom he was to give an account; at which I had thought to have flown upon him with my dagger in my hand, and he clapt hand to his sword, when in an instant fifteen or twenty gentlemen of mine leapt upon him, and there was enough to do to save him from being killed.

Monsieur de Burie took my part in a very high manner, and rattled him to some purpose, insomuch that some friends of his thurst him out of the hall to save him, for everyone had his sword drawn, and he had not a party sufficient to make it an equal match against the friends I had present there; and this was the occasion of the hatred they say he bears me, for before we were very good friends; but 'tis the least of my care.

But to return to our justice, the Countess of Arein, who was at Assier, sent me a letter by one of her gentlemen, called la Brun, wherein she entreated me to see justice duly performed, to which I writ her answer back, that I would by no means obstruct it, where I saw there was reasonable and just cause, and that Monsieur de Burie and I were there for no other end. The next day he returned to me again, and in private entreated me that I would further the execution of the commissioners' sentence, and that in return of so good an office I should not fail of ten thousand *francs*.

He made me this offer in the presence of a merchant that sold pistolets, which he himself chose out for me, telling me that he was privy to the affair, and would immediately disburse the sum. I told him he did me a very great pleasure, but that I would leave them in his hands, being to go to Monsieur de Burie to supper, whose lodging was hard by.

By the way as I went, I began to consider with myself from whence these ten thousand *francs* should come; but could not possibly imagine, though I was satisfied there must be malice and knavery in the case. After supper, when it grew late, I retired to my lodging at the Archdeacon Redoul's house, where by the way I met Madam de Longua, and Madame de Viole hard by the house, who passionately weeping, said to me these words, 'Oh Sir, Monsieur de Viole is going to be put to death, if you do not stand his friend, for sentence is past upon him, and this night there is order given to strangle him in prison, and in the morning to present him dead upon the Scaffold.'

All the forementioned lords and gentlemen had sent away post to the king about this business, but the messenger had returned too late, if I had not been. I dismist them with the best comfort I could, telling them that I would take care to prevent execution; to which end I appointed certain *gens d'armes* of my own company to ride the patronille before the prison and before the commissioners' lodgings, and never put off my cloths myself of all that night. It was very late before the Archdeacon Redoul come home, when so soon as I heard he was come into his chamber, I sent for him to talk with him about the business.

He had been privately enquiring after the affairs of Monsieur de Viole and the other prisoners, who were all people of good quality, and brought this account that they were all condemned to dye, and that for fear of scandal, and that no commotion might arise, they were to be dispatched secretly in prison by torchlight, and that by their process and judgment they had divided the city into three distinct corporations, to wit, the church into one, the magistracy into another, and the third estate into the last; all which three distinct bodies were sentenced to a fine of six-score thousand *francs*: whereupon it presently came into my head that the ten thousand *francs* of which la Brun had made me a tender was certainly to come from hence; and the said archdeacon wept, saying that the city of Cahors was ruined for ever, and that though all the goods of the city moveable and immoveable should be sold, they could not make up that sum.

Whereupon I advised him not to afflict himself, but leave it to me, for that out of the love I bore to Monsieur de Viole and the rest I would keep so good watch that I would trap them before they could do their execution, and as to the fines you speak of, said I, it is not the king's intention that your city should be destroyed, for it is his, and assure yourself he will remit them.

'Alas Sir,' said he, 'if the fines went into the king's purse, we should have some hope that His Majesty would not see us destroyed; but he is not to have one peny of them.'

'Why who then,' said I?

''Tis the Count Rhinegrave,' said he, 'who lent the king fifty thousand *francs* upon the county, and we have had a tryal with the said count about the fines of Tholouze, where he has cast us, it being proved that he had as good title to the fines and amerciaments as to any other part of the revenue, and that is the reason why we have no other remedy but to abandon the city, to go live in some other place, and leave him all we have.'

Hearing this I was ready to run mad to think that these two rogues should ruine one of the king's cities for one particular man. I past over the whole night in great anger and impatience, and in the morning Monsieur de Burie sent for me to hear the judgment of the process; but by the way, I thought to prevent them from pronouncing sentence, which being once pronounced, there was no possible way to save the city but that the Count Rhinegrave would have had the fines, who though he was a stranger, yet he was one the king had very often occasion to use. In this heat I came to Monsieur de Burie's chamber, where I found them all already set, and the bags upon the table.

They perceived very well by my countenance what I had in my stomach, but I said nothing, but took a little stool and placed myself at the end of the table, for they had taken up all the room round about it, and there the said Campain in a learned oration began to lay open the offence that had been committed in the city, enlarging himself upon the hainousness of the fact, and remonstrating to us, how many women and children had lost their husbands and their fathers in this bloody massacre, and that the king and queen had sent us thither to do this justice, which was equitable and right (his harangue lasted for half an hour at least) and that those offenders they had already put to death would signifie nothing if they did not also execute the principal authors of this sedition, which would serve for an exemple to the whole kingdom of France, concluding that therefore they would read the sentence before us, to have it afterwards executed in prison, entreating us to lend our assistance in the seeing it accordingly performed, and thereupon began to draw the sentence out of the bag.

I looked upon Monsieur de Burie, to see if he would speak, for it was for him to speak before me, but seeing he suffered him to proceed without interruption, and the other beginning to open the sentence to read it, I said to him, 'Hold Monsieur de Campain, proceed no further, till you have first answered what I have to demand of you.'

To which he made answer that after he had read the sentence, he would answer my questions, but that he would first read that, before he did anything else. Whereupon I said to Monsieur de Burie (rapping out a great oath) 'Sir, at the first word that comes out of his mouth, I will kill him if he do not first satisfie me in such things as I shall in your presence demand of him.'

At which Monsieur de Burie said to him, 'Monsieur de Campain, you must hear what he has to say to you, for perhaps he may have heard something, that I know not of,' and then I perceived my gentleman to turn pale, and upon my word he had good reason. I then asked him, 'Whose is the city of Cahors?'

To which he answered, 'It is the king's.'

'And whose is the judicature?' said I.

'The king's,' said he.

'And whose is the church?' said I.

To which he made answer that he could not tell. Whereupon I said to him, 'do you deny that the church is not the kings as well as the rest?'

To which he made answer that he did not concern himself about it.

I then said to him, 'Have you divided the city into three corporations, that is to say, the church, the judicature, and the city separate by itself, and imposed fines severally upon them all?'

To which he made answer that I should give ear to the sentence, and that would inform me, whether he had or no. Whereupon I began to thou him, saying, 'Thou shalt here declare before Monsieur de Bury and me what I demand of thee, or I will hang thee with my own hands, for I have hanged twenty honester men than thyself or those who have assisted at thy sentence'; and thereupon start up from my stool, at which Monsieur de Burie said, 'Speak Monsieur Campain, and say if you have done it or no.'

'Yes sir,' answered he, 'I have'.

Whereupon I said, 'O thou damned confounded villain, traytor to thy king, thou wilt ruine a city belonging to the king, for the profit of one particular man; were it not for the respect I bear to Monsieur de Burie, who is here the king's lieutenant, I would hang both thee and thy companions at the windows of this chamber;' saying to Monsieur de Burie, 'for God's sake let me kill these accursed rogues, that are traytors to their king for another's profit and their own;' and thereupon drew my sword halfway, and had they let me alone I had ordered them for ever making more sentences or arrests; but Monsieur de Bury leaped to me and caught hold of my arm, entreating me not to do it, whilst in the meantime they recovered the door, and fled away in so great a fright that they leaped the stairs without staying to count the steps.

I would fain have followed after to have killed them, but Monsieur de Burie and Monsieur de Courre, his nephew, held me so fast that I could not break from them, the rage wherein I was not permitting me to be master of myself; It ought not then to appear strange, if I call them so often rogues in my relation.

This being done. Monsieur de Burie, Monsieur de Courre, and I went into a garden, where the said Sieur de Bury told me that besides that I had preserved this city from total ruine, I had saved his honour also, for the king and the queen and all the world would infallibly have concluded that he had taken money, whereas he protested that he knew not one syllable of all this, and then it was that I told him which way I came to discover it, and do really believe there was no intelligence on Monsieur de Burie's side.

I dined with him and do think he did not eat four bits, and all that day observed him to be melancholy and displeased, sending word to all the commissioners not to proceed any further in anything whatsoever till the king should first be enformed of all that had past. I also sent to Judge Mage and the rest to forbid them that they should not be assisting in anything should be done by Campain and Gerard upon forfeiture of their lives.

They came in the evening one after another, I mean the judge's assistants, to excuse themselves to Monsieur de Burie, confessing to him that they had not foreseen the ruine this sentence would have inevitably have brought upon the city, which would also have been the undoing both of them and their posterity; but they durst never speak a word to me, nor so much as come where I was.

Monsieur de Burie told me all, but whatsoever the matter was, not one of them durst come in my sight; which if they had, upon my conscience I think I should have strangled one or another of them.

About five or six days after came the courrier that the relations and friends of Monsieur de Viole had sent to the king, who brought an injunction to the commissioners not to proceed any further in any manner whatsoever against the said Sieur de Viole, nor concerning this sedition, commanding them to set the said Sieur de Viole and the other prisoners at liberty, upon bail to appear when and so often as they should be summoned so to do. It is not to be wondered at if the city of Cahors have a kindness for me, as indeed they have to such a degree that by the respect they pay me, and the entertainments they caress me withal, it seems as if the king himself or some of his brothers were come into their city.

★★★★★★

Now Monsieur de Burie having: himself seen that these two brave commissioners did not go franckly to work, and that their only drift was to execute justice upon the Catholicks only, and not upon the Hugonots also, he sent in all haste to Bourdeaux, for Messieur d'Aleson the elder, and Ferron, counsellors in the Court of Parliament, and men that very well understood their business, that he might joyn with them to these commissioners of ours for a counterpoise to balance their wicked inclinations, and so we went straight to Ville-Franche de Rovergue, when hearing by the way that the Hugonots from all parts drew together in great numbers.

Monsieur de Burie sent for the companies of the Mareschal de Termes, of Messieurs de Randan, de la Vauguyon, and de Jarnac, for before we had no more than our own two companies; and found at Ville-Franche Monsieur the Cardinal of Armagnac, who staid there expecting our coming, to complain of the churches had been violated and defaced in his jurisdiction, and particularly at Ville Franche, a member of his Bishoprick of Rhodes; when so soon as he saw us draw near, the consuls seized of four or five of the principal of the seditious, whom we found prisoners.

The next day after our arrival came the above named Sieurs d'Alesme and de Ferron, of whom our commissioners would by no means allow, saying they had not the king's patents, though in the end we over-ruled them whether they would or no.

Monsieur de Burie had entreated me to do them no harm at our departure from Cahors, for they desired nothing more than to be gone; and at last they began to try these four or five that the Cardinal of Armagnac had caused to be taken: but it was impossible to persuade Campain and Gerard to consent to their execution, notwithstanding that an infinite number of rapines and violations, besides those of churches, was by the testimony of the most eminent persons of the city evidently proved against them. They continued eight or ten days in this dispute, evermore concluding that they ought to be releast, and although Monsieur de Ferron's wife and family were of that religion, he nevertheless affirmed with Monsieur d'Alesme, that they ought to dye.

The Cardinal of Armagnac and all the officers were in despair to see that justice was not executed, expecting nothing but all sorts of violence so soon as our backs should be turned, if some example were not made. In the end Messieurs d'Alesme and de Ferron came to my lodging to tell me that it was not to be hoped that these people would ever execute justice upon those of their own religion, and that therefore seeing no good was to be done with such men, they were resolved to return home. I then entreated them not to leave us; to which Monsieur d'Alesme made answer, 'Will you then do an act worthy your integrity and courage, and cause them to be hanged at the windows of the town house where they are prisoners, by which means you will put the business out of dispute, and without that there is no hope that justice shall be done.'

'Are you both of this opinion,' said I.

They answered me they were. Enough was said, I called to me Monsieur de Sainctorens's sergeant, saying to him in their presence, 'Go fetch me the goaler hither'; which he did, to whom I said, 'Deliver thy prisoners to this man; and you serjeant, take my two hangmen, and go hang them presently at the windows of the town hall.'

Whereupon he immediately departed, and in less than a quarter of an hour, we saw them hanged at the windows. The commissioners were furiously enraged at this action, and endeavoured to make Monsieur de Burie disapprove of it, which the next day I reproached them with, telling them in the presence of the said Sieur de Burie that Monsieur de Burie and I should agree well enough in despite of all their endeavours to divide us; 'And I doubt not,' said I, 'but to make you hang yourselves before the game be done and that we go out of this commission. There is a rumour that the Prince of Conde has taken arms and possest himself of the city of Orleans, which if it prove true, hope for no other but that I will be as good as my word.'

It was not two hours before Rance, the King of Navarre's secretary, arrived, and brought news to Monsieur de Burie that the Prince of Conde was in arms and had seized of Orleans, telling wonders of the prodigious forces the said prince had with him, in comparison of those of the king, and that the King of Navarre, the constable, Monsieur de Guise, and the Mareschal de S. Andre were together, who could not all raise so much as one man, with a thousand other flim flam stories. Whereupon the said Sieur de Burie expressly forbad him to speak a word to anyone else, telling him it would be as much as his life was worth should I come to hear the least whisper of it:

He sent also privately to the commissioners to get away before the news should be published, for otherwise it would not be in his power to save them from being put to death; and he was in the right, for I would infallibly have done their business. They needed not to be bid twice, but immediately sneaked away in great secrecy, so that I knew nothing of their departure till the next day, and searched very diligently for Monsieur Rance, who had he fallen into my hands, I think I should have taught him to carry news.

A Strange Dream

We went upon the Saturday from Cassaigne to go lie at Monsieur de Panias's house, taking two tassels of goshawks along with us, wherewith to pass away the time at the baths: and the very night that we came thither in my first sleep I dreamt a dream that did more discompose and weaken me than if I had four dayes had a continual fevor, which I will here set down, because there are many living to whom I told it, for these are no tales made for pleasure.

I dreamt that all the kingdom of France was in rebellion, and that a stranger prince had seized upon it, and had killed the king, my lords his brothers, and the queen, and that I was flying night and day on every side to escape; for me thought I had all the world in search of me to take me:

Sometimes I fled to one place, and sometimes to another, till at length I was surprised in a house, and carried before the new king, who was walking betwixt two great men in a church. He was low of stature, but gross and well knit, and had on his head a square velvet cap, such a one as they wore in former days. The archers of his guard were clad in yellow, red, and black, and me-thought as they led me prisoner thorough the streets, all the people ran after me crying, '*Kill the villain*'; one presented a naked sword to my throat, and another a pistol to my breast: those that led me, crying out, '*do not kill him for the king will have him hanged in his own presence.*'

And thus they carried me before the new king, who was walking, as I said before. There was in the church neither image nor altar; and so soon as I came before him, he said to me in Italian; '*Veni que forfante, tu m'ai fatto la guerra, Er a quelli i quali Suomo mai servitori, is ti faro apicquar adesso, adesso.*'

To which I made answer in the same language (for me-thought I spoke Tuscan as well as when I was in Sienna), '*Sacra Maesta, is servito al mio Re, si come Suono obligati fari tutti gli huomini de bene, su Maesta ne deve pigliar ques to a male.*'

At which, enflamed with fury, he said to the archers of his guard, '*Andate andate, menate lo adpicar quel forfante, que mi farebbe ancor a la guerra.*'

Whereupon they would have led me away; but I stood firm, and said to him, '*Io supplico su Maesta voler mi salvar la vita, poi che il Re mio signire é morto ensiemigli Signiori Susi fratelli: Io vi prometto che vi serviro con medesima fidelta con la qu'ale io servito il re mentre viveva.*'

Upon this the lords who were walking with him begged of him to save my life: upon whose intercession, looking steadfastly upon me, he said to me, '*Porometti tu ques to del cuore? or Su io ti de la vita per le pregiere di quelli che mi pregaro, fie mi fidele.*'

These lords me thought spoke French, but we two spoke Italian; whereupon he commanded them to take me a little aside, and that he would by and by talk to me again. They then sent me by a chest that stood hard by the church door, and those who were to look to me fell to talking with the archers of the guard.

As I was there standing by this chest, I began to think of the king, and repented me of the oath of fidelity I had taken; for that peradventure the king might not be yet dead, and that if I could escape away I would rather wander alone and on foot throughout the world to seek the king if he were yet alive; and thereupon took a resolution to run away.

Thus resolved I went out of the church, and being got into the street began to run, and never thought of my hip, for methought I ran faster than I would, when on a sudden I heard a cry behind me, '*Stop the villain*;' whereupon some came out of their houses to take me, and others stood in my way; but still I escaped both from the one and the other, and recovered a pair of stone stairs that went up to the wall of the town, where coming to the top, I lookt down, and methought the precipice was so great that I could hardly see to the bottom.

They mounted the stairs after me, and I had nothing wherewith to defend myself but three or four stones that I threw at them, and had a great mind to make them kill me; for me-thought they would put me to a cruel death; when having nothing left to defend my self withall, I threw myself headlong from the battlements, and in falling awaked and found myself all on a water, as if I had come out of a river, my shirt, the sheets, the counterpain all wringing wet, and I fancied that my head was bigger than a drum.

I called my *valet de chambre*, who presently made a fire, took off my wet shirt, and gave me another. They went also to Madam de Panias, who commanded another pair of sheets to be given them, and herself rose and came into my chamber, and saw the sheets, blankets, and counterpain all wet, and never departed the room till all was dried; which whilst they were in doing, I told her my dream, and the fright I had been in, which had put me into this sweat; She remembers it as well as I, the dream I dreamt of the death of King Henry my good master and this put me into a greater weakness than if I had had a continued fever for a whole week together.

The physitians told me that it was nothing but force of imagination, my mind being wholly taken up with these thoughts: And I do believe it was so; for I have fancied myself in the night fighting with the enemy, dreaming of the mishaps and the successes also I afterwards saw come to pass. I have had that misfortune all my life, that sleeping or waking I have never been at rest, and was always sure when I had anything working in my head that I was to do, not to fail to dream all that night: which is very troublesome.

RABASTENS AND 'THAT GREAT HARQUEBUZ SHOT'

But as men design, and God disposeth as seemeth best to him the events of things, he was pleased to order it very much contrary to what we proposed to ourselves: for the fifth day of the siege, the 23, of July, in the year 1562, upon a Sunday about two of the clock in the afternoon, I resolved to give an assault, the order whereof was after the manner following. That Monsieur de Sanctorens, Mareschal de Camp, should lead the companies one after the other up to the breach, which that he might the better do without confusion, I ordered all the companies to be drawn by four and four together out of the town, which upon pain of death were not to stir from their places till Monsieur de Sanctorens should come to fetch them, who was to stay three quarters of an hour betwixt every leading up, and in that manner to conduct all the companies one after another; and it was also ordered that the two captains who were upon the guard by the breach, which were l'Artigues and Salles of Bearn, should go on first to the assault.

As I was setting down this order one came in haste to tell me that the two canons that battered the flanck and that had been removed in the night were forsaken, and not a man durst shew himself upon the battery, by reason the artillery itself had ruined all the gabions. I therefore left it to Messieurs de Gondrin and de Sainctorens to conclude the order of the fight, that is to say that the companies should go on successively one after another, which was to be set down in writing, and myself ran on the outside to the hole of the wall, when I found only ten or twelve pioneers squat with their bellies close to the ground; for Tibanville, the commissary of the artillery, who had the charge of those two pieces of canon, had been constrained to quit them, and even Monsieur de Basillac himself.

Seeing then this disaster, I unbethought myself of a great number of bavins I had the day before caused to be brought into the town, and said to the gentlemen who were with me these words: 'I have heard, and alwayes observed, that there is no labour nor danger that gentlemen will ever refuse; follow me therefore I beseech you, and do as you shall see me do?'

They did not stay to be entreated, and so we went in great haste directly to the bavins that were within the town and lay in the middle of a street there where not a man durst abide, and there I took a bavin and laid it upon my shoulder, as also every gentleman took one, and there were a great many who carried two a piece; after which manner we returned out of the town by the same way we entred in, and thus I marcht before them till we came to the hole. By the way as we were going I had given order that they should bring me four or five halbardeers, which at my return I found already arrived at the hole, and made them enter into it. We threw them the bavins into the hole, which they took with the points of their halberts, and ran to throw them upon the gabions to raise them.

I dare be bold to affirm with truth that we were not above a quarter of an hour about this work, and so soon as ever the canon was covered, Tibanville and the other canoneers returned into the battery, where they began to shoot with greater fury than of all the dayes before, every clap almost overtaking another, everyone assisting them with great cheerfulness. If, captains, you shall do the same, and yourselves first put your hands to the work, you will make everyone follow your example, for shame will push and force them out, and when the service is hot in any place, if the chief do not go in person, or at least some eminent man, the rest will go very lamely on, and murmur when a man sends them to slaughter. And if you covet honour, you must sometimes tempt danger as much as the meanest souldier under your command.

I will deprive no man of his due honour; for I think I have assisted at as many batteries as any man this day alive, and must needs say this, that I never saw commissaries of the artillery more diligent and adventurous than both Fredeville and Tibanville shewed themselves during the whole five dayes that the battery continued, in my whole life; for they themselves both levelled and fired, though they had as good canoneers as ever I saw handle linstock in my dayes; and I dare be bold to say that of a thousand canon shot we made against this place not ten failed of their effect, or were spent in vain.

In the morning I sent for Monsieur de Gohas, who was at Vic-Bigorre, and the captains who were set to have an eye on Montamat, and the succour expected by him, writing to him to come away that he might be with me at the assault, by reason that Captain Paulliac, colonel of the infantry, was so dangerously wounded, and we had no hopes of his life. He received his shot at the time when I went overnight to carry Messieurs de Leberon and de Montant to cut off the great counterscarp, which shot went quite through his body. My son Fabian was also shot in the chin, and two souldiers close by my side.

I there committed a very great error, for I went in the evening before it was dark, and I believe they were aware that we intended to cut the counterscarp, for all their harquebuzeers were run together to that place; and the reason why I committed this error was that having computed with myself how many hours the night was long, I found that it was not above seven hours or thereabouts; and on the other side

I saw that in half an hour I should lose all that I had done, if the counterscarp was not pulled down by break of day, and that in case I should think fit to give an assault that day, they would be so strongly rampired and fortified, that with as many more canon shot as I had made against the place, it would be a matter of very great difficulty to enter.

This was the reason why I made so much haste to go and begin the work, that I might have it perfected by break of day; where I recommended the care of it to Messieurs de Leberon and de Montant, and the two captains upon the guard, by telling them that in their diligence our victory wholly consisted. And in truth they slept not, as I have already said, for by break of day the artillery began to play, and the counterscarp was wholly pulled down.

O comrades, you who shall go to besiege places, you cannot but confess that both here and in several places my enterprises and victories have succeeded more from my vigilancy and prompt execution than any valour, and I on my part am willing to confess that there was in the camp braver men than I. But no one can be a coward that has these three things; for from these three all the combats and victories proceed, and all valiant men choose to follow captains that are provided with these three qualities.

And on the other side he cannot be called hardy, let his heart be never so good, if he be tardy, backward, and slow in execution: for before he has fixt his resolution, he has been so long deliberating about it that the enemy is advertised of what he intends to do, and consequently is provided to prevent his design: but if he be quick he shall even surprize himself.

So that there is no great confidence to be reposed in a chief that is not endued with these three qualities, vigilancy, promptitude, and valour. If a man examine all the great warriors that have ever been, he will find that they had all those qualities. Alexander did not in vain bear the device I have mentioned before. Examine Caesar's *Commentaries*, and all the authors that have writ of him, you will find that in his life he fought two and fifty battels without ever losing any, saving that of Dirachium; but within thirty dayes he had a sufficient revenge against Pompey, for he won a great battel and defeated him. You will not find that in these two and fifty battels he ever fought three times in his own person, that is, with his own hand, though he was alwayes present there; by which you will understand that all his victories were the effects of his conduct, by being diligent, vigilant, and a prompt executer of his designs.

But for all this, these qualities are rarely found, and I believe we Gascons are better provided of them then any other people of France, or perhaps of Europe, and many good and great captains have gone out of it within these fifty years. I shall not compare myself to them, but this I will say of myself, because it is true, that my master never lost anything by my sloth or remissness.

The enemy thought me a league off when I came to beat up his quarters. And if diligence be required in all exploits of war, it is much more in a siege, for a very little thing will serve to overthrow a great design. If you press your enemy you redouble his fear, he will not know where he is, nor have leisure to recollect himself. Be sure to wake whilst others sleep, and never leave your enemy without something to do.

I shall now return to the assault; our order being set down, I went and placed myself at the gate of the town near unto the breach, where I had all the gentlemen with me, of which there might be six or seven score, and still more came up to us, for Monsieur de la Chappelle Lawzieres, who came from Quercy, brought a great troop of gentlemen along with him. I shall here relate one thing of my own presage, which is perfectly true, That it was impossible for all the friends I had to dispossess me of an opinion I had that I should in this assault be killed or wounded by a shot in some part of my head; and out of that conceipt was once half in a mind not to go to the assault, knowing very well that my death would at this time be of ill consequence, if not to the enterprise in hand, yet to the general design upon that country; this fancy therefore still running in my head the morning before the assault was to be given, I said to Monsieur de Las the king's advocate at Agen, who was of our council, these words:

Monsieur de Las, there are some who have exclaimed and do yet cry out that I am very rich; you know of all the money I have to a *denier*, for by my will, to which you are a witness, you are sufficiently enformed of my estate. But seeing the world are not otherwise to be perswaded but I have a great deal of money, and that consequently, if by accident I should die in this assault, they would demand of my wife four times as much as I am worth, I have here brought a particular of all the money I have at this day in the whole world, as well abroad at interest, as at home in the custody of my wife. The account of my steward Barat's drawing, and signed by my own hand. You are my friend,

I beseech you therefore if I dye that you and the Councillor Monsieur de Nort will transfer your love and friendship to my wife and my two daughters, and that you will have a care of them, especially Charlotte Catherine, who had the honour to be christened by the king and the queen his mother.'

Which having said, I delivered the scrowl into his hands, and very well perceived that he had much ado to refrain weeping. By this you may judge if I had not the misfortune that befel me before my eyes. I have no familiar spirit, but few misfortunes have befallen me in the whole course of my life that my mind has not first presaged. I still endeavoured to put it out of my fancy, resigning all things to the good will of God, who disposes of us as seems best to his own wisdom, neither did I ever do otherwise, whatever the Hugonots my enemies have said or written to the contrary against me.

So soon as two of the clock, the hour prefixt for the assault, was come, I caused eight or ten bottles of wine, that Madam de Panjas had sent me, to be brought out, which I gave the gentlemen, saying, 'Let us drink comrades; for it must now soon be seen which of us has been nurst with the best milk. God grant that another day we may drink together; but if our last hour be come, we cannot frustrate the decrees of fate.'

So soon as they had all drunk, and encouraged one another, I made them a short remonstrance in these words, saying, 'Friends and companions, we are now ready to fall on to the assault, and every man is to shew the best he can do. The men who are in this place are of those who with the Count de Montgommery destroyed your churches and ruined your houses; You must make them disgorge what they have swallowed of your estates. If we carry the place, and put them all to the sword, you will have a good bargain of the rest of Bearn. Believe me they will never dare to stand against you. Go on then in the name of God, and I will immediately follow.'

Which being said I caused the assault to be sounded, and the two captains immediately fell on; where some of their souldiers and ensigns did not behave themselves very well. Seeing then that those were not likely to enter, Monsieur de Sainctorens marcht up with four ensigns more, and brought them up to the breach, which did no better than the former, for they stopt four or five paces short of the counterscarp, by which means our canon was nothing hindred from playing into the breach, which made those within duck down behind it. I then presently perceived that somebody else and other kind of men than the foot must put their hands to the work; which made me presently forget the conceit I had of being killed or wounded, and said to the gentlemen these words.

Comrades, nobody knows how to fight but the nobless, and we are to expect no victory but by our own hands, let us go then, I will lead you the way, and let you see that a good horse will never be resty. Follow boldly, and go on without fear, for we cannot wish for a more honourable death. We deferre the time too long, let us fall on.

I then took Monsieur de Gohas by the hand, to whom I said, 'Monsieur de Gohas, I will that you and I fight together, I pray therefore let us not part; and if I be killed or wounded, never take notice of me, but leave me there and push forward, that the victory however may remain to the king': and so we went on as cheerfully as ever I saw men go on to an assault in my life, and looking twice behind me, saw that the gentlemen almost toucht one another they came up so close. There was a large plain of an hundred and fifty paces over or more, all open, over which we were to march to come up to the breach, which as we passed over, the enemy fired with great fury upon us all the way, and I had six gentlemen shot close by me.

One of which was the Sieur de Besoles; his shot was in his arm, and so great a one that he had like to have died of his wounds; the Viscount de Labatut was another, and his was in his leg: I cannot tell the names of the rest, because I did not know them. Monsieur de Gohas had brought seven or eight along with him, and amongst the rest Captain Savaillan the elder, of which three were slain, and the said Captain Savaillen wounded with a harquebuze shot quite through the face. There were also hurt one Captain du Plex, another Captain la Bastide, both kinsmen of mine about Villeneufue, who had alwayes served under Monsieur de Brissac, one Captain Rantoy of Damasan, and Captain Sales of Bearn, who had before been wounded with the thrust of a pike in the eye. There were two little chambers about a pike height or more from the ground, which chambers the enemy so defended both above and below, that not a man of ours could put up his head without being seen; however, our people began to assault them with a great shower of stones, which they poured in upon them, and they also shot at us, but ours throwing downwards had the advantage of this kind of fight.

Now I had caused three or four ladders to be brought to the edge of the grasse, and as I turned about to call for two of them to be brought to me, a harquebuze-shot clapt into my face, from the corner of a *barricado* joyning to the tower, where I do not think there could be four harquebuzeers, for all the rest of the *barricado* had been beaten down by our two canon that played upon the flanck. I was immediately all over blood, for it gusht out at my mouth, nose, and eyes; whereupon Monsieur de Gohas would have caught me in his arms, thinking I would fall, but I said, 'Let me alone, I shall not fall, follow your point.'

Upon this shot of mine, almost all the souldiers and the gentlemen began to lose courage, and to retire, which made me cry out to them, though I could scarce speak, by reason of the torrent of blood that pasht out of my mouth and nose; 'Whither will you go, gentlemen, whither will ye go? will ye be terrified for me? do not flinch or forsake the fight, for I have no hurt, and let everyone return to his place'; in the meantime hiding the blood in the best manner I could: and to Monsieur de Gohas I said, 'Monsieur de Gohas, take care I beseech you that the souldiers be not discouraged, and renew the assault.'

I could no longer stay there, for I began to faint, and therefore said to the gentlemen, 'I will go get my self drest, but if you love me, let no one follow, but revenge me.'

Which having said I took a gentleman by the hand, I cannot tell his name, for I could scarce see him, and returned by the same way I came, where by the way I found a little horse of a souldiers, upon which by the gentleman's assistance I mounted as well as I could, and after that manner was conducted to my lodging; where I found a chirurgeon of Monsieur de Gohas, called Maistre Simon, who drest me, and with his fingers (so wide were the orifices of the wound) pulled out the bones from my two cheeks, and cut away a great deal of flesh from my face, which was all bruised and torn.

Monsieur de Gramond was upon a little eminence hard by, looking on at his ease, who being of this new religion, though he had never born arms against the king, had no mind to meddle amongst us. He was aware how upon my hurt all the souldiers were disheartened, and said to those who were with him, 'There is some eminent person slain, see how the souldiers are discouraged, I am afraid it is Monsieur de Montluc,' and therefore said to one of his gentlemen, called Monsieur de Sart, 'Go run and see who it is, and if it be he, and that he is not dead, tell him that I entreat him to give me leave to come and see him.'

The said Sieur de Sart is a Catholick, who accordingly came, and at his entring into the town he heard that it was I that was hurt, and coming to my lodging found my people weeping for me, and me tumbled upon a pallet upon the ground; where he told me that Monsieur de Gramond begged leave that he might come to see me. To which I made answer that there was no unkindness betwixt Monsieur de Gramond and me, and that if he pleased to come, he would find that he had as many friends in our camp, and peradventure more than in that of their religion. He was no sooner gone from me, but Monsieur de Madaillan my lieutenant, who had marcht on the one hand of me when I went on to the assault, as Monsieur de Gohas did on the other, came to see if I was dead, and said to me:

Sir, cheer up your spirits, and rejoyce, we have entred the castle, and the souldiers are laying about them, who put all to the sword; and assure yourself we will revenge your wound.

I then said to him:

Praised be God that I see the victory ours before I dye. I now care not for death. I beseech you return back, and as you have ever been my friend, so now do me that act of friendship not to suffer so much as one man to escape with life.

Whereupon he immediately returned, and all my servants went along with him, so that I had nobody left with me but two pages, Monsieur de Las, and the chirurgeon. They would fain have saved the minister, and the governor, whose name was Captain Ladon, to have hanged them before my lodging, but the souldiers took them from those who had them in their custody, whom they had also like to have killed for offring to save them, and cut them in a thousand pieces. They made also fifty or threescore to leap from the high tower into the moat, which were there all drowned. There were two only saved who were hid, and such there were who offered four thousand crowns to save their lives, but not a man of ours would hearken to any ransom; and most of the women were killed, who also did us a great deal of mischief with throwing stones.

There was found within, a Spanish merchant whom the enemy had kept prisoner there, and another Catholick merchant also, who were both saved; and these were all that were left alive of the men that we found in the place, namely the two that someone helpt away, and the two Catholick merchants. Do not think, you who shall read this book, that I caused this slaughter to be made so much out of revenge for the wound I had received, as to strike terror into the country, that they might not dare to make head against our army. And in my opinion all souldiers in the beginning of a conquest ought to proceed after that manner, with such as are so impudent as to abide canon; he must bar his ears to all capitulation and composition, if he do not see great difficulties in his enterprise, and that his enemy have put him to great trouble in making a breach. And as severity (call it cruelty if you please) is requisite in case of a resolute opposition, so on the other side mercy is very commendable and fit, if you see that they in good time surrender to your discretion.

Monsieur de Gramond then came to visit me, and found me in a very ill condition, for I had much ado to speak to him, by reason of the great quantity of blood that issued from my mouth; Monsieur de Gohas also immediately after him came back from the fight to see me; saying, 'Take comfort *Monsieur*, and cheer up, upon my word we have sufficiently revenged you, for there is not one man left alive.'

He thereupon knew Monsieur de Gramond, and saluted him, who after they had embraced, entreated him to carry him to the Castle, which he did, where Monsieur de Gramond found the taking of it exceeding strange, saying he could never have believed this place had been near so strong, and that had I attaqued Navarreins it would have been more easily taken. He would then needs see all the removes I had made of the canon, which having seen, he said it had not been requisite that we should have omitted anything of the battery. About an hour after he returned, where he offered me a house of his hard by, and all other things in his power, and has since told me that at that time, and in the condition he then saw me, he never thought I could have lived till the next day, and believed he had taken his leave of me for ever.

Monluc Takes Leave of His Readers

Behold now (fellows in arms) you who shall read my life, the end of the wars in which I have served five and fifty years together that I had the honour to be in command for the kings my masters. From which services, that I might not forget them, I brought away seven harquebuzeshots for a memorandum, and several other wounds besides, there being not a limb in all my body that has escaped, my right arm only excepted. But I have by those wounds purchased a renown throughout Europe, and my name is known in the remotest king-doms, which I esteem more than all the riches in the world; and by the Grace of God, who has ever been assisting to me, I will carry this reputation along with me to my Grave.

This is a marvelous contentment to me when I think upon it, and call to mind how I am step by step arrived to this degree of honour, and thorough so many dangers am come to enjoy the short repose that remains to me in this world, in the calm and privacie of my own house, that I may have leisure to ask God forgiveness for the sins I have committed.

Oh if his mercie was not mfinitely great, in how dangerous a con-dition were all those that bear arms, especially that are in command; for the necessity of war forces us in despite of our own inclinations to commit a thousand mischiefs, and to make no more account of the lives of men than of a chicken: to which the complaints and outcries of the people, whom we are constrained in despite of us every day to swallow up and devoure, and the widows and the fatherless that we every day do make, load us with all the curses and execrations, misery and affliction can help them to invent, which by importuning the Al-mighty, and daily imploring the assistance of the saints, 'tis to be feared lye some of them heavie upon our heads.

But doubtless kings shall yet have a sadder account to make than we; for they make us commit those evils (as I told the king in discourse in Tholouze) and there is no mischief whereof they are not the cause: for seeing they will make warres, they should at least pay those who venture their lives to execute their passions, that they may not commit so many mischiefs as they do. I think my self then exceedingly happy in that God has given me leisure to think of the sins I have committed, or rather that the necessity of war has enforced me to commit.

For I am not naturally addicted to mischief; above all I have ever been an enemie to the vice of impurity, and a sworn adversary to all disloyalty and treason. I know very well and confess that my passion has made me say and do things for which I now cry *Mea Culpa*; but 'tis now too late to redress them, and I have one that lies heavier upon my heart than all the rest. But had I proceeded otherwise everyone would have flirted me on the nose, and the least consul of a village would have clapt too his gates against me, had I not alwaies had the canon at my heels; for everyone had a mind to lord it. God knows how fit I was to endure such affronts; but all's done and past; my hand was ever as prompt as my tongue, and it was but a word and a blow. I could have wisht, could I have perswaded myself to it, never to have worn a sword by my side, but my nature was quite otherwise, which made me carry for my device, *Deo Duce, Ferro Comite.*

One thing I can truly say of myself, that never any king's lieutenant had more commiseration of the ruine of the people than I, in all places where ever I came. But it is impossible to discharge those commands without doing mischief, unless the king had his coffers crammed with gold to pay his armies; and yet it would be much to do. I know not if those that succeed me will do better; but I do not believe it. All the Catholicks of Guienne can witness if I did not alwaies spare the people: for I appeal from the Hugonots, I have done them too much mischief to give me any good testimonie; and yet I have not done them enough, nor so much as I would; my good will was not wanting. Neither do I care for their speaking ill of me, for they will say as much or more of their kings.

But before I put an end to this Book of mine, which my name will cause to be read by many, I shall desire all such as shall take the pains to read these *Commentaries*, not to think me so ingrate that I do not acknowledg, after God, to hold all I have of estate and preferment of the kings my masters, especially of my good master King Henry, whom God absolve. And if I have in some places of my book said that wounds were the recompence of my service, it is not at all intended to reproach them with the blood I have lost in their quarrels. On the contrary I think the blood of my sons who died in their service very well employed. God gave them to me, and he took them from me.

I have lost three in their service: Marc Anthony my eldest, Bertrand (to whom I gave the name of Peyrot (which is one of our Gascon names) by reason that Bertrand did not please me), and Fabian, Seigneur de Montesquieu. God gave me also three others. For of my second son I had Blaize, and of my youngest Adrian and Blaize, whom God preserve that they may be serviceable to their kings and country, without dishonouring their race; that they may well study my book, and so imitate my life, that, if possible, they may surpass their grandsire; and I beseech your Majestie be mindful of them. I have left them, amongst my papers, the letter your Majestie was pleased to write to me from Villiers dated the 3. of December 1570, which contains these words.

Assure yourself that I shall ever be mindful of your many and great services, for which if you shall in your own person fall short of a worthy recompence, your posterity shall reap the fruits of your merit; as also they are such, and have so well behaved themselves in my service, that they have of themselves very well deserved my acknovdedgment, and that I should do for them what I shall be very ready to do whenever an opportunity shall present itself Sir, this is your Majesties promise, and a king should never say or promise anything but he will perform.

I do not then by any means reproach my masters; and I ought also to be satisfied, though I am not rich, that a poor cadet of Gascony is arrived at the highest dignities of the kingdom. I sent several at this day who murmur and repine at their Majesties, and for the most part those who have done little or nothing make the greatest complaints.

In others who have really deserved something it is a little more pardonable: all that we have, of what degree so ever we are, we hold it of the kings our masters. So many great princes, lords, captains, and souldiers, both living and dead, owe to the king the honours they have received; and their names shall live by the employments they have received from the kings they served, and were not only enterred with those honourable titles, but have moreover honoured those who are descended of them, and mention will be made of their virtue whilst any records of honour remain in the world.

I have listed a good number in my book, and have myself had souldiers under my command, who have been no better in their extraction, than the sons of poor labouring men, who have lived and died in a reputation as great and high as they had been sons of lords, through their own virtue, and the esteem the kings and their lieutenants had of them.

When my son Marc Antony was carried dead to Rome, the Pope and all the cardinals, the Senate and all the people of Rome payd as much honour to his hearse as if he had been a prince of the blood. And what was the cause of all this, but only his own valour, my reputation, and my king, who had made me what I was? So that the name of Marc Antony is again to be found in the Roman annals. When I first entred into arms out of my page-ship in the House of Lorrain, there was no other discourse but of the great Gonsalvo, called the great captain.

How great an honour was it to him (which also will last for ever) to be crowned with so many victories? I have heard it told that King

Lewis and King Ferdinand being together, I know not at what place, but it was somewhere where they had appointed an interview, these two great princes being sat at table together, our king entreated the King of Spain to give leave that Gonsalvo might dine with them; which he accordingly did, whilst men of far greater quality than he stood waiting by. So considerable had the king his master's favour and his own valour made him. This was the honour he received from the King of France, who in recompence for his having deprived him of the Kingdom of Naples put a weighty-chain of gold about his neck. I have heard Monsieur de Lautrec say that he never took so much delight in looking upon any man, as upon that same.

O how fair an example is this for those who intend to advance themselves by arms! When I went the second time into Italy, as I passed through the streets of Rome, everyone ran to the windows to see him that had defended Sienna, which was a greater satisfaction to me than all the riches of the earth. I could produce several exemples of French men of very mean extraction, who have by arms arrived at very great preferments: but out of respect to their posteritie I shall forbear; but it was the bounty of their kings that so advanced them for the recompence of their brave services.

It is then just that we confess, we could be nothing without their bountie and favour, if we serve them, 'tis out of obedience to the commandment of God, and we ought not to try to obtain rewards by importunities and reproaches; and if anyone be ill rewarded, the fault is not in our kings, but in them who are about them, that do not acquaint them who have served well or ill (for there are many of both sorts) to the end that His Majestie's largess should be rightly placed. And there is nothing that goes so much to the heart of a brave and loyal subject, as to see the king heap honours and rewards upon such as have served him ill. I am sure it is that that has vext me more than any disappointment of my own.

I have often heard some men say the king or the queen have done this and that for such a one, why should they not do as much for me? I know also that their Majesties have said, 'They will no more commit such oversights, we must wink at this one fault': but it was the next day to begin the same again. However a man ought never to stomack anything from his prince. The honour of such men lies in a very con-temptible place, since they more value a reward or a benefit than their own reputation or renown, and are so ready to take snuff if they fail of their expectation.

And moreover (as I have already said) they are commonly men that have never strook three strokes with a sword, and yet will vapour what dangers they have passed, and what hardships they have endured. If a man should strip them naked, one might see many a proper fellow that has not so much as one scar in all his body. Such men, if they have born arms any while, are very fortunate, and at the day of judgment if they go into Paradise, will carry all their blood along with them, without having lost one dram of their own, or having shed one drop of any others here upon earth.

Others I have heard, and of all sorts of men even to the meanest, complain that they have served the king four, five or six years, and notwithstanding have not been able to get above three or four thousand *livers* yearly rent: poor men they are sore hurt. I speak not of the souldiers only, but of all other conditions of men His Majestic makes use of. I have heard my father, who was an old man, and others older than he, report that it was a common saying at court, and throughout the whole kingdom in the reign of Lewis the Twelfth.

Chastillon, Bourdillon,
Galliot, & Bonneval,
Governent le Sang Royal,

And yet I dare be bold to say, that all these four lords who governed two kings, put them all together, never got ten thousand *livers* yearly revenue. I have formerly said as much to the Mareschal de Bourdillon, who thereupon returned me answer, that his predecessor was so far from getting 3000 *livers* a year, that he sold 1500, and left his family very necessitous. Should anyone ask the admiral to shew what his predecessor, who governed all, got by his favour, I durst lay a good wager he could not produce 2000 *livers* yearly revenue. As for Galliot he lived a great while after the others, and he peradventure might in that long time rake together three or four thousand *livers* a year. For what concerns Bonneval; Monsieur de Bonneval that now is and Monsieur de Biron are his heirs, and I believe they can boast of no great estates.

O happy kings that had such servants. 'Tis easie to discern that these men served their masters out of the love and affection they bore to their persons and the crown, and not upon the account of reward; and I have heard that they evermore rather begged for the king's own domestick servants, than for themselves. They are gone down to their graves with honour, and their successors are not nevertheless in want.

Since I have spoken of others, I will now say something of myself.

Some perhaps after I am dead will talk of me, as I talk of others. I confess that I am very much obliged to the kings I have served, especially to Henry my good master, as I have often said before, and I had now been no more than a private gentleman, had it not been for their bounty, and the opportunities they gave me to acquire that reputation I have in the world; which I value above all the treasure the earth contains, having immortalized the name of Montluc.

And although during the long time that I have born arms I have acquired but very little wealth, yet has no one ever heard me complain of the kings my masters: marry I have spoke by mouth of those about them, when in these late troubles I was calumniated by them, as if I could have done all things with nothing.

Believe me the wounds I have received have administred more comfort than affliction to me; and one thing I am sure of, that when I am dead they can hardly say that at the resurrection I shall carry all the blood, bones, and veins I brought with me into the world from my mother's womb, along with me into Paradise. As for riches I have enough. It is true, that had I been bred up in the school of the Baylif of Esperon I should have had more; the story is not amiss, and therefore I shall insert it here.

Lewis the Twelfth going to Bayonne lay in a village called Esperon, which is nearer to Bayonne than to Bourdeaux. Now upon the great road betwixt these two places, the *baylif* had built a very noble house. The king thought it very strange, that in a country so bare and barren as that was, and amongst downs and sands that would bear nothing, this *bayliff* should build so fine a house, and at supper was speaking of it to the chamberlain of his household; who made answer that the *baylif* was a rich man: which the king not knowing how to believe, considering the wretched country his house was seated on, he immediately sent for him, and said to him these words.

'Come on *baylif*, and tell me why you did not build your fine house in some place where the country was good and fertile?'

'Sir,' answered the *baylif*, 'I was born in this country, and find it very good for me.'

'Are you so rich,' said the king, 'as they tell me you are?'

'I am not poor,' replied the other, 'I have (blessed be God) where withal to live.'

The king then askt him, how it was possible he should grow so rich in so pitiful a barren country.

'Why, very easily Sir,' replyed the *baylif*.

'Tell me then which way,' said the king.

'Marry sir,' answered the other, 'because I have ever had more care to do my own business. that! that of my master, or my neighbours.'

'The Devil refuse me,' said the king (for that was alwaies his oath) 'thy reason is very good; for doing so, and rising betimes, thou couldst not choose but thrive.'

O how many sons has this *baylif* left behind him to inherit this virtuous humour! I was never any of those. I do really believe that there is never a little pedlar in the world, who, having trotted, run, and moyled as I have done, but would have enricht himself to a merchant. And there is never a treasurer nor a receiver (let him be as honest as he would) in the kingdom, that had had so much money pass through his hands, as has done through mine, but more would have stuck to his fingers.

I have been seven or eight times captain of foot, which is none of the worst commands for getting of money; and I have known several captains in my time, who have enricht themselves meerly out of their souldiers pay. I was not so ignorant, nor so raw a souldier, neither did I want dexterity, but that I could have done the feat as well as they: neither was it any such hard matter to learn, for with a good quarter-master and some few other little helps the business had been done.

I have since been three times camp-master, in which employment God knows I might have had skip-jacks enow to have made muster, and intelligence enough with the commissaries. I could have discovered where anything was to be got, as soon or sooner than any men in the army, I had nose good enough. I was often governor of a place, where I could have had fourscore or a hundred men at my devotion to have passed muster, as *Messieurs les Governeurs* know well how to do: by which means having been so long in these commands as I have been, and made so many musters as I have done in my life, with a little good husbanding. Good God! what a mountain of gold might I have had! I never think of it but it makes me wonder at my own honesty that could resist so many temptations.

I was moreover the king's lieutenant in Sienna, and another time in Montalsin; where I had wayes enow to have lined my pockets, as others in the like commands have done: for it had been no more but to have had intelligence with three or four merchants, who should have affirmed that the corn of the garrison had been bought by them, and taken up upon their credit, and it had been done. God knows what profits are made of these magazines. I could then have made demands upon the account of borrowing, and have deputed some who would have been ready to have taken the employment upon them, to have brought in a hundred or two hundred thousand *francks* in debentures.

But instead of this His Majesty owed us five payes when we came out of Sienna, whereof I found means to acquit him of three so soon as we came to Montalsin. Afterwards the second time that I was sent thither, in the place of Monsieur de Soubize, I stayed six weeks by the king's command at Rome with the Pope, and his Majestie's ambassadors and agents. It was at the time when the Duke of Alva made war with his Holiness, and all the sea-coast was ready to be abandoned, and Grossette was not able any longer to subsist, having not a grain of corn, no more then the other garrisons.

I found at Rome some Siennois gentlemen, that marcht out of Sienna with me, who brought me acquainted with a banquer called Julio d'Albia, a Siennois also, who upon my own bare word lent me 600 *mogues* of corn, which are 300 tuns or barrils, at twelve *muids* the barrel, conditionally that I should monthly pay him 600 crowns at every muster.

This money I could no way raise but out of the deductions I received from the musters, and instead of putting it into my own pocket, I accordingly paid him all, the last payment only excepted; for there was no more money, nor means to have any; so that we made no muster. I might have made my advantage of this, for I furnisht several places that stood in need, according to the authority I was invested withal; and I saved half the corn, which I lent to the country people, who were more distrest for bread than the souldiers.

There it was that I began to play the usurer; but it was at the expence of the king's conscience; for, for every *muid* that I lent them then, I received two at the harvest; and indeed it was double worth at the time when I lent it, and yet a penny of this profit never came into my purse, for I left it all to the king. I stayed yet seven months longer in these parts, without receiving so much as one pay; during four months of which I made my men live of twenty ounces of bread a day out of the profits I made of the corn, saving so much as in me lay my master's money. The other three months I paid the souldiers with good words and the liberality of my bonnet, as I had done at Sienna. Sometime after Don Francisco arrived, who found corn yet in the magazine.

I moreover dealt with the Dutchess of Castro, wife to the duke who was slain at Piacenza, who knew Monsieur de Valence my brother at the time when he was in the service of Pope Paul Farnese. Pope Paul Caraffa had made a prohibition that no manner of grain should be carried out of Romania; but this dutchess underhand permitted certain merchants to bring it by night into our territories, where our merchants met, and bought it of them. I carried this practice very close, of which I could have made a very great advantage to my own private profit; but never so much as one *liard* came into my purse.

I could have brought the king a bill of two or three hundred thousand *francs* debt, as did Signior Jourdano Corso, and others whom I shall forbear to name, who were well paid. I was neither so simple, nor my opportunities were not so few, but that I could have done it as well as any of them. I have been His Majestie's lieutenant in this province of Guienne, and have been much up and down abroad in the world, but never saw any country equal to it, either in riches or convenience of living. And having such an employment, I could have had intelligence with the receiver of the province (those kind of men desire no better) and have stufft my own coffers; for what upon musters, garrisons, and equipages of the artillerie, I could have made infinite advantages.

How many impositions might I have laid upon the county? for the king had given me power to do it, which would have turned to my particular benefit: for although His Majesty in that commission doubtless intended those levies for his own service, I could if I would have put the charge upon him, and have converted a great part of them to my own proper use. I could if I would have fired towns, and have sent a will with the wisp up and down to the towns and villages to whisper the principal Inhabitants in the ear, that they must either give me money to free them, or that otherwise I would cause them to be undone, and come quarter souldiers upon them, who should eat them to the very bones: for they know men of our trade are seldom weary of ill doing.

I could also have sent to tell the Hugonots, who lived at home under the protection of the edict, that unless they greased me in the fist, I would cause them all to be ruined and pulled in pieces; and what would they not have given me to have secured their lives and estates? for they did not greatly confide in me, hearing how I had handled them before. But instead of making use of such artifices of these to enrich myself, I let the captains and *gens d'arms*, and others who served the king, and askt it of me, take all; reserving very little or nothing to

231

my own benefit. And even that which I had at Clairoe I took by the king's permission. Let others therefore rest content. If God would please to let me be once cured of this great harquebuze-shot in my face, I think yet, that should the war break out again, I should be one to mount to horse; and I think it is not far off; for so long as there are two religions, France will evermore be in division and trouble. It cannot otherwise be, and the worst on't is 'tis a war that will not be ended of a long time.

Other quarrels are easily composed, but that for religion has no end. And although the martial sort of men are not very devout, they however side, and being once engaged stick to their party. In the posture that affairs now stand, I do not think we are at an end. However I have this satisfaction in myself, that I have to my utmost opposed it, and done my best endeavour to settle the peace of the kingdom. Would to God that all those who have been in command had connived no more than I. But we must let God work his own will. After he has sufficiently scourged us for our sins he will burn the rod.

And now, you lords and captains, who shall do me the honour to read my book, let me beseech you not to read it with prejudice, but believe that I have delivered the truth, without depriving any one of his due and merited honour. I make no question but that some will bring some things that I have here related into dispute, to see if they can catch me tripping in point of truth; forasmuch as they will find that God has never more accompanied the fortune of any man, for the employments I have gone through, then he did mine.

But let me assure such that I have omitted an infinite number of passages and particularities, by reason that I never committed anything to writing, nor ever kept any memorial, as never suspecting myself to become a writer of books. I ever thought myself unfit for that employment, but in the time of my last hurt, and during my sicknesses I have dictated this that I leave you, to the end that my name may not be buried in oblivion; nor so many other gallant men, whom I have seen perform so many and so brave exploits: for the historians write only of kings and princes.

How many brave gentlemen have I here set down, of whom these people make no mention, no more than if they had never been? He who has writ the Battle of Cerisolles, though he does name me, yet it is but slightly, and *in transitu* only; and yet I can honestly boast that I had a good hand in that victory; as also at Bullen and Thionville. Which they take no notice of at all, no more than of the valour and gallant behaviour of a great number of your fathers and kindred, whose names you will find here. Do not then think it strange if I have been so fortunate as I have written, for I never minded anything but my command, and have ever acknowledged that all my successes came from God, into whose hands I ever resigned myself and all my affairs; although the Hugonots were pleased to report me for an Atheist. They are my profest enemies, and you ought not to believe them.

And although I have had my imperfections and my vices, and am no more a Saint than other men, (they had their share too though they pretended holiness and mortification) yet I have ever placed my hope in God, evermore acknowledging that from Him alone I was to expect my good or evil fortune, attributing to his bounty and assistance all the successes of my life.

Neither was I ever in any action whatever wherein I have not implored his Divine assistance, and never passed over day of my life, since I arrived at the age of man, without calling upon his Name, and asking pardon for my sins. And many times I can say with truth that upon sight of the enemy I have found myself so possest with fear, that I felt my heart beat and my limbs tremble (let us not make ourselves braver than we are; for every man upon earth apprehends death when he sees it before his eyes) but so soon as I had made my prayer to God, I felt my spirits and my strength return. The prayer which I continually used, from my first entring into arms, was in these very words.

My God, who hast created me, I most humbly beseech Thee to preserve my judgment entire, that this day I may not lose it; for it is thou that gavest it me, and I hold it from no other but thee alone. If thou hast this day appointed me to die, grant that I may fall with the resolution of a man of honour, which I have sought for through so many dangers. I ask thee not my life, for I desire nothing but what pleases thee. Thy will be done. I resigne all things to thy divine wisdom and bounty.

After which having said my little Latin prayers, I declare and protest in the presence of God and men, that I suddenly felt a heat creep over my heart and members, so that I had no sooner made an end, but that I found myself quite another man than when I began. I was no more afraid, and my understanding again returned to perform its office, so that with promptitude and judgment I discerned what I had to do, without ever losing it after in any engagement wherein I have ever been.

How many are departed this life, who were they now living could witness if ever they saw me astonisht or lose my judgment in any action of war, whether at an assault, or in any other recounter or battel. Messieurs de Lautrec, de l'Escut, de Barbezieux, de Montpezat, de Termes, du Bié, de Strozzy, de Bourdillon, de Brissac, d'Anguien, de Boitieres, and de Guise could have given testimony of me; for they had all had me under their command, and have all seen me in a thousand and a thousand dangers, without the least sign of fear or amazement. Who, could they again return to life, would be good witness of the truth of what I have delivered; and yet they are not all dead under whom and by whom I had the honour to serve and to be commanded, who although they were with much younger captains than I, it was nevertheless fit I should obey them.

Monsieur le Duc d'Aumale, and the Mareschaux de Coffé and de Vielle Ville are of this number; and I beseech you (my noble lords if my book peradventure fall into your hands) to do me right, and declare whether what I have here delivered be true or false; for you have been eye-witnesses of part of it; and I fancie that after my death you will be curious to see what I have writ.

There are others also who are able to give me the lye, if I have said ought but true; namely Signior Ludovico de Biraga and Monsiur le President le Birague, who never abandoned that brave Mareschal de Brissac. Several others are yet living who have been my companions in arms, and many others who have served under my command; all which are able to affirm the truth of what I have said, and whether whenever there was a debate about any execution I did not always think nothing impossible; but on the contrary concluded things feasible, which others concluded impossible to be effected.

I undertook it, and brought it about, having evermore that stedfast assurance in God, that he would not forsake me, but open the eyes of my understanding to see what was to be done to make my enterprise succeed. I never thought anything impossible but the taking of Thionville, of which the honour is to be attributed to Monsieur de Guise alone, and in truth there was more of fortune than reason in that success, though the said Sieur de Guise was ever confident he should carry it, and so he did.

Fellows in arms, how many and how great things shall you perform if you put your whole trust in God, and set honour continually before your eyes? discoursing with yourselves that if it be determined you shall end your dayes in a Breach 'tis to much purpose to stay behind in the Grasse. *Un bel morir* (says the Italian) *tuta la vita honara*. 'Tis to die like a beast for a man to leave no memory behind him. Never go about to deprive another man of his honour, nor even set avarice and ambition in your prospect: for you will find that it will all come to nought, and end in misery and disgrace. I do not say this that I have any mind to play the preacher, but merely out of respect to truth. How many are there in the world, who are yet living, and whom I shall forbear to name, that have had the reputation of valiant men, and yet have been very unfortunate in their undertakings?

Believe me the hand of God was in this, and though they might implore his divine ayd, their devotion was not right, which made the Almighty adverse to them. If therefore you would have God to be assisting to you, you must strip yourselves of ambition, avarice, and rancour, and be full of the love and loyaltie we all owe to our prince. And in so doing although his quarrel should not be just, God will not for all that withdraw his assistance from you: for it is not for us to ask our king if his cause be good or evil, but only to obey him. And if you are not rewarded for the services you have performed, you will not stomack your being neglected, by reason it was not your intention nor design to fight upon the score of ambition and greatness, nor out of a thirst of riches; but upon the account of fidelity and duty that God has commanded you to bear to your prince and sovereign.

You will rejoyce to find yourselves esteemed and beloved by all the world, which is the greatest treasure a man of honour ought to covet. For great estates and high titles persish with the body, but a good reputation and renown are immortal as the soul. I now see my-self drawing towards my end, and languishing in my bed towards my dissolution, and 'tis a great consolation to me, that in spite of death my name shall live and flourish, not only in Gascony, but moreover in foreign nations.

This then is the end of my book, and of thus far of my life, which if God shall please longer to continue to me, some other may write the rest, if ever I shall again be in place where I shall perform anything worthy of myself; which nevertheless I do not hope for, finding myself so infinitely decayed that I never again expect to be able to bear arms. I have however this obligation to the harquebuze shot, which has pierced through and shattered my face, that it has been the occasion of writing these *Commentaries*, which I have an opinion will continue when I am dead and gone.

I entreat all those who shall read them not to look upon them as proceeding from the pen of an historian, but of an old souldier, and a Gascon, who has writ his own life truly, and in the rough stile of a souldier. All such as bear arms may take example by it, and acknowledge that from God alone proceed the successes or the misfortunes of men. And seeing we ought to have recourse to him alone, let us beseech him to assist and advise us in all our afflictions, for in this world there is nothing else of which the great ones have their share as well as the meanest of us all. Wherein he manifesteth his own greatness, in that neither king nor prince are exempted from his correcting hand, and who stand not continually in need of him and his divine assistance.

Do not disdain, you who desire to follow arms, instead of reading *Amadis de Gaule*, and *Launcelot du Lake*, to spend sometimes an hour in reading what I have done, and in taking notice of what I have been, in this treatise that I leave behind me. By which means you shall learn to know yourselves, and betimes to form yourselves to be souldiers and captains; for you must first learn to obey, that you may afterwards know how to command. This is not for silkworms and spruce courtiers to do; nor for those that are in love with their ease, but for such as by the ways of virtue and at the price of their lives will endeavour to immortalize their names, as I hope in despite of envy I have done that of Montluc.

LEONAUR

ALSO FROM LEONAUR
AVAILABLE IN SOFTCOVER OR HARDCOVER WITH DUST JACKET

OFFICERS & GENTLEMEN *by Peter Hawker & William Graham*—Two Accounts of British Officers During the Peninsula War: Officer of Light Dragoons by Peter Hawker & Campaign in Portugal and Spain by William Graham .

THE WALCHEREN EXPEDITION *by Anonymous*—The Experiences of a British Officer of the 81st Regt. During the Campaign in the Low Countries of 1809.

LADIES OF WATERLOO *by Charlotte A. Eaton, Magdalene de Lancey & Juana Smith*—The Experiences of Three Women During the Campaign of 1815: Waterloo Days by Charlotte A. Eaton, A Week at Waterloo by Magdalene de Lancey & Juana's Story by Juana Smith.

JOURNAL OF AN OFFICER IN THE KING'S GERMAN LEGION *by John Frederick Hering*—Recollections of Campaigning During the Napoleonic Wars.

JOURNAL OF AN ARMY SURGEON IN THE PENINSULAR WAR *by Charles Boutflower*—The Recollections of a British Army Medical Man on Campaign During the Napoleonic Wars.

ON CAMPAIGN WITH MOORE AND WELLINGTON *by Anthony Hamilton*—The Experiences of a Soldier of the 43rd Regiment During the Peninsular War.

THE ROAD TO AUSTERLITZ *by R. G. Burton*—Napoleon's Campaign of 1805.

SOLDIERS OF NAPOLEON *by A. J. Doisy De Villargennes & Arthur Chuquet*—The Experiences of the Men of the French First Empire: Under the Eagles by A. J. Doisy De Villargennes & Voices of 1812 by Arthur Chuquet .

INVASION OF FRANCE, 1814 *by F. W. O. Maycock*—The Final Battles of the Napoleonic First Empire.

LEIPZIG—A CONFLICT OF TITANS *by Frederic Shoberl*—A Personal Experience of the 'Battle of the Nations' During the Napoleonic Wars, October 14th-19th, 1813.

SLASHERS *by Charles Cadell*—The Campaigns of the 28th Regiment of Foot During the Napoleonic Wars by a Serving Officer.

BATTLE IMPERIAL *by Charles William Vane*—The Campaigns in Germany & France for the Defeat of Napoleon 1813-1814.

SWIFT & BOLD *by Gibbes Rigaud*—The 60th Rifles During the Peninsula War.

www.ingramcontent.com/pod-product-compliance
Lightning Source LLC
Chambersburg PA
CBHW032044080426
42733CB00006B/193